Course 4

TEST GENERATOR
COMPUTER SOFTWARE

Question Manual

GLENCOE
McGraw-Hill

New York, New York   Columbus, Ohio   Woodland Hills, California   Peoria, Illinois

Glencoe/McGraw-Hill

A Division of The **McGraw·Hill** *Companies*

Send all inquiries to:
Glencoe/McGraw-Hill
936 Eastwind Drive
Westerville, OH 43081

Printed in the United States of America.

ISBN 0-02-827612-4

2 3 4 5 6 7 8 9 10 11 12 069 05 04 03 02 01 00 99

CONTENTS

TO THE TEACHER

This test bank contains true/false, multiple choice, completion, matching, and short answer questions as well as problems covering all chapters in the *Science Interactions, Course 4* text. The questions are grouped by type (short answer, multiple choice, etc.) within each chapter. These questions and the test generator software have been prepared to assist you in developing objective-based tests for your students.

LEARNING OBJECTIVES

Learning objectives are suggested outcomes of what your students may be capable of achieving during or after your teaching. The objectives for each chapter (the same ones found in the Teacher Wraparound Edition of the text) are listed before the questions in this manual.

LEVELS OF DIFFICULTY

In addition to being correlated to the objectives, each test question is designated with one of two levels of difficulty based on Bloom's Taxonomy. All the questions are evaluations within the cognitive domain. Affective and psychomotor domains are best evaluated on an individual basis in the classroom setting.

Questions are designated as basic (B) level or advanced (A) level. Basic questions are those on the knowledge and comprehension levels of Bloom's taxonomy. These questions ask students to define or recognize specific facts relating to whom, what, or when. Students may also be asked to choose, classify, or describe an event or phenomenon. Advanced questions are represented by the application, analysis, synthesis, and evaluation levels. These questions ask students to predict, solve, decide, or tell why something happens. Advanced questions often require the students to form an answer that may be different for each student.

Below each question is a code that gives you both the objective number and the level of difficulty for that question. The objectives are listed and numbered on pages CO-1 to CO-6. Use this information when you select questions to help you tailor your test to the exact needs and abilities of your students.

COMPONENTS

- *Science Interactions, Course 4* Test Bank Question Manual
- Glencoe Test Generator User's Manual (Windows)
- Glencoe Test Generator User's Manual (Macintosh)
- Diskettes (Windows/Macintosh)

The *Science Interactions, Course 4* Test Bank consists of a Question Manual and a set of floppy disks (the program disk, the test bank data disks, and a set of disks containing graphics that may accompany some questions). The *User's Guide* is a separate booklet. It contains instructions for the setup and use of the software. Be sure to use the correct booklet for your system (Windows or Macintosh). The program disk contains a program that lets you retrieve the questions you want and print tests. It also lets you edit and add questions as needed.

The Question Manual contains a printed listing of all the questions in the test bank. Use this manual to preview the available questions and to make your choices for inclusion on tests; or, if you prefer, you may view and select questions on-screen using the included computer program.

SITE LICENSE

Your adoption of *Glencoe Science Interactions, Course 4* entitles you to site-license duplication rights for all components of this test bank with the restriction that all copies must be used within the adopting schools. This license shall run for the life of the adoption of the accompanying text.

USING THE TEST BANK

Before you begin, follow the directions in the *User's Guide* to make backup copies of all the disks. Then, set up your computer and printer and configure the software following the instructions. The *User's Guide* contains all the instructions on how to use the software. Refer to this Question Manual as needed to preview and select questions for your tests.

Some questions require the student to examine a drawing or chart. If you have a compatible printer, the program can print the graphic with the questions. The Question Manual also contains blackline masters of all the figures referenced by the test questions. These figures are grouped by chapter to simplify the process of copying and collating them with the copies of your tests if you don't have a compatible printer.

SOFTWARE SUPPORT HOTLINE

Should you encounter any difficulty when setting up or running the programs, contact the Software Support Center at Glencoe Publishing between 8:30 A.M. and 4:00 P.M. Eastern Time. The toll-free number is 1-800-437-3715.

INTRODUCTION

This package includes a test generator program called *ExamView*–an application that enables you to quickly and easily create tests, enter your own questions, and customize the appearance of the tests you create. The *ExamView* test generator program offers many unique features. Using the QuickTest wizard, for example, you are guided step-by-step through the process of building a test. Numerous options are included that allow you to customize the content and appearance of the tests you create.

As you work with the *ExamView* test generator, you may use the following features:

- an "interview" mode or a "wizard" to guide you through the steps to create a test in less than five minutes
- five methods to select test questions
  – from a list
  – random selection
  – by criteria (difficulty code or objective–if available)
  – while viewing questions
  – all questions
- the capability to edit questions or to add an unlimited number of questions
- a sophisticated word processor
  – streamlined question entry
  – toolbar
  – cut, copy, paste, undo
  – tabs (center, left, right, decimal, leaders)
  – fonts and text styles (bold, underline, color, etc.)
  – support for symbols and foreign characters
  – tables
  – borders and shading
  – paragraph formatting (justification, spacing, hanging indent, etc.)
  – pictures or other graphics within a question, answer, or narrative
  – find/replace commands
- numerous test layout and printing options
  – scramble the choices in multiple choice questions
  – organize matching questions in a one- or two-column format
  – print multiple versions of the same test with corresponding answer keys
  – print an answer key strip for easier test grading
  – change the order of questions
  – print a test with or without space for students to record their answers
  – specify the layout of a test to conserve paper
  – print a comprehensive answer sheet
- the ability to link groups of questions to common narratives
- password protection
- extensive help system

INSTALLATION AND STARTUP INSTRUCTIONS

The *ExamView* test generator software is provided on one or more floppy disks or on a CD-ROM depending on the size of the question bank. The disks include the program and all of the questions for the corresponding textbook. Before you can use the test generator software, you must install it on your hard drive or network. The system requirements, installation instructions, and startup procedures are provided below.

SYSTEM REQUIREMENTS

To use the *ExamView* test generator, your computer must meet or exceed these minimum hardware requirements:

- 486, 50 MHz computer
- Windows 3.1, Windows 95, or Windows 98
- color monitor (VGA-compatible)
- high-density floppy disk drive
- hard drive with at least 5 MB space available
- 8 MB available memory *(16 MB memory recommended)*
- mouse
- printer *(optional, but recommended)*

INSTALLATION INSTRUCTIONS

Follow these steps to install the *ExamView* test generator software on a hard drive or network. The setup program will automatically install everything you need to use the *ExamView* test generator software.

Step 1
Turn on your computer.

Step 2
Insert the *ExamView* installation disk into Drive A. If the program is provided on a CD-ROM, insert the disc into your CD-ROM drive.

Step 3
Windows 3.1: While in the Program Manager, choose *Run* from the **File** menu.
Windows 95/98: Click the **Start** button on the *Taskbar* and choose the *Run* option.

Step 4
If you are installing the software from floppy disks, type **a:\setup** and press **Enter** to run the installation program. If the *ExamView* software is provided on a CD-ROM, use the drive letter that corresponds to the CD-ROM drive on your computer (e.g., **e:\setup**).

   Note: The installation program is configured to copy the software to *c:\examview* on your hard drive. You can, however, change this location. For example, you can select a location on your network server.

Step 5
Follow the prompts on the screen to complete the installation process. If the software and question banks are provided on more than one disk, you will be prompted to insert the appropriate disk when it is needed.

Step 6
Remove the installation disk from the disk drive when you finish.

GETTING STARTED

After you have completed the installation process, follow these instructions to start the *ExamView* software. This section also explains the options used to create a test and edit a question bank.

Startup Instructions

Step 1
Turn on the computer.

Step 2
Windows 3.1: Locate the *ExamView* program icon. Double-click the program icon to start the test generator software.
Windows 95/98: Click the **Start** button on the *Taskbar*. Highlight the **Programs** menu and locate the *ExamView* folder. Select the *ExamView* option to start the software.

Step 3
The first time you run the software you will be prompted to enter your name, school/institution name, and city/state. You are now ready to begin using the *ExamView* software.

Step 4
Each time you start *ExamView,* the **Startup** menu appears. Choose one of the following options:
- Create a new test using the QuickTest Wizard.
- Use the *ExamView* Test Builder to:
  - Create a new test.
  - Open an existing test.
- Use the *ExamView* Question Bank Editor to:
  - Create a new question bank.
  - Open an existing question bank.

Step 5
Use *ExamView* to create a test or edit questions in a question bank.

The *ExamView* program is divided into two components: Test Builder and Question Bank Editor. The **Test Builder** includes options to create, edit, print, and save tests. The **Question Bank Editor** lets you create or edit existing question banks. Both the Test Builder and the Question Bank Editor have unique menus and options to work with tests and question banks.

As you work with *ExamView,* you can easily switch between these components using the *Switch to...* option in the **File** menu. Be sure to save your work before you switch between components.

Important: Whenever you need assistance using *ExamView,* access the extensive help system. Click the **Help** button or choose an option from the **Help** menu to access step-by-step instructions and detailed descriptions of the features of *ExamView.* If you experience any difficulties while you are working with the software, you may want to review the troubleshooting tips in the user-friendly help system.

Test Builder

The Test Builder will empower you to create tests from an existing question bank or you can create a new test on your own.

- *If you want ExamView to choose questions randomly from an existing question bank,* choose the QuickTest Wizard option to create a new test. Then, follow the step-by-step instructions to (1) enter a test title, (2) choose the question bank from which to select questions, and (3) identify how many questions you want on the test. The QuickTest Wizard will automatically create a new test and use the Test Builder to display the test on screen. You can print the test as is, remove questions, add new questions, or edit any questions.

- *If you want to create a new test on your own,* choose the option to create a new test. Then identify a question bank from which to choose questions by using the *Question Bank...* option in the **Select** menu. You may then add questions to the test by using one or more of the following question selection options: *Randomly, From a List, While Viewing, By Criteria,* or *All Questions.*

After you create a test, you can customize the appearance of the test by changing the order of the questions, editing test instructions, specifying the font and style for selected test elements, and choosing whether to leave space for students to write their answers directly on the test. The customizing changes you make to the questions will not change the original question bank; your changes are made only to the copy of the questions on the test you just created.

When you have finalized the content and appearance of your test, you can print it and/or save it. To print a test, you may choose how many copies of the test you want, whether you want all the copies to be the same, and whether you want to scramble the questions and the multiple choice options. If you scramble the questions, *ExamView* will print a custom answer sheet for each variation of the test.

Question Bank Editor

The Question Bank Editor will empower you to edit questions in an existing publisher-supplied question bank or to create new question banks. Always use the Question Bank Editor if you want to change a question permanently in an existing question bank.

You may edit questions in a question bank or add new questions by using the built-in word processor. The word processor includes many features commonly found in commercially available word processing applications. These features include the following: fonts, styles, tables, paragraph formatting, ruler controls, tabs, indents, and justification.

A question bank may include up to 250 questions in a variety of formats including multiple choice, true/false, modified true/false, completion, yes/no, matching, problem, essay, short answer, case, and numeric response. You can assign a difficulty code, a page reference, and two objectives to each question.

SOFTWARE SUPPORT

Glencoe provides toll-free telephone assistance for instructors who experience difficulty while using *ExamView*. Before calling for assistance, please check the following:

- Is your computer working properly? Try some other software, which you know is working, on the same computer.
- Can you repeat the problem? Does the problem occur at the same point each time?

In order for the Support Center to help you as quickly as possible, before calling for assistance have the following at hand:

- exact title and ISBN number from the disk label or package.
- brand, model, and configuration of the computer you are using.
- system version (Windows 3.1, Windows 95, or Windows 98) installed on your computer.
- the exact wording of any error message.

The Glencoe Support Center toll-free number is **800-437-3715**. The Support Center is available from 8:30 A.M. to 4:00 P.M. Eastern Time. You can also send an e-mail to the following address **glentech@mcgraw-hill.com** to contact the Support Center.

WINDOWS USER'S GUIDE

MACINTOSH TEST GENERATOR
INTRODUCTION

With the *Glencoe Test Generator* you can quickly and easily create tests, enter your own questions, and customize the test layout to meet your needs. The *Glencoe Test Generator* program offers many features not found in other test generators. Using the *QuickTest* option, for example, the software guides you step-by-step through the process of building a test. For the more advanced user, the software includes numerous options that give you complete control over the content and appearance of the tests you create.

As you work with the *Glencoe Test Generator*, you will use these features:

- an "interview" mode to guide you through the process of having the software create a test

- five methods to select test questions yourself
  - from a list
  - random selection
  - by criteria (difficulty code, objective, or topic)
  - while viewing questions
  - all questions

- the capability to edit or add an unlimited number of test questions

- a word processor with many distinctive features
  - text manipulation functions (undo, cut, copy, paste, clear, and select all)
  - tabs (center, left, right, decimal)
  - text styles (bold, underline, italic, subscript, superscript, and condensed) and sizes
  - extended character support («» ½ ¼ α β Γ π Σ σ μ τ ϕ θ Ω ÷ ≈ ° ·· $\sqrt{}$ ^{n} ...) using fonts
  - find/replace (within a question or the entire question bank)
  - include graphic images within a question, answer, or narrative

- numerous test formatting options
  - scramble the choices in multiple choice questions
  - print an answer strip
  - modify printing order for the question types
  - select the printing order based on difficulty, objective, or topic
  - provide space on the test for students to write their answers or remove all answer areas for tests completed on scanner sheets
  - specify layout for multiple choice questions (traditional or alternative to conserve paper)
  - print a comprehensive answer sheet (answer, topic, objective, etc.) or just the answer

- the ability to link groups of questions to common narratives

- password protection

- extensive on-line help

WHAT'S ON THE DISK

The *Glencoe Test Generator* software is provided on one or more disks depending on the test bank. If the test bank is on one disk, it contains both the program and the question banks. When supplied on multiple disks, Disk 1 is the test generator program and the other disk(s) contain the question banks corresponding to your textbook.

WHAT YOU NEED

To use the *Glencoe Test Generator* software, you need the following equipment:

- Any Macintosh computer with at least 2Mb of memory
- System 6.0.5 or higher
- A hard drive or two floppy drives

INSTALLATION

Follow these steps to install the program and the question bank files on your hard drive. Although you can run the program from floppy drives, installing the software on your hard drive is recommended.

Step 1
Switch your computer on (if it's not already on).

Step 2
When the Desktop appears, insert the program disk (Disk 1) into a drive.

Step 3
Drag the disk icon to your hard drive to create a new folder and copy the test generator.

Step 4
Eject the disk from the drive.

Step 5
If the test bank is provided on more than one disk, insert the next disk into a drive. Drag the files to the test generator folder to copy the question banks to your hard drive.

Step 6
Eject the question bank disk. (Repeat Step 5 for each additional question bank disk.)

GETTING STARTED

If you installed the software on your hard drive, double-click the test generator folder at this time. If you are running the software from a floppy drive, insert the program disk into a drive.

Step 1

Double-click the test generator icon.

The *Glencoe Test Generator* software starts and the opening screen appears. If the opening screen does not appear, check the Troubleshooting section of this manual (pp. M-25 to M-26).

Step 2

Click the mouse button to display the **Main** menu.

The Main menu, shown in Figure 1-1, appears on your screen. The software is divided into three parts: *QuickTest, Build/Print Test,* and *Edit Question Banks.* A brief description of each of the parts is given below.

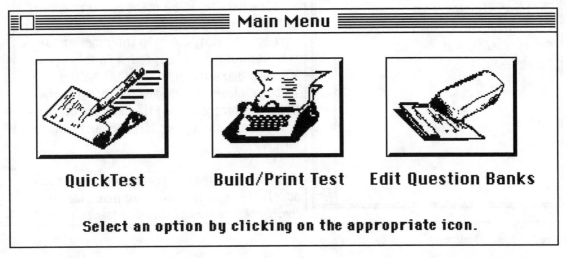

Figure 1-1 Main Menu

QuickTest

If you want the software to select the questions randomly, then *QuickTest* is just the thing for you! With *QuickTest,* you can build a test containing up to 250 questions from as many as thirty question banks in less than one minute.

Build/Print Test

Although *QuickTest* provides a quick and simple way to create tests, many times you will want to create a test with specific questions or questions that match specific criteria. The *Glencoe Test Generator* allows you to do just that. Using the *Build/Print Test* option, there are five different ways to select questions. You are also given a way to change the question type order, change the test layout options, edit headers and instructions, and edit questions even after they have been included in your test. Once tests have been built, you have the option of saving them to disk and retrieving them at a later time.

Edit Question Banks

In addition to using the supplied question banks, you also have the option of creating your own. The *Glencoe Test Generator* contains a powerful word processor with many distinctive features that allows you to add questions to existing question banks or create entirely new question banks. Question banks can contain up to 250 questions from a variety of question types. Each question can be assigned an objective, a page reference, a difficulty index, and a topic. Questions can include a picture (graphic) and/or be linked to a narrative (specialized instruction).

HELP

Context-sensitive help is available from anywhere within the software by choosing *Help* from the **Apple** () menu. A window appears on your screen as shown in Figure 1-2.

A list of help topics appears in the window. The software attempts to determine the most likely topic based on where you are in the program. Use the up and down arrow keys or the mouse to highlight the topic about which you want more information.

MACINTOSH USER'S GUIDE

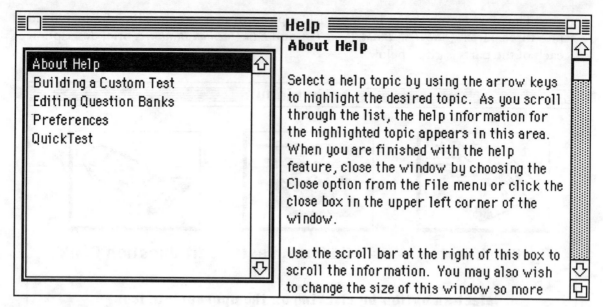

Figure 1-2 Help Window

As you move through the list of help topics, the program displays the help information in a box on the right side of the help window. If the help text is too long to fit on the screen at one time, you can use the mouse to scroll through the remainder of the information. When you are through reviewing the help information, close the window.

PREFERENCES

Choose *Preferences* from the **Edit** menu. The software lets you set the default font and size for all new questions, headers, instructions, and question numbers. The supplied question banks are in Courier 12. Unless you need to change the question banks to a different font, there is no need to change the default font and size.

If you enter a password in the Password field, each time you start the software you will be prompted to enter the password. Make sure that if you enter a password, you record it in a safe place.

If you want the software to select the questions randomly, then *QuickTest* is just the thing for you! With *QuickTest*, you can build a test containing up to 250 questions from many question banks in less than a minute.

When you choose the *QuickTest* option, the software leads you step-by-step through the process of building a test. Extensive prompt messages tell you exactly what to do and which buttons to press. There is no need to choose anything from the menus.

To begin *QuickTest*, start the software and choose *QuickTest* from the **Main** menu.

CHOOSING QUESTION BANKS

The dialog box shown in Figure 2-1 appears on your screen.

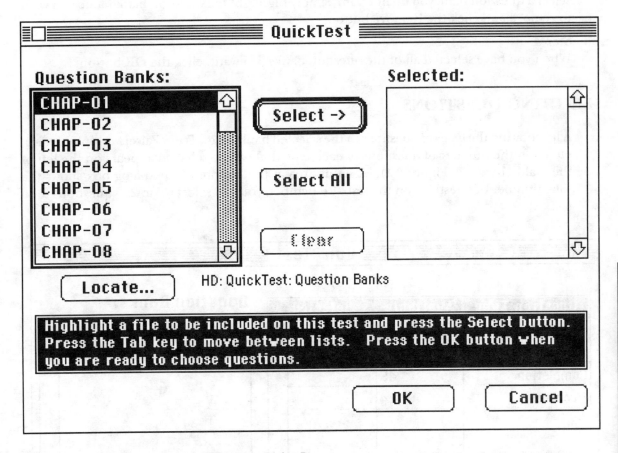

Figure 2-1 QuickTest Question Bank Selection Dialog Box

MACINTOSH USER'S GUIDE

Step 1
A list showing question bank files appears at the left. Depending on whether you are working on a floppy drive system or a hard drive, follow the appropriate steps below:

Floppy Drives   Make sure the disk containing the question banks is in a drive. If the question banks are on separate disks, insert a question bank disk into another drive. Click the **Locate** button, select the question bank disk, and then click the **Done** button. The question banks on that disk will appear in the list. If, after selecting question banks from this disk, you decide that you want to select questions from another question bank disk, simply click the **Locate** button again, eject the disk, and insert the new disk in the drive.

Hard Drive   When you installed the question banks on the hard drive, you placed them in the test generator folder. Click the **Locate** button, double-click the folder name, and click **Done**. The question bank names appear in the list.

Step 2

Use the up and down arrow keys or the mouse to highlight the first question bank file to include on your test. Once the bank name is highlighted, click the **Select** button. When you click the button, notice how *QuickTest* inserts the name of the question bank into the *Selected* list on the right of the screen. As a shortcut, you can simply double-click on a question bank name to select it.

Step 3

Select the other question banks to use for the test in the same manner. If you inadvertently select a question bank you do not want, simply highlight the question bank name you want to remove and click the **Remove** button.

Step 4

When you have selected all of the question banks you want, click the **OK** button.

SELECTING QUESTIONS

A list showing the types of questions in the selected banks (e.g., True/False, Multiple Choice, etc.) and the number of questions of each type that can be selected appears on the left of the dialog box (see Figure 2-2). A status area at the bottom of the dialog box shows the total number of questions on the test. Remember, you can select up to 250 questions for a test.

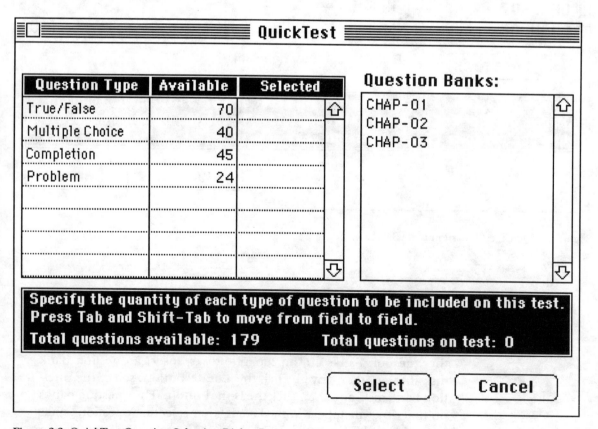

Figure 2-2 QuickTest Question Selection Dialog Box

If you notice that you forgot to include a question bank, simply click the **Cancel** button to return to the previous screen, select the question bank, and click **OK** again.

Step 1
In the spaces provided, key the number of questions of each type you want to include on your test. After you press **Return** for each entry, the status area is updated.

Step 2
When you are satisfied with the makeup of your test, click the **Select** button. The software will now automatically select the questions for your test.

QUICKTEST SUMMARY

Once the *Glencoe Test Generator* has completed the question selection process, the dialog box shown in Figure 2-3 appears on your screen. The summary shows you how many questions are on the test, which question banks were used in selecting questions, and how many questions of each question type have been selected. At this time, you can print the test, save it, change the test layout, or cancel the selections and begin again.

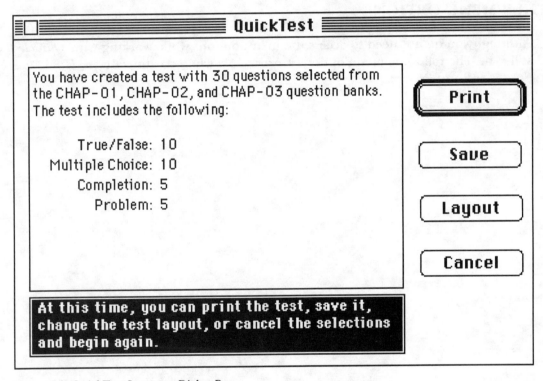

Figure 2-3 QuickTest Summary Dialog Box

Step 1
Review your selections.

Step 2
To continue, click the **Print** button. Once your test has been printed, the software returns you to the test summary screen.

Changing the Test Layout

If you prefer, you may change the test layout or print multiple variations of your test. The question order within each question type will be different for each variation. To print multiple variations, enter a number greater than one in the field using the *Layout* option.

Many test layout options, discussed in detail in Section 3–Build/Print Test, are available. To change any of the options, click the **Layout** button. Remember, you can get on-line help at any time by pressing **⌘+H**. After changing the options, click the **OK** button to continue.

Saving Your Test

You may, if you like, choose to save your test to disk. Click the **Save** button. Use the controls to set the drive and/or folder on which to save. Key-enter a name for your test and click the **Save** button. Once a test has been saved, you can use the *Build/Print Test* option, discussed in Section 3, to retrieve the test from disk. The test can then be modified using the features discussed in that section.

EXIT TO MAIN MENU

At any time while working with *QuickTest*, you may choose to quit. To exit, simply press **⌘+Q**. Return to the **Main** menu by choosing **⌘+W** or by clicking the close box to close the QuickTest window. When the software asks if you want to select new questions from the current question banks, click the **No** button.

OTHER MENU OPTIONS

Although you do not need to access the menu options while working with *QuickTest*, you still can. The following menu options are available when creating a test: *Help, Close, Page Setup, Quit,* and *Preferences*.

Although *QuickTest* provides a quick and simple way to create tests, many times you will want to create a test with specific questions or questions that match specific criteria. The *Glencoe Test Generator* allows you to do just that. Using the *Build/Print Test* option, there are five different ways to select questions. You are also given a way to change the question type order, change the test layout options, edit headers and instructions, and edit questions even after they have been included in your test.

To begin building a new test, follow these steps:

Step 1
Start the *Glencoe Test Generator* software.

Step 2
From the **Main** menu, select the *Build/Print Test* option.

BUILDING A TEST

Once you have selected the *Build/Print Test* option, the "visual test" is displayed on your screen. If you do not want to build a new test, you can choose the *Open Test* option from the **File** menu to retrieve a previously saved test from disk.

The Visual Test

While you are building your test, the window shown in Figure 3-1 (referred to as the "visual test") will always reflect the current composition of the test. The program displays the first page header, instructions, narratives, and the questions in the order they will be printed on the test. Use the arrow keys or the mouse to scroll through the list of questions. A status line appears at the bottom of the window showing the current question bank name, current item highlighted [e.g., First Page Header, Instructions, TF (1 of 20), etc.], and the total number of questions on the test.

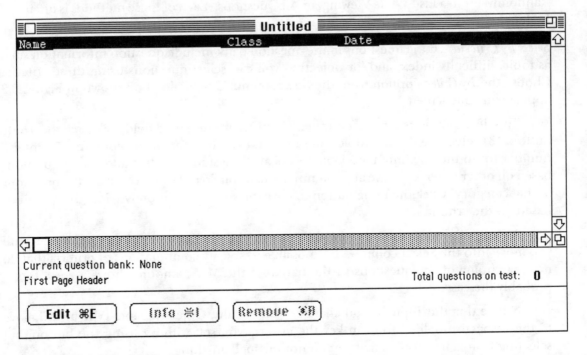

Figure 3-1 Visual Test Window

Selecting a Question Bank

The first thing you will want to do when you begin a new test is select a question bank from which to select questions. Choose the *Question Bank* option from the **Select** menu. The dialog box shown in Figure 3-2 will appear. Use the controls shown to set the drive and/or folder where your question bank files are located. Select the desired question bank from the list. Click the **Open** button to open the selected question bank file.

Only one question bank file may be open at a time, although questions from many question banks may be contained on a single test. Select questions from one question bank, then open a different question bank and select additional questions.

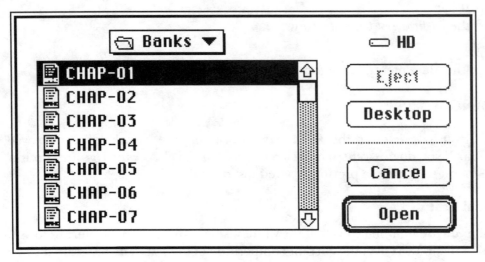

Figure 3-2 Question Bank Selection Dialog Box

Selecting Questions

Once you have selected a question bank, you are now ready to select questions for your test. As was mentioned above, you can select questions in five different ways: By Criteria, Randomly, From a List, While Viewing, or All Questions. Each of these methods is discussed in detail.

Select By Criteria. If the questions in the question bank include question information such as topic, difficulty index, and/or objective, you can select questions using these criteria. Choose the *By Criteria* option from the **Select** menu. The dialog box shown in Figure 3-3 appears on your screen.

To select questions on a given topic: (1) move to the Topic field, (2) click the **Topic** button, (3) select the desired topic from the list, (4) tab to the Select column, (5) enter a number up to the maximum available. Repeat these steps to select additional questions based on other criteria. Leave any column blank if you do not want to restrict the questions in that category. Click the **Done** button to have the software randomly select the questions based on the criteria set.

As you will notice when you use this feature, the MAX amount does not appear until you move into the Select column. It is possible to specify combinations of criteria that do not match any of the questions in the bank. If the MAX amount shows a zero, this is probably the case.

Notice that the **Topic** button changes to Difficulty, Objective, and Type as you move to the respective fields. You can key the criteria yourself without using the button, but selecting from a list ensures that you do not misspell anything.

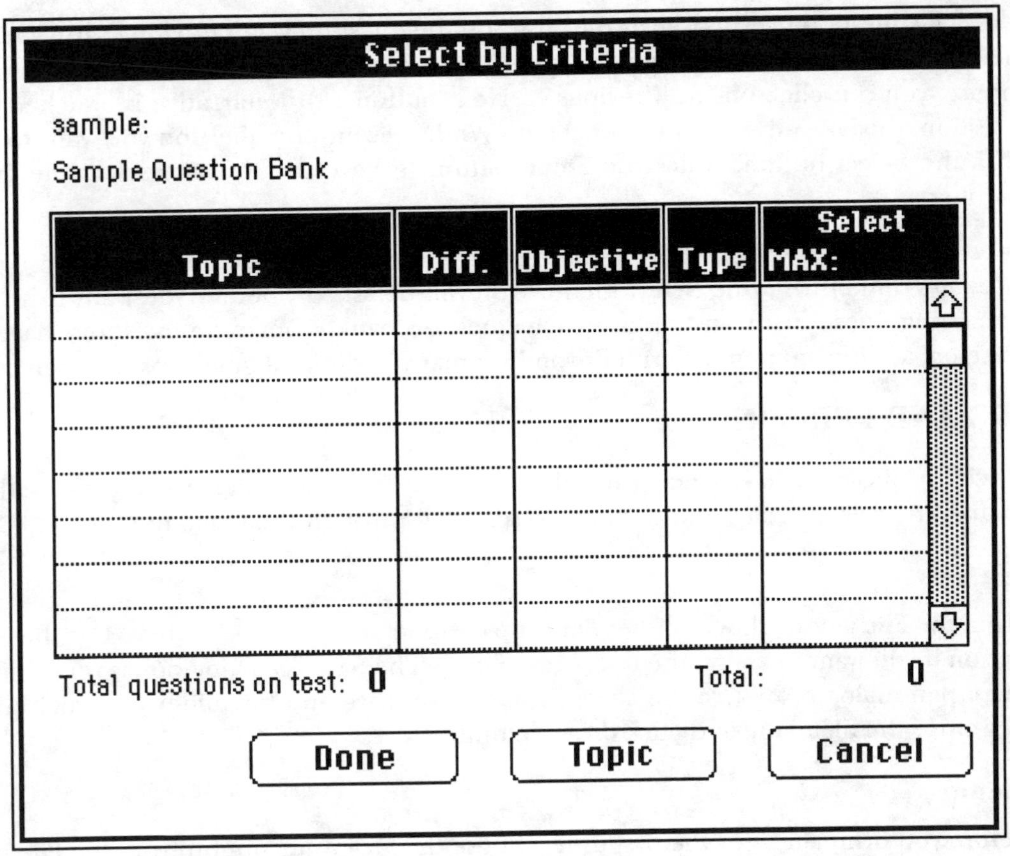

Figure 3-3 Select by Criteria Dialog Box

Multiple groups of questions can be selected at any one time. For example, on the first line select three True/False questions with Topic 1 and difficulty index 2, and on the second line select five Multiple Choice questions with Topic 3 and difficulty index 4.

Note: This selection method is applicable only if the question banks include topics, objectives, or difficulty codes.

Select Randomly. Questions can also be selected randomly by question type, much as they were using *QuickTest*. Choose the *Randomly* option from the **Select** menu. For each question type, the number of questions available and the number already selected is shown. Enter the number of additional questions of each type that you want to add to the test. Click the **Done** button to have the software randomly select the questions.

Select From a List. Often, you will select questions while looking at a printout of the question bank. If you are selecting questions in this way, this is probably the best option for you to use. Choose the *From a List* option in the **Select** menu.

The software displays a list showing the question type, narrative number (if any), difficulty index, and topic for each of the questions in the bank. Click on a question to select it. A check mark appears to the left of the question information to indicate this question is now selected. To unselect a question, simply click on the line again. Click the **Done** button to have the software select the marked questions.

Select While Viewing. If you want to be able to see the questions before selecting them, then you will want to use the *While Viewing* option. Choose the *While Viewing* option from the **Select** menu.

The question text (as well as the answer if the question is not too long) appears in the viewing window. Move through the questions using the arrow keys. If you are using a mouse, you can click on the **Previous** or **Next** buttons. If a narrative is attached to the question, the **Narrative** button is enabled. While viewing the question you want to select, click the **Select** button. Click the **Done** button to have the software select the marked questions.

Select All Questions. To include all of the questions from a question bank, choose the *All Questions* option from the **Select** menu. You will be asked whether you want to select all remaining questions from the particular question bank. Once the questions have been selected, an informational alert tells you how many additional questions were selected.

SAVING AND PRINTING

Once the questions have been selected, the *Glencoe Test Generator* allows you to save the test to disk. Review the selected questions by scrolling through the visual test.

Saving a Test

From the **File** menu, choose either *Save* or *Save As* to save your test to disk. Use the *Save As* option if you want to assign the test a new name. The Save As dialog box is very similar to the Open dialog box. Use the controls to set the drive and/or folder on which to save. Key-enter the file name and click the **Save** button.

Page Setup

Before you print a test for the first time, choose the *Page Setup* option from the **File** menu. Verify that the appropriate options are set.

Printing a Test

To print a test, choose the *Print Test* option from the **File** menu. Set the options and click the **Print** button.

Opening a Test

Choose the *Open Test* option from the **File** menu to open tests that have already been saved. In the Open Test dialog box, there are controls to change drives and folders to locate your tests. Choose a test by highlighting the name from the list and clicking the **Open** button. Files can also be opened by double-clicking on the file name.

MISCELLANEOUS FEATURES

In addition to those features already mentioned, the *Glencoe Test Generator* offers the following features while working with the *Build/Print Test* option. Use any or all of these features to customize your test.

Question Type Order

Questions on a test must be grouped by question type (True/False, Multiple Choice, etc.). The default order in which question types will appear on a test is as follows: True/False, Multiple Choice, Yes/No, Completion, Matching, Short Answer, Problem, and Other.

You can change the question type order for the current test only, or save the question type order for use with all new tests. Choose the *Question Type Order* option from the **Select** menu. Specify the order in which you want the question types to appear. To move a question type to another place in the list, drag it to its new location. Click the **OK** button to change the order for the current test only. Use the **Save** button to change all subsequent tests as well as the current test.

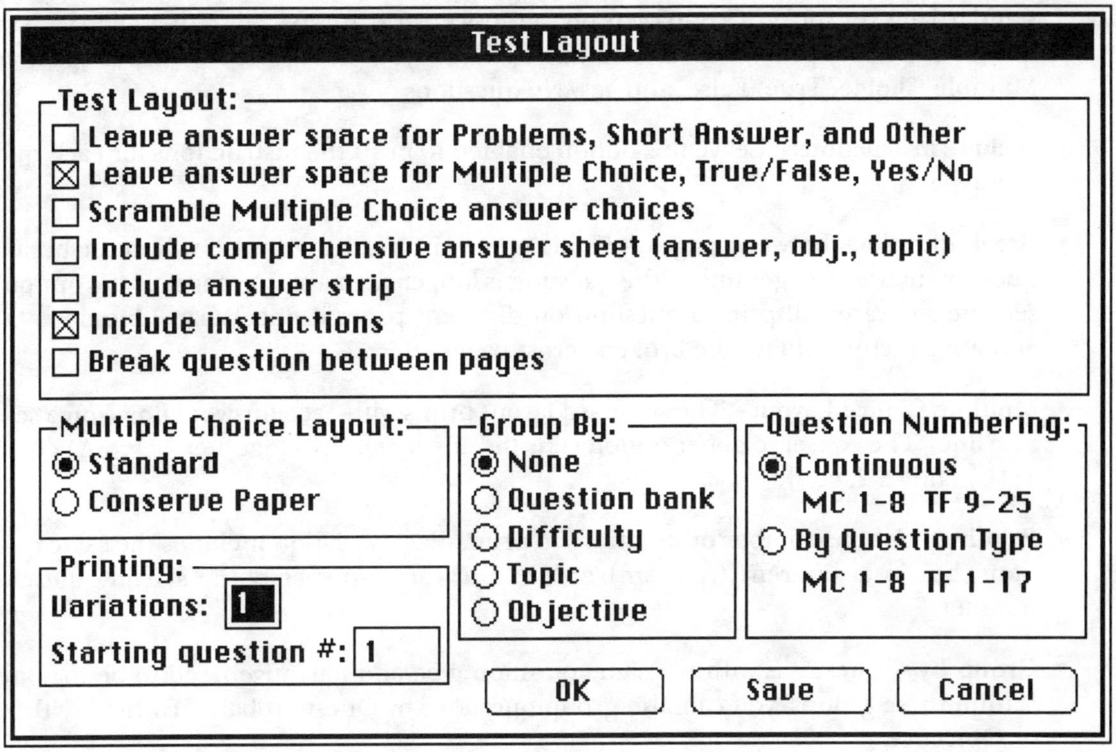

```
┌─────────────────────────────────────────────────────────────┐
│                        Test Layout                          │
├─────────────────────────────────────────────────────────────┤
│ ┌─Test Layout:─────────────────────────────────────────────┐ │
│ │ ☐ Leave answer space for Problems, Short Answer, and Other│ │
│ │ ☒ Leave answer space for Multiple Choice, True/False, Yes/No│ │
│ │ ☐ Scramble Multiple Choice answer choices                │ │
│ │ ☐ Include comprehensive answer sheet (answer, obj., topic)│ │
│ │ ☐ Include answer strip                                   │ │
│ │ ☒ Include instructions                                   │ │
│ │ ☐ Break question between pages                           │ │
│ └──────────────────────────────────────────────────────────┘ │
│ ┌─Multiple Choice Layout:─┐ ┌─Group By:──┐ ┌─Question Numbering:─┐│
│ │ ◉ Standard              │ │ ◉ None     │ │ ◉ Continuous       ││
│ │ ◯ Conserve Paper        │ │ ◯ Question bank│   MC 1-8  TF 9-25 ││
│ │                         │ │ ◯ Difficulty│ │ ◯ By Question Type ││
│ ┌─Printing:───────────────┐│ ◯ Topic     │ │   MC 1-8  TF 1-17  ││
│ │ Variations: [ 1 ]       ││ ◯ Objective │ └────────────────────┘│
│ │ Starting question #: [1]│└─────────────┘                       │
│ └─────────────────────────┘   ( OK )  ( Save )  ( Cancel )       │
└─────────────────────────────────────────────────────────────┘
```

Figure 3-4 Test Layout Dialog Box

Clear All Selections

If you want to remove all of the questions from the test—not just those in the current question bank—select the *Clear All Selections* option from the **Select** menu. You will be asked if you want to clear all questions in the current test. Respond appropriately.

Test Layout

Numerous test layouts are available for customizing your test. Select the *Test Layout* option from the **Special** menu. A dialog box as shown in Figure 3-4 appears.

The options available are listed on pages M-13 and M-14.

- **Leave answer space for Problems, Short Answer, and Other** – Set this option to include space on the printed test for the students to write their answers. The blank space provided on the test will be slightly more than the amount of space that the correct answer requires.

- **Leave answer space for Multiple Choice, True/False, Yes/No** – Set this option to include a space to the left of the question for the students to write their answers.

- **Scramble Multiple Choice answer choices** – Set this option to scramble the answer choices for multiple choice questions when you print multiple variations of your test. Some answer choices should not be scrambled (e.g., **d. All of the above**). To prevent these choices from being scrambled on questions you create, insert the # symbol after the answer letter (e.g., **d.# All of the above**). This symbol will not be printed on the test.

- **Include comprehensive answer sheet** – Enable this option to print a comprehensive answer sheet including the answer, topic, objective, and difficulty code for each question.

- **Include answer strip** – Set this option to print an answer strip for True/False, Multiple Choice, and Yes/No questions. The software prints the answer strip in addition to the standard answer sheet. The answers on the answer strip are spaced so they align with the questions on the printed test. Use this option if you elect to leave answer space for Multiple Choice, True/False, and Yes/No questions.

- **Include instructions** – Leave this option enabled to print the instructions for each question type.

- **Break questions between pages** – If this option is off, the software will never break a question between pages unless the question is longer than a single page. If the option is set, the software will print a question on different pages if necessary. Questions that contain a picture will not be broken across pages.

- **Multiple Choice Layout** – The standard layout prints with each answer choice on a separate line. The conserve paper option runs the answer choices together [e.g., (A) choice 1, (B) choice 2, etc.].

- **Printing** – Set the number of variations to print. Each variation includes the same questions, but in a different (random) order. You can also specify the starting question number.

- **Group By** – Questions with the same question type and narrative need to be together. Within these groups, you can also group questions by Question bank, Difficulty, Topic, or Objective.

- **Question Numbering** – Choose to number questions continuously (MC 1-8 TF 9-25) or by question type (MC 1-8 TF 1-17).

Click the **OK** button to change the test layout options only for the current test. Use the **Save** button to save the test layout options for use with subsequent tests.

Headers

Each test contains two headers, one that prints at the top of the first page, and another for subsequent pages. Headers may be edited and saved with the current test only or saved to disk for use with all new tests. Choose the *Test Headers* option from the **Special** menu to edit the headers.

When editing the headers, you can use any of the features of the word processor. These features are discussed in Section 4–Edit Question Banks. Headers should be limited to about six lines.

The placeholder **[PG]** can be included in either of the headers. When this placeholder is encountered during printing, it will be replaced with the current page number (e.g., *Page [PG]* will be printed as *Page 1*).

Instructions

Default instructions are provided for each question type (e.g., True/False, Multiple Choice, etc.). Instructions may be edited and saved with the current test only or saved to disk for use with all new tests. Choose the *Instructions* option from the **Special** menu to edit the instructions.

For each question type, there are two sets of instructions–one that appears if you choose to leave space for the answers on the test, and one that appears if you do not. The instructions that you can edit depend on the current test layout settings.

When editing the instructions, you can use any of the features of the word processor. These features are discussed in Section 4–Edit Question Banks. Instructions should be limited to about six lines.

Summary

At any time while building a test, you can choose the *Summary* option from the **Special** menu. A test summary appears on your screen. The summary shows you how many questions are on the test, which question banks you used in selecting questions, and how many questions of each question type you selected.

Editing Questions

Usually, if you want to make changes to a question, you will make them using the *Edit Question Banks* option (see Section 4). From time to time, though, you may want to change a question for just one test.

To make changes to a question after you include it on a test, you first need to highlight the question on the visual test. Highlight the question and click the **Edit** button. Edit the question with the word processor. To edit the answer, click the **Answer** button. For a detailed description of all of the word processor options, refer to Section 4. After you make the desired changes, click the **OK** button.

Question Info

To view the question information for a particular question, you first need to highlight the question on the visual test. Once the question has been highlighted, click the **Info** button.

The Question Info dialog box includes question information such as question bank source (where you selected the question from), objective, page reference, difficulty index, topic, and narrative.

The question information cannot be changed at this point. To change the question information, you must edit the original question using the *Edit Question Banks* option.

SECTION 4–EDIT QUESTION BANKS

In addition to using the supplied question banks, you also have the option of creating your own. The *Glencoe Test Generator* contains a powerful word processor with many distinctive features that allows you to add questions to existing question banks or create entirely new question banks. Question banks can contain up to 250 questions from a variety of question types. Each question can be assigned an objective, a page reference, a difficulty index, and a topic. Questions can include a picture or be linked to a narrative (specialized instruction).

EDITING QUESTION BANKS

To begin editing question banks, follow these steps:

Step 1
Start the *Glencoe Test Generator* software.

Step 2
From the **Main** menu, select the *Edit Question Banks* option.

After you choose this option, the program displays the Open Question Bank dialog box.

Open Question Bank

Use the Open Question Bank dialog box to open an existing question bank. Choose a question bank by highlighting the name from the list and clicking the **Open** button. If you do not want to open a question bank, click the **Cancel** button.

Question Window

As you can see, the first question appears on the screen (see Figure 4-1). The bottom of the window indicates the current question number, the answer to the question (for True/False, Multiple Choice, Yes/No, and Completion questions), and the total questions currently in this bank. Buttons for editing the question, changing the answer, changing the question information (objective, page reference, narrative, etc.), and creating a new question appear at the bottom of the screen.

It is quite easy to move from question to question using the *Glencoe Test Generator*. To move between questions, simply press the up and down arrow keys or click the **Previous** or **Next** buttons. There are also options in the **Question** menu for moving between questions.

Previous (⌘+1)	Moves to the previous question in the question bank.
Next (⌘+2)	Moves to the next question in the question bank.
First (⌘+3)	Moves to the first question in the question bank.
Last (⌘+4)	Moves to the last question in the question bank.
Goto (⌘+G)	By choosing the *Goto...* option, you can go to any question in the question bank if you know the question type and question number. When this option is chosen, a dialog box appears on the screen. Select the appropriate question type from the pop-up menu, and enter the question number. Click the **OK** button to view the selected question.

You can also use the *Find* option from the **Edit** menu to locate a particular word or phrase in any question. See the "Find" section in this manual (p. M-20) for more information.

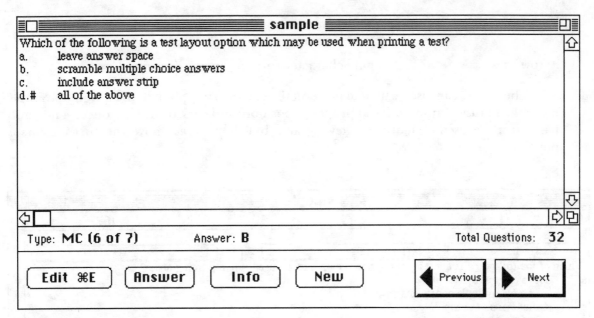

Figure 4-1 Question Window

Editing a Question

To edit a question, simply display the question in the main window and click the **Edit** button.

Creating a New Question

To create a new question, click the **New** button in the main window. The Add New Question dialog box appears. Use the pop-up menu to select the desired question type and click the **OK** button. The program adds the new question to the end of the group of questions with the same type. Key the question, answer, and information. Use the buttons provided to switch among these elements.

WORD PROCESSOR

The word processor for the *Glencoe Test Generator* appears on your screen as shown in Figure 4-2 when you edit an existing question or choose to add a new question. There are scroll bars for moving through the question. A ruler at the top of the screen indicates the margins, tab settings, spacing, and justification for the current paragraph.

Key your questions as you would with any word processor. Text will wrap when it reaches the right margin (as shown on the ruler). Questions should be limited to 100 lines in length, although most will be far less. At any time while keying, you can click the **Record** button to record your changes and return you to the main window. To make further changes to the question, simply click the **Edit** button from the main window.

Use the following keystrokes to move through the document if you have an extended keyboard.

Use This Key Command:	To Move to:
Home	The beginning of the question.
End	The end of the question.
Page Up	The previous page if the question requires more than one screen.

Page Down	The next screen if the question exceeds the bottom of the current screen.
Arrow keys	One character (or line) in any direction.

The mouse can also be used to position the cursor at any point in the question. Simply move the mouse pointer to the appropriate position, and click the mouse once. The scroll bar(s) can be used to move the viewing area but they do *not* move the current cursor position.

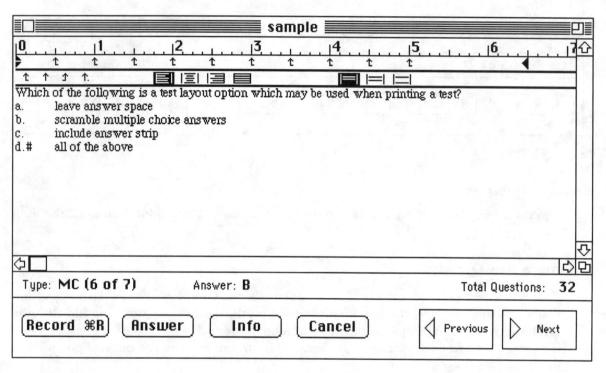

Figure 4-2 Word Processor

Selecting Text

Select a block of text when you want to perform an editing operation (Copy, Cut, Paste, or Clear). Selected text will be shown in a highlight color. Text can be selected in the following ways:

* Use any of the arrow keys while holding down the Shift key.

* Hold the mouse button down and *drag* the mouse pointer over the desired text.

* Highlight a word by double-clicking the mouse on it.

* Highlight a paragraph by triple-clicking (clicking the mouse three times quickly in the same location).

* Choose *Select All* from the **Edit** menu to select the entire question.

Once selected, you can use the following editing options (found on the **Edit** menu).

Cut (⌘+X)	Removes the highlighted text and copies it to the Clipboard.
Copy (⌘+C)	Leaves the highlighted text in place and copies it to the Clipboard.
Clear (Delete)	Removes the highlighted text without copying it to the Clipboard.

Also, if you press a key while text is highlighted, that character will replace the highlighted text. Any of the editing operations can be reversed by choosing *Undo* from the **Edit** menu. Once text has been copied to the Clipboard using either *Cut* or *Copy*, the cursor can be placed in a different position and the *Paste* option can be chosen to place the copied text in the new location.

To remove the highlight from the text, simply use the arrow keys to move the cursor, or click the mouse button once in the text.

Ruler Settings

As was mentioned earlier, the ruler shows the margins, tabs, indent position, and other format settings for the current paragraph. Each paragraph can have its own ruler, although this is not a requirement. Ruler settings can only be changed using the mouse.

Set Tab	Drag any one of the four tab types shown at the bottom left of the ruler to the desired position on the ruler.
Move Tab	Drag any of the current tab positions to the desired position on the ruler.
Delete Tab	Drag any of the current tab positions off the ruler.
Spacing	Highlight the selected paragraph and click the *Single Space, One and a Half,* or *Double Space* option.
Justification	Choose *Left Justify, Center Justify, Full Justify,* or *Right Justify.*
Set Margins	Drag any of the margin indicators to the desired position.

Note: It is recommended that you do not change either the left or right margin positions since extra space is required on each line when a question is printed.

To change the ruler settings for more than one paragraph, highlight all of the desired paragraphs and change the settings.

The **Format** menu includes several other options for working with rulers and formatting the question text.

Copy Ruler	Copies the ruler settings from the current ruler.
Apply Ruler	Applies the copied ruler settings to the selected paragraph(s).
Clear All Tabs	Removes all of the tabs from the current ruler. Affects all selected paragraphs.
Character Format	Displays a dialog box allowing you to change several attributes of the selected text at the same time (font, style, size, and color).
Paragraph	Displays a dialog box allowing you to set off an individual paragraph with lines on any side or entirely enclose the paragraph in a shadowed box.
Color	Displays a dialog box allowing you to set the color of the selected text. If you have a color printer, the *Glencoe Test Generator* software will print the question in color.
Show Codes	While editing a question, you may sometimes insert a carriage return or tab characters in places where you don't want them. Since these characters do not normally appear on your display, it can be frustrating trying to remove them. To make this easier, you can choose the *Show Codes* option. When you choose this option, hard carriage returns are displayed as "¶" and tabs appear as "→". To turn this option off, choose *Hide Codes.*

Fonts, Sizes, and Styles

The *Glencoe Test Generator* allows you to enter text in any font and in a wide variety of text styles (Plain, **Bold**, <u>Underline</u>, *Italic*, Outline, SHADOW) and sizes (9, 10, 12, 14, 18, 24, or any size from 8 to 72 points using the *Other Size* option). Other styles are available by choosing the *Other Style* option (Strikethru, Boxed, Dotted Underline, Double Underline, Superscript, and Subscript). Fonts, sizes, and styles may be changed while you are keying. For example, key "This text is going to be in <⌘+B>Bold<⌘+B>." Changes can also be applied to existing text by highlighting a block and choosing the appropriate font, size, and/or style from the menus. Format changes can be reversed by using the *Undo* option in the **Edit** menu.

Find

Sometimes when editing a longer question, you may want to find a word or phrase quickly. Choose the *Find* option from the **Edit** menu. The dialog box as shown in Figure 4-3 appears on your screen. Enter the text you want to find, set the other options, and click the **Find** button. If the text is found, it will be shown in the main window. If the text appears more than once and you want to search again, simply click the **Find** button again. Click the **Done** button to return to the editing window.

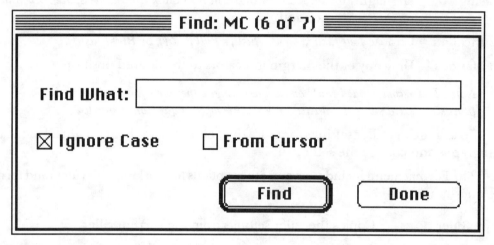

Figure 4-3 Find Dialog Box

Replace

To find and replace text while editing a question, choose the *Replace* option from the **Edit** menu. Enter the text you want to find and the text to replace it with. The software will either ask you before it replaces an occurrence of the text, or not, depending on the Confirm Replace check box setting. You can either elect to replace only the first occurrence (**Replace** button), or every occurrence in this question (**Replace All** button). When you are finished, click the **Done** button.

Replace Font

If you decide that you want to change the font and/or size for a question or all of the questions in a question bank, you can choose the *Replace Font* option. For example, to change the font for every question, answer, and narrative in a bank to Times, and the size to 14, follow these steps:

- Make sure that you are not in editing mode. If you are, the font and size will be changed for just that question.

- Choose the *Replace Font* option.

- Leave the "Replace" font and size set to "Any font" and "Any size" respectively.
- Set the "With" font and size to "Times" and "14" respectively.
- Click the **OK** button. You will be warned and given a chance to cancel the operation. It is important to be careful when using this option, since it cannot be undone.

WORKING WITH QUESTIONS

Once a question has been entered and recorded, the *Glencoe Test Generator* provides a variety of options to work with the questions in the question bank.

Changing an Answer

While viewing or editing a question, click the **Answer** button. If the question type is True/False, Multiple Choice, or Yes/No, a dialog box will appear with a pop-up menu containing valid answer choices. Simply press the letter of the answer (for example, **F** for false, **D** for choice D, **N** for no) and click the **OK** button.

For all other question types, edit the answer in much the same way as you would edit a question. Use any of the editing features mentioned earlier. When you are finished editing the answer, click the **Record** button.

Changing the Question Info

Although not required, each question can be assigned an objective, page reference, difficulty index, and topic. Questions can also be linked to narratives that will be automatically included in the test when printed. To change the question information, click the **Info** button while viewing a question.

The dialog box as shown in Figure 4-4 appears on your screen. Change any or all of the information. If you want to attach a narrative to a question, simply enter the narrative number in the corresponding field. See the "Narratives" section in this manual (p. M-22) for more information.

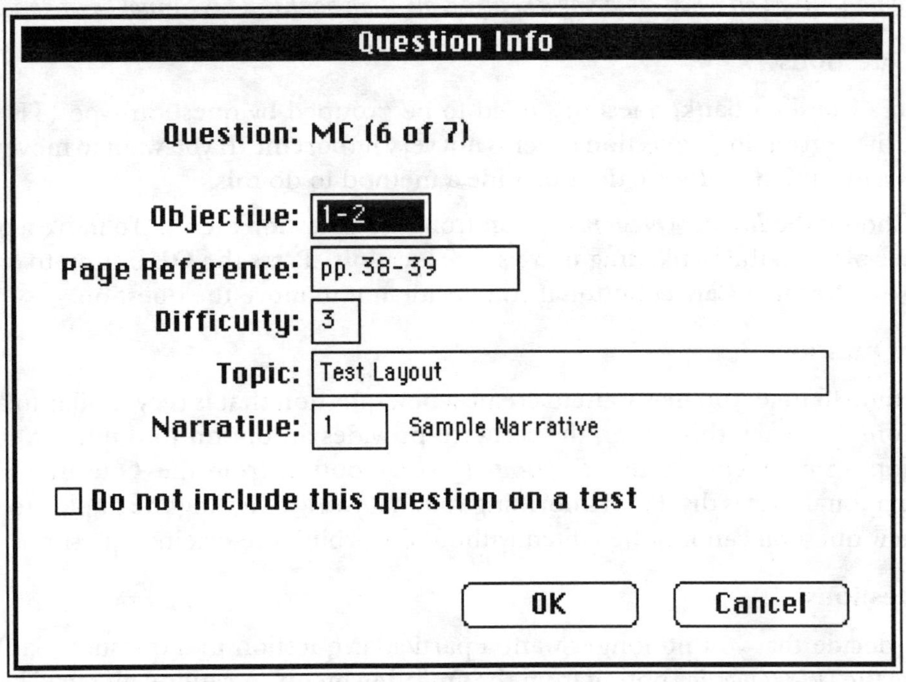

```
┌─────────────────────────────────────────────────────┐
│                   Question Info                      │
│                                                       │
│   Question: MC (6 of 7)                              │
│                                                       │
│        Objective: │1-2 │                             │
│   Page Reference: │pp. 38-39 │                       │
│       Difficulty: │3 │                               │
│            Topic: │Test Layout                    │  │
│        Narrative: │1 │  Sample Narrative             │
│                                                       │
│   ☐ Do not include this question on a test           │
│                                                       │
│                        ( OK )    ( Cancel )          │
└─────────────────────────────────────────────────────┘
```

Figure 4-4 Question Information Dialog Box

In the Question Info dialog box, there is also a check box stating "Do not include this question on a test." If this option is set, the *Glencoe Test Generator* will not select this question for a test when randomly selecting questions. You can use this option if you want to keep a question in the bank but, at least for the time being, do not want to include it on any test.

Narratives

Often, you will want to enter a group of questions that refer to the same descriptive paragraph (narrative) or specialized instruction. The *Glencoe Test Generator* provides an easy but powerful way to do just that. Choose the *Narratives* option from the **Question** menu.

Each narrative consists of a narrative number (1-20), a description (25 characters), and the narrative itself. Up to twenty narratives may be included in any one question bank.

It is important that the description you enter for each narrative be unique. When the software builds a test from selected questions, it uses the narrative description to decide whether or not a particular narrative has already been included in the test.

Once you have entered a narrative description, click the **Add** button to add a new narrative. Enter a narrative as you would enter a question. Click the **OK** button to record the narrative.

If you find that a narrative that was previously entered is no longer needed, use the **Delete** button. To edit an existing narrative, highlight the entry and then click the **Edit** button. Click the **Done** button when you are through working with this dialog box.

Find/Replace

The *Glencoe Test Generator* provides a way to find and/or replace text across multiple questions within a question bank. Use the same options you used when finding and/or replacing text within a question. The software will search through all of the questions in the question bank, displaying them if necessary when it finds the indicated text. To find/replace text across multiple questions, make sure that you are not editing a question when you choose the *Find* or *Replace* options from the **Edit** menu.

Note: Be very careful when using the Replace All button with the Confirm Replace option turned off when replacing text across question banks. This cannot be undone.

Reorder Questions

Within a question bank, questions need to be grouped by question type (TF, MC, etc.). Inside these groupings, question order is not very important. If you want to move a question within a group, the software does provide a method to do this.

Choose the *Reorder Questions* option from the **Question** menu. To move a question to another place in the bank, drag it to its new location. Press the **OK** button to confirm the changes. Press the **Cancel** button if you decide not to move the question.

Duplicate Questions

From time to time, you may want to create a new question that is very similar to an existing question. To make this easier, the software provides an option to duplicate the current question. Simply choose the *Duplicate Question* option from the **Question** menu. An informational alert is displayed informing you that you are viewing the duplicated question. The new question can now be edited without disturbing the original question.

Delete Questions

If you decide that you no longer want a particular question in a question bank, you can choose the *Delete Question* option from the **Question** menu. A caution alert will be displayed asking you to confirm that you want to delete the question. Respond appropriately.

SAVING AND PRINTING

After you edit questions or create new ones, the *Glencoe Test Generator* allows you to save the question bank to disk. Also, you can print a question bank to be used as a reference sheet when selecting questions to build a test.

Saving a Question Bank

From the **File** menu, choose either the *Save* option or the *Save As* option to save your question bank to disk. Use the *Save As* option to assign a new file name or change the location of the file. Key-enter the name and click the **Save** button.

Printing a Question Bank

Printing a question bank is not the same as printing a test. A printed question bank is used more for a reference when building a test. To print a question bank, choose the *Print* option from the **File** menu. Print the entire question bank or the current question.

MISCELLANEOUS FEATURES

In addition to those features already mentioned, the *Glencoe Test Generator* offers the following features while working with the *Edit Question Banks* option. Review the information below.

Context-Sensitive Help

At any point while running the program, you can select the *Help* option from the **Apple** menu. Help can also be brought up using the help key (**⌘+H**). Close the window after viewing the help information.

Get Picture

Pictures (graphic images) can be included right in with the question, answer, or narrative using the *Glencoe Test Generator* software. To retrieve a picture (PICT file) from disk, choose the *Get Picture* option from the **Special** menu while you are in editing mode. Once loaded from disk, the picture will be automatically inserted into the question. To reposition the picture, click on it and drag it to the desired position. If the picture is positioned within a text block, the text will wrap around the picture on all sides.

To resize the picture, click on one of the resize handles as shown in Figure 4-5 and drag it until the picture is the desired size. To reduce the amount of white space surrounding a picture without changing the size of the picture frame, hold down the **Option** key while dragging one of the resize handles.

Pictures can also be cut, copied, or pasted to and from the Clipboard. You can also undo any editing operation on a picture.

New Question Bank

Choose this option (accessed from the **File** menu) to begin an entirely new question bank. Once this option is chosen, you will be prompted to enter the question bank title. Enter any name you want and click the **OK** button. The software displays the main window. Use the **New** button to add questions to the question bank.

Preferences

As in the other program modules, you can use the *Preferences* option from the **Edit** menu to change the software's password and/or the default font. If you do not want to use a password, simply leave the Password field blank.

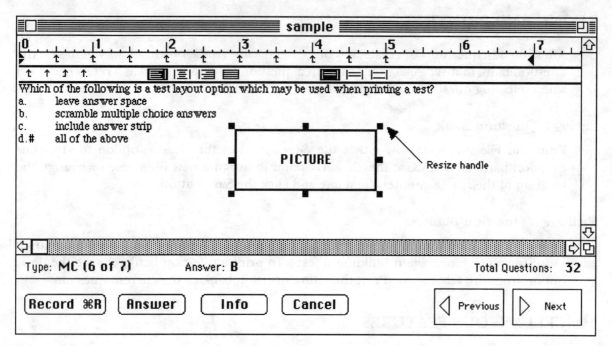

Figure 4-5 Get Picture

Bank Title

When the question bank was originally created, you were asked for a question bank title. If the title was entered incorrectly, or you just want to change it, use the *Bank Title* option from the **Special** menu.

MACINTOSH USER'S GUIDE

SECTION 5–TROUBLESHOOTING

The following troubleshooting guidelines are provided to assist you if you have difficulty using the *Glencoe Test Generator*. If you need further assistance, the Software Support toll-free number is also provided.

COMMONLY ASKED QUESTIONS OR PROBLEMS

I can't locate the question banks or tests on disk.

Use the *Open Question Bank* option in the **File** menu to display the Open dialog box. Change the drive and/or folder.

I can't select question banks from multiple disks while using QuickTest.

After selecting question banks from one disk, click the **Locate** button, eject the question bank disk, and insert the next disk. To tell the software that you switched disks, click the **Done** button. The software will now display the question banks on the new disk.

A menu option is dim and can't be selected.

All of the menu options are not active at all times. For example, the *Close* option in the **File** menu is available only when a window is currently open. Often, while you work in a dialog box, many of the menu options will be inactive.

Printing a test produces an error message or a garbled printout.

If you experience problems printing a test, verify that the printer is on-line, the paper is inserted and aligned properly, and the printer cables are not loose. Try to print again. If the printer does not respond this time, the problem is most likely a hardware problem and not a software issue.

If the printout is garbled, check the *Page Setup* option in the **File** menu. Verify that the correct printer is specified.

Can graphics be created from scratch and used with the test generator?

Yes. Any graphic used with the test generator must be created using a paint program that saves graphics in a PICT format. Use the *Get Picture* command in the **Special** menu to retrieve a picture from disk or simply paste it from the paint program.

I received an error message trying to save a file.

Verify that your data disk has been properly formatted and that it is in the appropriate drive. If you receive a disk full message, remove any unneeded files and then try to save the file again. Also, the disk should not be write-protected. Slide the write-protect switch to the closed position.

There is not enough memory to run the program.

If you receive this error message when you start the program, you must free additional memory. Quit any other open application. A minimum of 900K **free** memory is required to run the program.

There is not enough memory for an operation.

If you create very large question banks or tests, you may encounter this message. Question banks or tests larger than 60 pages should probably be split into smaller units. Large tests can be separated by using the beginning question number option in the Print Test dialog box. If your computer has extra memory, choose the *Get Info* option from the Finder and increase the Preferred size for the program.

MACINTOSH USER'S GUIDE

I am unable to select by criteria.

Not all supplied question banks contain question information (topics, objectives, etc.).

I cannot change the starting question number when printing a test.

The question number cannot be changed if the current test layout option for question numbering is not set to continuous (e.g., MC 1-8 TF 9-25).

Narratives are not printing with the test questions.

If you create your own narrative, you must link the narrative to each of the questions that refer to it. Choose to edit the question information and enter the appropriate narrative number in the field.

A narrative also may not print if you gave it the same name as another narrative already included in the test. Narrative names must be unique.

SOFTWARE SUPPORT CENTER

Glencoe provides toll-free telephone assistance for teachers who experience difficulty while using our software or templates. Before calling for assistance, please check the following:

- Is your computer working properly? Try some other software, which you know is working, on the same computer.
- Are you certain the software is not working properly? Try the software on another computer.
- Can you repeat the problem? Does the software seem to malfunction at the same point each time?

In order for the Support Center to help you as quickly as possible, have the following information at hand before calling for assistance:

- the exact title and ISBN number from the disk label or package
- the brand, model, and configuration of the computer you are using
- the version of the operating system installed on your computer

The Glencoe Support Center toll-free number is **800/437-3715**. The Support Center is available from 8:30 a.m. to 4:00 p.m. Eastern Time.

MACINTOSH USER'S GUIDE

INDEX (MACINTOSH TEST GENERATOR)

CHAPTER OBJECTIVES

CHAPTER 1

1. Measure and record weather data.
2. Predict weather conditions based on observations and measurements.
3. Explain how satellites provide weather data.
4. Describe how radar provides weather data.
5. Explain how Doppler radar works.
6. Interpret a weather map.
7. Predict weather using a weather map.

CHAPTER 2

1. Explain how energy is moved through the atmosphere.
2. Explain how solar energy causes the formation of global winds.
3. Describe the circulation patterns of global winds.
4. Explain the stages of a thunderstorm.
5. Describe some of the consequences of thunderstorms.
6. Describe the formation of a hurricane.
7. Explain how a hurricane moves and weakens.

CHAPTER 3

1. Identify those natural disasters that people can be forewarned about.
2. Determine the source of a hurricane's energy and what happens when the storm leaves its energy source.
3. Explain the different ways that wind associated with a storm causes damages.
4. Determine the other forms of damage associated with the passage of a storm.
5. Explain the effects of natural disasters on the local economy.
6. Describe how periodic disturbances can alter the ecosystem.
7. Identify possible health hazards resulting from the disasters.

CHAPTER 4

1. Recognize that some ecosystems include a larger variety of species than others.
2. Demonstrate that populations of living organisms differ in size and composition.
3. Identify some of the abiotic factors that affect life.
4. Describe how water dissolves substances that are essential for life.

CHAPTER 5

1. Describe the components of an organism's habitat and niche.
2. Relate feeding relationships of organisms to the flow of energy in ecosystems.
3. Identify the different trophic levels in an ecosystem.
4. Compare and contrast the ways carbon, water, and nitrogen cycle through ecosystems.

CHAPTER 6

1. Compare and contrast linear growth and exponential growth.
2. Describe how environmental factors place limits on population growth.
3. Recognize how species' interactions regulate population size.
4. Sequence the events that occur in ecological succession.
5. Describe some effects of human activity on ecosystems.

CHAPTER 7

1. Explain how the basic laws of chemistry apply to life processes.
2. Relate Calories to the energy content of foods.
3. Identify three categories of nutrients.
4. Compare the chemical structures of carbohydrates, lipids, and proteins.
5. Operationally define the lock-and-key model of enzyme activity.
6. Explain how enzymes increase the rate of chemical reactions.
7. Identify how enzyme reactions can be controlled.
8. Explain the process of digestion.
9. Classify the breakdown products of carbohydrate, fat, and protein digestion.

CHAPTER 8

1. Demonstrate the law of conservation of matter through a balanced equation.
2. Describe how carbon is cycled through the environment.
3. Discuss the importance of nitrogen and phosphorus atoms to organisms.
4. Explain how nitrogen and phosphorus atoms are recycled in the ecosystem.
5. Sequence the steps that occur in photosynthesis.
6. Distinguish between anabolic and catabolic reactions.
7. Compare and contrast photosynthesis and respiration.

CHAPTER 9

1. Describe soil.
2. Explain the role of weathering in soil development.
3. Describe how physical and chemical weathering differ.
4. Describe the important factors in soil formation and composition.
5. Compare and contrast the different soil horizons.
6. Describe three methods that can be used to maintain soil fertility.
7. Explain deforestation and its effects.
8. List the essential elements needed for productive soil.

CHAPTER 10

1. Differentiate among various types of pesticides.
2. Compare and contrast the benefits and risks of pesticide use.
3. Compare and contrast organic and nonorganic pest-control methods.
4. Classify chemical preservatives as inhibitors or antioxidants.
5. Explain the process and purpose of pasteurization.
6. Recognize the effects of heat on food.
7. Compare and contrast methods of heating food.

CHAPTER 11

1. Distinguish between renewable and nonrenewable resources.
2. Describe ways in which the sun's energy can be used to generate power.
3. Identify ways of reusing and recycling items to conserve natural resources.
4. Describe the benefits of recycling natural resources.

CHAPTER 12

1. Describe the origins, features, and types of igneous rocks.
2. Explain how igneous rocks can be a useful resource.
3. Describe the origins and types of sedimentary rocks.
4. Identify sources of minerals for automobiles within sedimentary rocks.
5. Identify the various types of metamorphism.
6. Discuss metamorphic rocks as sources for automotive minerals.
7. Compare origins of the classes of rock using the rock cycle.

CHAPTER 13

1. Explain what petroleum is and how it forms.
2. Relate properties of rocks to migration and trapping of petroleum.
3. Classify and sequence steps in the search for oil.
4. Compare and contrast oil-exploration methods.
5. Determine the composition of petroleum.
6. Describe petroleum refining.
7. Describe many petroleum products and their uses.

CHAPTER 14

1. Evaluate the costs and benefits of the three main final destinations for solid waste.
2. Discuss conditions that help determine whether a product is recyclable.
3. Trace the process of recycling a car.
4. Describe the methods used in recycling glass, steel, and plastics.
5. Discuss the advantages of recycling glass, steel, plastics, and other minerals.
6. Discuss three ways a person can help reduce solid wastes and conserve natural resources.
7. Identify four methods of source reduction.

CHAPTER 15

1. Classify the types of weathering and how they affect the selection of building sites.
2. Compare and contrast types of soil movement caused by gravity.
3. Classify and investigate factors that lead to flooding.
4. Infer how stream erosion can affect the selection of a home site.
5. Describe how wave action can make houses collapse.
6. Explain the hazards that earthquakes pose to buildings.
7. Describe ways to minimize earthquake hazards.

CHAPTER 16

1. Identify the forces that buildings must withstand.
2. Describe construction techniques that result in sturdy buildings.
3. Classify building materials as natural or artificial.
4. Compare building materials based on their properties.
5. Explain the electron-sea model for metallic bonding.
6. Demonstrate how an alloy is formed.
7. Identify modern materials that are used in buildings.
8. Explain the advantages and disadvantages of using modern materials.

CHAPTER 17

1. Compare and contrast weight and mass.
2. Explain why center of gravity is important in moving large objects.
3. Describe the causes and effects of contact forces.
4. Identify situations where work is being done on an object.
5. Explain the difference between work and power.
6. Distinguish between mechanical advantage and efficiency.
7. Identify the main purposes of simple machines.
8. Give examples and classify some commonly used simple machines.

CHAPTER 18

1. Compare and contrast the transfer of heat by conduction, convection, and radiation.
2. Differentiate between thermal conductors and insulators.
3. Explain the use of insulators in buildings.
4. Identify several types of conventional heating systems.
5. Describe how air conditioners and refrigerators transfer heat.
6. Distinguish between passive and active solar-heating systems.
7. Explain why water is a good material for storing thermal energy.

CHAPTER 19

1. Contrast direct current and alternating current.
2. Calculate the power and energy use of appliances in the home or school.
3. Explain the function of resistance in an electrical circuit.
4. Demonstrate that the currents in the paths of a parallel circuit are independent.

CHAPTER 20

1. Relate the concept of homeostasis to the causes of disease.
2. Review the functions of major organs and systems of the human body.
3. Describe how organisms cause communicable diseases.
4. Compare and contrast the primary characteristics of bacteria, protists, fungi, and viruses.
5. Explain how heart disease and skin cancer develop.
6. Determine how a genetic disease is passed from parent to offspring.

CHAPTER 21

1. Identify the body's defenses against infection.
2. Explain how the inflammatory response helps rid the body of pathogens.
3. Compare and contrast active and passive immunity.
4. Sequence the steps involved in developing antibody immunity.
5. Differentiate between antibody immunity and cellular immunity.
6. Explain how autoimmune disorders affect the body.
7. Explain how vaccines stimulate the development of active immunity.
8. Compare the effects on disease of chemical drugs, radiation, and other therapies.

CHAPTER 22

1. Name some common symptoms of disease.
2. Explain how external examination is used to diagnose disease.
3. Explain how the pathogen responsible for a disease is identified.
4. Distinguish between epidemic and endemic disease.
5. Explain how body fluids are used to diagnose disease.
6. Distinguish between passive transport and active transport.
7. Explain how electrophoresis is used to identify microorganisms and biological molecules.
8. Describe how a light microscope enlarges an image.
9. Explain how X rays, ultrasound, and magnetic resonance imaging are used to diagnose disease.

CHAPTER 23

1. Experiment with balanced forces resulting in constant speed. .
2. Describe how an unbalanced force produces acceleration.
3. Explain the concept of momentum.
4. Compare gravity and contact forces.
5. Explore the acceleration of a falling object.
6. Define weight.
7. Describe how an object reaches terminal speed.
8. Relate air drag to an object's shape.
9. Explore lift.

CHAPTER 24

1. Compare which bird flight structures are equivalent to the parts of an airplane.
2. Explain how the shapes of bird and plane wings vary with the fliers' sizes and the type of flying to be done.
3. Model how birds and planes change direction in flight.
4. Explain the various flight styles birds use to obtain thrust.
5. Describe how birds obtain the energy needed for flight.
6. Compare methods different aircraft use for providing thrust.
7. Describe some adaptations that allow seeds to be spread as widely as possible.
8. Distinguish between winged seeds and those that use parachutes.

CHAPTER 25

1. Describe the uses of space-based observations of Earth.
2. Explain the uses of space-based observations of the planets and stars.
3. Explain how a rocket accelerates a spaceship.
4. Compare the kinds of propellants used in liquid- and solid-fuel rockets.
5. Describe the speeds required for travel in space and means of attaining those speeds.

CHAPTER 1—WEATHER PREDICTION

MULTIPLE CHOICE

1. A knot is a unit commonly used to measure wind speed and equals _____.
   a. 1 mile per hour
   b. 10 miles per hour
   c. 1.5 miles per hour
   d. 0.5 mile per hour

   ANS: C   DIF: A   OBJ: 1-1

2. The jet stream is _____.
   a. a high-altitude river of air
   b. the exhaust trail left behind a high-speed jet aircraft
   c. a slow-moving air mass over the Gulf of Mexico
   d. in the Pacific Ocean off California

   ANS: A   DIF: A   OBJ: 1-6

3. Meteorologists are scientists who study _____.
   a. meteorites
   b. weather
   c. the metric system
   d. metals

   ANS: B   DIF: B   OBJ: 1-7

4. Doppler radar systems are used _____.
   a. to locate storms
   b. to track weather balloons
   c. to determine air temperature
   d. to determine barometric pressure

   ANS: A   DIF: B   OBJ: 1-5

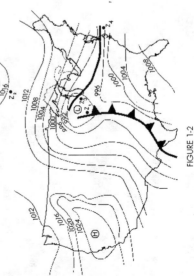

FIGURE 1-2

5. In Figure 1-2, which of the following describes the location of the cold front? _____
   a. extending south from the low
   b. extending east from the low
   c. covering an extensive part of Canada
   d. located in the northwest

   ANS: A   DIF: B   OBJ: 1-6

6. In Figure 1-2, the cold front is moving _____.
   a. to the east
   b. upward
   c. to the west
   d. nowhere

   ANS: A   DIF: B   OBJ: 1-6

7. At point Z_2 in Figure 1-2, the wind is blowing from the _____.
   a. north
   b. southwest
   c. east
   d. west

   ANS: A   DIF: B   OBJ: 1-6

8. What would the weather at point Z_1 in Figure 1-2 probably be like?
   a. gray, cloudy, rain or snow
   b. sunny, warm
   c. clear skies, cool
   d. sunny, very hot

   ANS: A   DIF: B   OBJ: 1-7

FIGURE 1-1

9. The cluster of symbols shown in Figure 1-1 is called _____.
   a. an isobar
   b. a weather forecast
   c. a satellite data point
   d. a station model

   ANS: D   DIF: B   OBJ: 1-6

10. The wind direction shown in Figure 1-1 is from the _____.
    a. north
    b. southwest
    c. southeast
    d. east

    ANS: C   DIF: B   OBJ: 1-6

3. A north wind is blowing _____ the north.

ANS: from   DIF: B   OBJ: 1-2

4. During the night, weather satellites receive data by means of _____ radiation to determine temperature differences.

ANS: infrared   DIF: A   OBJ: 1-3

5. Warm objects give off _____ infrared radiation than cooler objects.

ANS: more   DIF: B   OBJ: 1-3

6. _____ form when water vapor high in the air condenses.

ANS: Clouds   DIF: B   OBJ: 1-2

7. The _____ is reached when air cools to the temperature at which the water vapor in the air condenses.

ANS: dew point   DIF: A   OBJ: 1-1

8. A(n) _____ remains over, and takes pictures of, the same spot on Earth.

ANS: geostationary satellite   DIF: B   OBJ: 1-3

9. The phenomenon in which an approaching object produces a higher-pitched sound than an object that is moving away is called the _____.

ANS: Doppler effect   DIF: B   OBJ: 1-5

10. Winds may blow at more than 250 knots in the high-altitude river of air called the _____.

ANS: jet stream   DIF: A   OBJ: 1-2

11. _____ is always expressed as a percent and is equal to the amount of water vapor in the air/amount of water vapor the air can hold at that temperature times 100 percent.

ANS: Relative humidity   DIF: B   OBJ: 1-1

12. Lines called _____ connect areas of equal atmospheric pressure on a weather map.

ANS: isobars   DIF: B   OBJ: 1-6

13. As air molecules flow from areas of high pressure to areas of low pressure, _____ is created.

ANS: wind   DIF: B   OBJ: 1-2

11. The temperature in degrees Fahrenheit shown in Figure 1-1 is _____.
   a. 82
   b. 92
   c. 10
   d. not listed

ANS: A   DIF: B   OBJ: 1-6

12. What type of precipitation is shown in Figure 1-1?
   a. rain
   b. snow
   c. hail
   d. none

ANS: D   DIF: B   OBJ: 1-6

13. What is the barometric pressure shown by Figure 1-1?
   a. 305 millibars
   b. 1030.5 millibars
   c. 1082.0 millibars
   d. 1000.0 millibars

ANS: B   DIF: B   OBJ: 1-6

14. How much cloud cover is there shown by Figure 1-1?
   a. 100%
   b. 50%
   c. 75%
   d. 25%

ANS: D   DIF: B   OBJ: 1-6

15. According to Figure 1-1, what was the change in barometric pressure recorded in the last three hours?
   a. +10 millibars
   b. -10 millibars
   c. +10 degrees
   d. 82 millibars

ANS: A   DIF: B   OBJ: 1-6

COMPLETION

1. If an isobar is a line connecting points of equal atmospheric pressure, an isotherm is a line connecting points of equal _____.

ANS: temperature   DIF: B   OBJ: 1-2

2. Long-range (five- to six-day) weather forecasts are based on _____.

ANS: weather trends   DIF: A   OBJ: 1-2

14. The _____ pressure is the measure of the pressure caused by the weight of the atmosphere.

ANS: barometric   DIF: A   OBJ: 1-1

15. The cluster of symbols that describes the weather at a certain location on a weather map is called a(n) _____.

ANS: station model   DIF: B   OBJ: 1-6

16. A(n) _____ system can detect wind velocities and clear air disturbances, not just precipitation.

ANS: Doppler radar   DIF: B   OBJ: 1-5

MATCHING

Match each item with the correct statement below. Write the answer in the space provided.

a. cirrus clouds
b. psychrometer
c. nimbostratus clouds
d. cumulonimbus clouds
e. stratus clouds
f. barometer
g. thermometer
h. high-altitude satellite photographs
i. wind vane
j. anemometer

1. _____ Instrument that measures wind speed.
2. _____ Instrument that measures wind direction.
3. _____ Instrument that measures temperature.
4. _____ Used to track and model major storm systems.
5. _____ Instrument used to measure relative humidity.
6. _____ Large, tall clouds, commonly associated with thunderstorms.
7. _____ Low, flat, dark gray clouds producing rain.
8. _____ High, thin, fibrous clouds that often are the first signs of a storm.
9. _____ Sheetlike clouds.
10. _____ Instrument used to measure air pressure.

1. ANS: j   DIF: B   OBJ: 1-1
2. ANS: i   DIF: B   OBJ: 1-1
3. ANS: g   DIF: B   OBJ: 1-1
4. ANS: h   DIF: B   OBJ: 1-3
5. ANS: b   DIF: B   OBJ: 1-3
6. ANS: d   DIF: B   OBJ: 1-2
7. ANS: c   DIF: B   OBJ: 1-2
8. ANS: a   DIF: B   OBJ: 1-2
9. ANS: e   DIF: B   OBJ: 1-2
10. ANS: f   DIF: B   OBJ: 1-1

SHORT ANSWER

1. List six pieces of information that might be found on a station model.

ANS: temperature, dew point, cloud cover, types of clouds, barometric pressure, wind speed, wind direction, change in barometric pressure, type of precipitation, visibility

DIF: A   OBJ: 1-6

2. What does a weather map show?

ANS: where weather systems are and where they are likely to go

DIF: B   OBJ: 1-6

3. What information do meteorologists get from weather satellites?

ANS: extent of cloud cover, location, and size of storms

DIF: A   OBJ: 1-3

4. How can isobars give an indication of wind speed?

ANS: The closer together the isobars, the faster the winds.

DIF: A   OBJ: 1-6

5. Why do winds have higher speeds over oceans than over land?

ANS: Friction slows winds down, and there is less friction over water than over land.

DIF: A   OBJ: 1-2

6. What are microclimates?

ANS: isolated areas where the weather is different from the surrounding areas

DIF: A   OBJ: 1-2

7. Why does an accurate weather forecast require knowing distant climatic conditions?

ANS: Weather moves around the globe, bringing weather changes. Good forecasting requires these data.

DIF: A   OBJ: 1-2

8. A weather vane points to the southwest. How would you describe the wind that is blowing?

ANS: It is described as a southwest wind, blowing from the southwest toward the northeast.

DIF: B   OBJ: 1-2

16. Why does the air feel drier in the winter than in the summer?

ANS: Air generally holds less water vapor at colder temperatures than at warmer ones; therefore, the winter air feels drier than summer air as a result of its naturally lower relative humidity.

DIF: A   OBJ: 1-2

17. In a region with a mountain range oriented north-south and prevailing winds that move weather fronts from west to east, why will one side of the mountain range have more precipitation?

ANS: As air masses move up over the mountains, the air cools and cannot hold as much moisture. As the air mass cools, it drops its moisture on the west side of the mountains, and the air that reaches the east side is cooler and drier.

DIF: A   OBJ: 1-2

18. Explain the basic principle on which a Doppler radar system works.

ANS: As a sound wave approaches the receiver, the wavelength of the sound becomes crowded together and shorter. The shorter the sound wavelength, the higher the pitch or frequency of the sound. A Doppler radar system sends out a radio signal. If it is received back at a higher pitch, the object (usually a storm system) is moving toward the sender, and a lower pitch indicates it is moving away.

DIF: B   OBJ: 1-5

19. Why are you more hot and uncomfortable on a summer day when the relative humidity is high?

ANS: Your body's cooling mechanism is evaporation (sweating), a cooling process. When the humidity is high, the air is nearly saturated with water and your sweat evaporates much more slowly. Slower evaporation equals less cooling.

DIF: B   OBJ: 1-2

20. How does a thermometer work?

ANS: Matter expands where heated. When a thermometer warms, the liquid expands more than the glass of the tube, and the liquid level rises.

DIF: B   OBJ: 1-1

21. How are weather maps prepared?

ANS: Every six hours, weather stations all over the world transmit data to central locations. Meteorologists at each center plot these data on maps. Then they draw isobars and mark the locations of fronts and high- and low-pressure areas.

DIF: A   OBJ: 1-6

1-8

---

9. When does frost form?

ANS: when the dew point is reached at a temperature below the freezing level

DIF: A   OBJ: 1-2

10. Explain the relationship between isobars on a weather map and wind speed and direction.

ANS: Wind flows from areas of high pressure to areas of low pressure, hence from one isobar to the one closest to it. The closer the isobars, the faster the wind.

DIF: A   OBJ: 1-6

11. How is the weather information collected by satellites and by radar different?

ANS: Satellite pictures just show where clouds are. Radar can determine which clouds are producing precipitation.

DIF: A   OBJ: 1-4

12. Why is it better to exercise when the relative humidity is low?

ANS: In high relative humidity, the air is already nearly saturated with water vapor, causing your sweat to evaporate much more slowly, and decreasing the cooling effect normally provided by the perspiration.

DIF: A   OBJ: 1-2

13. How is Doppler radar different from conventional radar?

ANS: Doppler radar can provide data on the speed of moving objects within a storm, an improvement over conventional radar. Also, Doppler radar uses radio signals; conventional radar uses microwaves.

DIF: A   OBJ: 1-5

14. Why are weather satellites important meteorological tools?

ANS: Satellites provide an overall picture of huge weather systems. A series of these pictures shows the speed and direction of a storm system.

DIF: B   OBJ: 1-3

15. How do weather satellites distinguish cloud cover at night?

ANS: At night, satellites sense infrared radiation from Earth. Cloud tops are cooler than clear areas.

DIF: A   OBJ: 1-3

1-7

22. Why does a mass of air with low pressure bring a gray day?

ANS: Air with low pressure has a low density. Because of this, the air rises and cools until the air reaches its dew point. Water vapor in the air mass condenses, forming clouds.

DIF: A   OBJ: 1-7

23. What discovery led meteorologist Edward Lorenz to conclude that successful long-range weather forecasting was impossible?

ANS: He accidentally found that equations describing weather are extremely sensitive to initial conditions, that slight alterations will totally change final results. Lorenz concluded, therefore, that long-range forecasting was impossible.

DIF: A   OBJ: 1-7

24. How are relative humidity and the dew point related?

ANS: The dew point depends on the relative humidity. When relative humidity is high, water condenses at a higher temperature.

DIF: A   OBJ: 1-1

25. How do meteorologists use the isobars on a weather map?

ANS: Isobars indicate wind speed and direction and the location of high- and low-pressure areas.

DIF: A   OBJ: 1-7

26. Write a short weather forecast for your local area. Describe an approaching front system, and discuss wind speed, humidity and precipitation levels, and storm developments.

ANS: Variable. Example: The approaching warm front will bring thunderstorms and heavy rain by tomorrow night. Wind will be from the west at 5 to 10 miles an hour and humidity will increase to 80 percent. Tornadoes might be a possibility.

DIF: A   OBJ: 1-2

OTHER

If the underscored word or phrase makes the sentence true, write "true" in the space provided. If the underscored word or phrase makes the sentence false, write the correct term or phrase in the space provided.

1. If you are enjoying a beautiful day of sunshine and cloudless, blue skies, the barometric readings are probably high.

ANS: true   DIF: A   OBJ: 1-2

2. The barometric readings are generally high during gray, cloudy, and rainy days.

ANS: low   DIF: A   OBJ: 1-2

3. Air is generally drier in the summer.

ANS: wetter   DIF: B   OBJ: 1-2

4. A knot is a unit commonly used to measure wind speed.

ANS: true   DIF: B   OBJ: 1-1

5. The amount of infrared radiation an object gives off per unit of surface is related to its size.

ANS: temperature   DIF: A   OBJ: 1-3

6. High-altitude satellites provide data about wind direction, wind speed, and precipitation.

ANS: Doppler radar systems   DIF: B   OBJ: 1-5

7. Doppler radar systems send out microwaves to provide information about storms used by weather forecasters.

ANS: radio signals   DIF: B   OBJ: 1-5

CHAPTER 2—SEVERE WEATHER

MULTIPLE CHOICE

1. The energy transferred from an object at a higher temperature to an object at a lower temperature is called ____.
   a. temperature
   b. heat
   c. convection
   d. potential energy

   ANS: B   DIF: B   OBJ: 2-1

2. Global winds do not blow directly north or south because of ____.
   a. gravity, which is greater at the poles and deflects winds to the east and west
   b. the magnetic field of Earth, which deflects the winds
   c. the Coriolis effect
   d. the tilt of Earth's axis

   ANS: C   DIF: B   OBJ: 2-3

3. Global winds in the northern hemisphere appear to be turning ____.
   a. clockwise
   b. to the north
   c. counterclockwise
   d. to the left

   ANS: A   DIF: A   OBJ: 2-3

4. Hurricanes get their energy from ____.
   a. warm water
   b. tropical depressions
   c. friction over the ocean
   d. cumulonimbus clouds

   ANS: A   DIF: A   OBJ: 2-6

5. The cumulus stage of a thunderstorm is characterized by ____.
   a. violent lightning
   b. heavy rain
   c. rapid upward movement of warm, moist air
   d. formation of tornadoes

   ANS: C   DIF: B   OBJ: 2-4

6. Tropical air masses do NOT ____.
   a. have warm, moist air
   b. have strong winds in the center
   c. rise and produce high pressure
   d. turn into hurricanes

   ANS: C   DIF: B   OBJ: 2-6

7. Hurricanes ____.
   a. move opposite to the prevailing global winds
   b. gain even more power from warm land masses
   c. have interiors that are colder than the surrounding air
   d. have eyes with little or no winds

   ANS: D   DIF: B   OBJ: 2-7

8. Which statement is characteristic of a hurricane?
   a. The spinning, spiraling movement is caused by the Coriolis effect.
   b. Air rushes skyward in the storm's center.
   c. Moisture condenses into tiny droplets that form clouds.
   d. all of the above

   ANS: D   DIF: B   OBJ: 2-6

9. Hurricanes over land ____.
   a. gain a new source of energy
   b. lose their source of energy
   c. encounter decreased friction
   d. have a more organized air flow

   ANS: B   DIF: B   OBJ: 2-6

COMPLETION

1. ____ is the transfer of energy in the form of electromagnetic waves.

   ANS: Radiation   DIF: B   OBJ: 2-1

2. The condition of Earth's atmosphere at any particular place and time is called ____.

   ANS: weather   DIF: B   OBJ: 2-1

3. The ____ is the deflection of a moving object from its original position as seen by observers on Earth's surface.

   ANS: Coriolis effect   DIF: A   OBJ: 2-6

4. Only ____ percent of the total incoming solar radiation is transmitted through the atmosphere and absorbed at Earth's surface.

   ANS: 50   DIF: A   OBJ: 2-1

5. As the kinetic energy of the molecules of an object increases, the ____ of the object increases.

   ANS: temperature   DIF: B   OBJ: 2-1

6. Global winds are deflected to the east/west because of the ____.

   ANS: Coriolis effect   DIF: B   OBJ: 2-3

7. Cumulus, mature, and dissipating stages are characteristic of a _____ life cycle.

ANS: thunderstorm's   DIF: B   OBJ: 2-4

8. _____ may result when charges in a cloud become separated.

ANS: Lightning   DIF: B   OBJ: 2-5

9. Evaporation is a _____ process.

ANS: cooling   DIF: B   OBJ: 2-1

10. Hurricane season in the southeastern United States is commonly during the fall and _____ seasons.

ANS: summer   DIF: A   OBJ: 2-6

11. The center of a hurricane is characterized by _____ barometric pressures.

ANS: low   DIF: A   OBJ: 2-6

12. The _____ stage of a thunderstorm occurs when the storm contains only downdrafts and the clouds begin to dissolve.

ANS: dissipative   DIF: B   OBJ: 2-4

13. The sound wave formed by the rapid expansion and contraction of air caused by lightning is known as _____.

ANS: thunder   DIF: A   OBJ: 2-5

14. In the United States, the forecasting of dangerous weather situations such as severe thunderstorms, hurricanes, and tornadoes is the job of the _____.

ANS: National Weather Service   DIF: B   OBJ: 2-1

15. _____ are violent local disturbances that may develop during the mature stage of severe thunderstorms.

ANS: Tornadoes   DIF: A   OBJ: 2-5

16. The air mass over the Canadian Arctic is characterized by _____ and _____ air.

ANS: cold, dry   DIF: A   OBJ: 2-3

17. _____ occur in desert areas when several inches of rain fall after long periods without significant rainfall.

ANS: Flash floods   DIF: A   OBJ: 2-5

18. The area in the center of a hurricane that is clear and has little or no wind is the _____.

ANS: eye   DIF: B   OBJ: 2-7

19. Global winds such as the trade winds and the westerlies are called _____.

ANS: prevailing winds   DIF: B   OBJ: 2-3

20. The transfer of heat within a fluid by movement of the fluid from warmer areas to cooler areas is called _____.

ANS: convection   DIF: B   OBJ: 2-1

MATCHING

Match each item with the correct statement below. Write the answer in the space provided.

a. tornadoes
b. typhoon
c. convection
d. blocking high
e. radar
f. meteorologist
g. Coriolis effect
h. evaporation
i. heat
j. conduction
k. tropical depression
l. lightning
m. air mass
n. weather
o. radiation

1. _____ A transfer of heat within a fluid by movement of the fluid from warmer areas to cooler areas.
2. _____ radio detection and ranging
3. _____ hurricane in the Pacific Ocean
4. _____ scientist who studies weather
5. _____ local storms in which winds rotate rapidly around areas of low air pressure
6. _____ Earth's rotation deflecting global winds
7. _____ method of heat transfer allowing the sun to warm Earth
8. _____ energy transferred from a hotter object to a cooler object
9. _____ transfer of heat between objects in contact
10. _____ change of a liquid into a gas
11. _____ condition of Earth's atmosphere at any given time or place
12. _____ a large part of the atmosphere with similar characteristics
13. _____ air mass of low pressure just north or south of equator
14. _____ visible electrical emission from a charged cloud
15. _____ air mass able to stall or change movement of a tropical storm

1. ANS: c   DIF: B   OBJ: 2-1
2. ANS: e   DIF: B   OBJ: 2-4
3. ANS: b   DIF: A   OBJ: 2-6
4. ANS: f   DIF: B   OBJ: 2-3
5. ANS: a   DIF: A   OBJ: 2-5
6. ANS: g   DIF: B   OBJ: 2-7
7. ANS: o   DIF: B   OBJ: 2-1
8. ANS: i   DIF: B   OBJ: 2-1

9. ANS: j   DIF: B   OBJ: 2-1
10. ANS: h   DIF: B   OBJ: 2-1
11. ANS: n   DIF: B   OBJ: 2-2
12. ANS: m   DIF: A   OBJ: 2-7
13. ANS: k   DIF: B   OBJ: 2-4
14. ANS: l   DIF: B   OBJ: 2-5
15. ANS: d   DIF: A   OBJ: 2-7

SHORT ANSWER

1. Why is it necessary to add more energy to water at the boiling point in order to vaporize the water?

   ANS: A molecule of gaseous water has more energy than a molecule of liquid water at the same temperature.

   DIF: A   OBJ: 2-1

2. What happens to a hurricane that stays in the open ocean?

   ANS: It is eventually moved into the cool North Atlantic by the prevailing winds. There, evaporation is slower. The storm loses its source of energy. It is downgraded and eventually breaks up into a series of thundershowers.

   DIF: A   OBJ: 2-7

3. Explain briefly how the prevailing winds and blocking highs can affect the path of a typical Atlantic hurricane.

   ANS: The prevailing winds generally move the hurricanes westward across the Atlantic Ocean. Usually, as the storms near the eastern U.S., they move to the north because of the trade winds. If the hurricane encounters a large, high-pressure air mass (blocking high), it will be diverted around the high-pressure area, commonly due west.

   DIF: A   OBJ: 2-7

4. What commonly happens to a hurricane when it makes landfall?

   ANS: Friction over land is much greater, causing winds to decrease and the spiral wind pattern to be disrupted. Once over land, the storm is cut off from its energy source of warm, moist air and warm ocean water. Over land, the hurricane breaks up.

   DIF: B   OBJ: 2-7

5. How does a blocking high prevent a hurricane from moving into the high-pressure area?

   ANS: Air masses that contain high pressure produce strong winds that blow outward and keep a hurricane from advancing.

   DIF: A   OBJ: 2-7

6. How is the layer of air just above Earth warmed by solar radiation?

   ANS: Solar radiation is transmitted through the atmosphere and absorbed at the surface of Earth. The air is heated by contact with the warm earth. Conduction transfers heat from Earth to the molecules of the air.

   DIF: A   OBJ: 2-1

7. Explain in terms of energy why rising warm air eventually cools.

   ANS: As air rises, it expands. The energy needed for the molecules to move apart comes from the energy absorbed by the air molecules. As the molecules do the work of expanding, heat energy is used up and the air cools.

   DIF: B   OBJ: 2-2

8. How does a global convection cell work? Explain the full cycle.

   ANS: Air is warmed at the equator, gets less dense, is pushed upward, and moves northward or southward. The rising air expands, uses energy to expand, and cools. It becomes more dense and sinks back toward Earth.

   DIF: A   OBJ: 2-3

9. Why does water vapor condensing into rain cause the storm cloud to heat up?

   ANS: Heat absorbed by molecules when they change from liquid to gas is released as they change from gas to liquid.

   DIF: A   OBJ: 2-4

10. What causes the air at the edges of the thunderstorm to move downward?

    ANS: the weight of the rain

    DIF: A   OBJ: 2-5

11. Why is it difficult to predict a hurricane's path?

    ANS: Varying local weather conditions determine the path.

    DIF: B   OBJ: 2-7

FIGURE 2-1

12. Figure 2-1 shows an example of what concept?

ANS: the Coriolis effect

DIF: B   OBJ: 2-3

13. How is our weather affected by the process shown in Figure 2-1?

ANS: Winds blowing north and south appear to be turned by the spinning of Earth.

DIF: B   OBJ: 2-3

14. Explain the balance between solar radiation and Earth's radiation from pole to pole.

ANS: The greatest amount of solar radiation is received at the equator and the least at the poles. However, Earth also radiates energy from its surface. From the poles to about 40 degrees, the amount of energy radiated from Earth's surface is greater than the amount reaching it from the sun. From 40 degrees north latitude to 40 degrees south latitude, more solar energy reaches the surface than is radiated back from the surface.

DIF: A   OBJ: 2-1

15. If Earth did not rotate, what would the atmospheric circulation patterns most likely look like?

ANS: Global winds would blow directly north or south rather than curving to the left or right. There would still be the three major convection cells in each hemisphere.

DIF: A   OBJ: 2-3

16. What causes hail to form during a thunderstorm?

ANS: The rapid upward movement of air during the storm can reach heights of 25 km at speeds of up to 300 km/hr, and water freezes at the high altitudes. Ice pellets may make many trips up and down in the updrafts and downdrafts, adding a layer of ice on each trip, until they become too heavy and fall as hail.

DIF: A   OBJ: 2-5

17. What happens to the total incoming solar radiation on the way to Earth's surface?

ANS: Some is absorbed by the clouds and atmosphere (20 percent), and approximately 30 percent is reflected back to space from the atmosphere, the clouds, and the surface of Earth. The remaining 50 percent is transmitted through the atmosphere and absorbed at Earth's surface.

DIF: A   OBJ: 2-1

18. Why does the Coriolis effect make winds appear to curve to the right in the northern hemisphere?

ANS: Moving air at the equator has a higher eastward velocity than Earth's surface at higher latitudes. As air from the equator moves northward, because of inertia it travels farther eastward than Earth's surface at the higher latitudes. Therefore, the winds appear to curve to the right.

DIF: A   OBJ: 2-3

19. Compare the mature and dissipative stages of a thunderstorm.

ANS: The mature stage begins when rainfall starts, while the dissipative stage begins when the storm contains only downdrafts and clouds begin to dissolve. While the mature stage has mostly upward air movement, the dissipative stage has none.

DIF: A   OBJ: 2-4

20. Hurricane Allie hits land. At the same time, Hurricane Buster follows the Gulf Stream along the East Coast of Florida. Which hurricane will last longer and why?

ANS: Hurricane Allie will probably die out soon after hitting land because it no longer has access to warm water, its energy source. Hurricane Buster will last longer because it is moving over the warm water in the Atlantic Ocean.

DIF: A   OBJ: 2-7

21. How does the Coriolis effect influence the path of a hurricane?

ANS: The Coriolis effect from the spinning of Earth causes winds in the latitude where hurricanes form to blow from east to west. Many hurricanes form in the Atlantic Ocean off the west coast of Africa and are blown toward the west.

DIF: A   OBJ: 2-7

22. How does solar energy cause the formation of global winds?

ANS: More solar radiation is received near Earth's equator. The warm water at the equator warms the air, starting convection cells or global movements of air.

DIF: B   OBJ: 2-2

23. Hurricane Andrew struck Florida on the east coast, went across the land, traveled across the Gulf of Mexico, and struck the coast of Louisiana. Why didn't it die over Florida?

ANS: Wind circulation transports warm, moist air to all parts of the storm even when the storm is over land. Andrew must have been big enough to get energy from the Atlantic while over Florida. Then, because Florida is narrow, it began picking up energy from the warm water of the Gulf.

DIF: A   OBJ: 2-7

24. How does evaporation contribute to the development of storms?

ANS: Air that is moist or becomes moist through evaporation of water becomes less dense. Moist air is less dense than the surrounding air and rises until it cools. Then it can return to Earth in a storm. Also, the air absorbs energy as water evaporates. Energy is later released when water vapor condenses, giving the storm more energy.

DIF: A   OBJ: 2-4

MULTIPLE CHOICE

1. Which of the following natural disasters can NOT be accurately predicted with present technology?
   a. floods
   b. blizzards
   c. hurricanes
   d. earthquakes

   ANS: D   DIF: B   OBJ: 3-1

2. Floods can cause _____.
   a. loss of public services (electricity, gas, and phones)
   b. the spread of infectious disease
   c. the destruction of homes, roads, and bridges
   d. all of the above

   ANS: D   DIF: B   OBJ: 3-4

3. The forward speed of hurricanes is usually _____
   a. 12–14 mph
   b. 60 mph
   c. 35 mph
   d. 150 mph

   ANS: A   DIF: A   OBJ: 3-2

4. Hurricanes generally last _____.
   a. a few days
   b. a few hours
   c. a few minutes
   d. a month or more

   ANS: A   DIF: A   OBJ: 3-2

5. Severe storms such as hurricanes cause problems including _____.
   a. economic damage
   b. ecological damage
   c. health concerns
   d. all of the above

   ANS: D   DIF: B   OBJ: 3-5

6. Floods can cause disease by _____.
   a. cutting off clean water supplies
   b. causing forest fires
   c. destroying bridges
   d. raising the salinity

   ANS: A   DIF: B   OBJ: 3-7

OTHER

If the underscored word or phrase makes the sentence true, write "true" in the space provided. If the underscored word or phrase makes the sentence false, write the correct term or phrase in the space provided.

1. The transfer of heat between objects that are in contact is called <u>convection</u>. _____

   ANS: conduction   DIF: B   OBJ: 2-1

2. <u>Radiation</u> is the transfer of energy in the form of electromagnetic waves. _____

   ANS: true   DIF: B   OBJ: 2-1

3. <u>Condensation</u> is the change of a liquid into a gas. _____

   ANS: Evaporation   DIF: B   OBJ: 2-4

4. Air containing water vapor is <u>more</u> dense than dry air under similar pressure and temperature conditions. _____

   ANS: less   DIF: B   OBJ: 2-4

5. Global winds form <u>two</u> global convection cells in the northern hemisphere. _____

   ANS: three   DIF: B   OBJ: 2-3

7. Weather forecasters track hurricanes with _____.
   a. aircraft
   b. Doppler radar
   c. satellites
   d. all of the above

   ANS: D   DIF: B   OBJ: 3-1

8. Scientists from the _____ study and track hurricanes.
   a. International Red Cross
   b. National Hurricane Center
   c. Army Corps of Engineers
   d. Centers for Disease Control

   ANS: B   DIF: B   OBJ: 3-1

9. Thunderstorms occur _____.
   a. only in the Midwestern states
   b. only in the winter
   c. all over the country
   d. only on the Gulf Coast

   ANS: C   DIF: B   OBJ: 3-4

10. During floods, bridges are most commonly destroyed by _____.
   a. high winds
   b. runaway ships
   c. water eroding away the supporting structure
   d. earthquakes

   ANS: C   DIF: A   OBJ: 3-4

11. Where do most Atlantic Ocean hurricanes originate?
   a. in cold water of the North Atlantic near Iceland
   b. in warm tropical water west of Africa
   c. in Hudson Bay
   d. in warm tropical water in the Gulf of Mexico

   ANS: B   DIF: B   OBJ: 3-2

12. What ingredients contribute to the formation of a hurricane?
   a. low-pressure area, warm ocean, energy from water vapor condensation, rotation of Earth
   b. high-pressure area, warm ocean, thermal energy from water evaporation, Earth's rotation
   c. updrafts, cool air, low-pressure center, lightning, tropical ocean
   d. spiral winds, storm surge, tropical ocean, landfall

   ANS: B   DIF: B   OBJ: 3-2

13. The force of wind hitting a building depends on _____.
   a. the level of humidity
   b. the rate of evaporation
   c. the wind speed
   d. the diameter of wind spirals

   ANS: C   DIF: A   OBJ: 3-3

14. Which hurricane-caused phenomenon is responsible for the most deaths during a storm?
   a. inland flooding
   b. high-speed winds
   c. tornadoes
   d. storm surges

   ANS: D   DIF: B   OBJ: 3-4

15. One way in which thunderstorms and hurricanes differ is that _____.
   a. storm surges are associated more with thunderstorms than with hurricanes
   b. hurricane winds are not as strong as thunderstorm winds
   c. thunderstorms contain more evaporated precipitation than hurricanes
   d. hurricane winds spiral and thunderstorm winds blow in a straight line

   ANS: D   DIF: A   OBJ: 3-1

16. Wind speeds within the eye of a hurricane are _____.
   a. over 400 km/h
   b. extremely low
   c. at their maximum
   d. over 250 km/h

   ANS: B   DIF: A   OBJ: 3-3

17. The storm surge associated with a hurricane _____.
   a. can combine with high tide for maximum effect
   b. builds up in the high-pressure area on the outside of the hurricane
   c. affects communities far inland
   d. is less destructive when it is forced into a narrow channel such as a bay

   ANS: A   DIF: A   OBJ: 3-4

18. One benefit associated with storms is that they _____.
   a. keep pollutants high up in the air away from Earth's surface
   b. help create extremes of temperature in certain areas of Earth
   c. provide water for plants and animals
   d. in no way affect the sun's energy that reaches Earth

   ANS: C   DIF: A   OBJ: 3-6

19. Most physical damage caused by hurricanes results from wind and _____.
   a. lightning
   b. changes in salinity
   c. hail
   d. water

   ANS: D   DIF: A   OBJ: 3-4

20. As a hurricane approaches land, _____.
a. it gathers more energy from the warm ground
b. it transfers the energy carried by its winds to shallower water, creating huge waves that batter the shore
c. most of its energy returns to the sea and little is left to damage the land
d. its winds disappear and most inland damage is caused by flooding
ANS: B   DIF: B   OBJ: 3-2

21. The correct sequence of the following events in the life of a hurricane—A. Large waves batter shore; B. Hurricane approaches land; C. Removed from energy source, hurricane dies out; D. Wind energy no longer transferred to waves, blows directly over land; E. Energy carried by wind transferred to shallower water—is _____.
a. BEADC
b. ADCEB
c. EBDCA
d. BADEC
ANS: A   DIF: A   OBJ: 3-2

COMPLETION

1. The _____ causes the spiraling wind patterns characteristic of hurricanes.
ANS: Coriolis effect   DIF: A   OBJ: 3-2

2. Wind speeds normally _____ as a hurricane moves over land.
ANS: decrease   DIF: B   OBJ: 3-2

3. As wind speed doubles, the force exerted by the wind increases by _____ times.
ANS: four   DIF: A   OBJ: 3-2

4. Of all natural disasters, _____ occur most often and kill the most people worldwide.
ANS: floods   DIF: B   OBJ: 3-1

5. _____ are disease-causing agents.
ANS: Pathogens   DIF: B   OBJ: 3-7

6. Crop destruction resulting from floods, hurricanes, and thunderstorms can cause _____ to increase all over the country.
ANS: food prices   DIF: A   OBJ: 3-5

7. _____ is used to distinguish the forward speed of a hurricane from the wind speed within the hurricane.
ANS: Doppler radar   DIF: A   OBJ: 3-3

8. Wind speeds decrease over land because of _____.
ANS: friction   DIF: B   OBJ: 3-2

9. _____ is a dangerous disease caused by bacteria commonly found in soil.
ANS: Tetanus   DIF: B   OBJ: 3-7

10. The International Red Cross helps local authorities to _____ people from areas threatened by floods or hurricanes.
ANS: evacuate   DIF: B   OBJ: 3-5

11. Hurricanes form over _____, moist oceans.
ANS: warm   DIF: B   OBJ: 3-1

12. Some species of plants and animals need _____, often started by lightning, to survive.
ANS: forest fires   DIF: B   OBJ: 3-6

13. Firefighters who parachute into forests from airplanes are called _____.
ANS: smoke jumpers   DIF: B   OBJ: 3-6

14. Soil dams called _____ are constructed along rivers to control flooding.
ANS: levees   DIF: B   OBJ: 3-4

15. Beachfront homes are often damaged when waves cause _____, which undermines their foundations.
ANS: erosion   DIF: B   OBJ: 3-4

MATCHING

Match each item with the correct statement below. Write the answer in the space provided.

a. erosion   f. pathogen
b. salinity   g. counterclockwise
c. flash flood   h. storm surge
d. tetanus   i. typhoon
e. gust   j. evacuate

1. _____ term for disease-causing bacteria or viruses
2. _____ large, violent storm originating in the Pacific Ocean
3. _____ unusually high rise in level of ocean during a hurricane that can create a wall of water
4. _____ sudden rise in a stream or river often causing severe damage to the surrounding country
5. _____ wearing away of soil or rock by natural forces such as wind and water
6. _____ sudden increase in the wind

7. _____ concentration of salt in the environment
8. _____ deadly disease caused by bacteria in the soil
9. _____ describes the direction of hurricane winds in the northern hemisphere
10. _____ to leave a threatened area

1. ANS: f   DIF: B   OBJ: 3-7
2. ANS: i   DIF: B   OBJ: 3-1
3. ANS: h   DIF: B   OBJ: 3-4
4. ANS: c   DIF: B   OBJ: 3-4
5. ANS: a   DIF: B   OBJ: 3-6
6. ANS: e   DIF: B   OBJ: 3-3
7. ANS: b   DIF: B   OBJ: 3-6
8. ANS: d   DIF: B   OBJ: 3-7
9. ANS: g   DIF: B   OBJ: 3-2
10. ANS: j   DIF: B   OBJ: 3-1

SHORT ANSWER

1. List four physical characteristics that can affect an ocean ecosystem if the system is disrupted too much.

ANS: any four of these: salinity, temperature, wave energy, mineral content, amount of sediment in water, pollution (fertilizers, sewage, pesticides)

DIF: A   OBJ: 3-6

2. During a hurricane, homeowners are often instructed to fill their bathtubs with water. Why?

ANS: to provide safe, clean drinking water if water supplies are cut off or contaminated

DIF: A   OBJ: 3-7

3. What type of damage besides water damage results from a hurricane?

ANS: major wind damage: power lines and trees are downed and buildings are blown apart by the extremely high winds (120–321 km/hr)

DIF: B   OBJ: 3-4

4. Do hurricanes along the Gulf Coast of Florida cost people in other parts of the country money? If so, how?

ANS: Yes, because insurance rates go up. Higher taxes are needed to rebuild roads, bridges, airports, and other structures. Crops and factories that are damaged or destroyed result in higher prices for food and other products.

DIF: A   OBJ: 3-5

5. Describe two instances in which you might expect tornadoes to form.

ANS: during the mature stage of thunderstorms and along the outer edges of hurricanes

DIF: A   OBJ: 3-4

6. Historically, the country of Bangladesh has suffered greatly from hurricanes (typhoons). Explain why this country is so vulnerable to severe storms.

ANS: Bangladesh is located at the head of the Bay of Bengal, which funnels the storm surges, causing more flooding.

DIF: A   OBJ: 3-4

7. Over land, a hurricane loses force and dies out. Why does this occur?

ANS: Land cuts the hurricane off from its energy supply—the warm ocean water.

DIF: A   OBJ: 3-2

8. Why are flooded rivers very dangerous?

ANS: As with wind, the force of moving water increases as the speed increases.

DIF: A   OBJ: 3-4

9. Why does income from tourism decrease in an area hit by a hurricane?

ANS: damaged cities and tourist attractions; fearful vacationers

DIF: A   OBJ: 3-5

10. Explain how hail forms.

ANS: During severe thunderstorms, violent updrafts carry water to high altitudes, where it freezes. In extremely severe storms, the hailstones ride the updrafts and downdrafts several times, adding a layer of ice each trip and growing larger. When the hail does fall to Earth, it can fall from an altitude of several kilometers and cause a great deal of damage.

DIF: A   OBJ: 3-4

11. Explain how a storm surge is formed in a major hurricane.

ANS: The high winds within the hurricane form a mound of water. Over the open ocean, this simply causes high waves. However, when the hurricane reaches shallow coastal areas, the waves have no place to go. The water builds up into a huge storm surge, which is magnified if it arrives at the coast during normal high tide.

DIF: B   OBJ: 3-4

12. How are hurricanes formed?

ANS: They form off the west coast of Africa, in the warm tropical ocean, as a wave of low pressure. As the storm builds, it draws warm, moist air into the central low-pressure area and forces it up into the cooler, upper atmosphere. As the water cools, it condenses, releasing energy, which warms the surrounding air. Cool, dense air from high altitudes flows down and under the warm air, pushing the warm air upward. The Coriolis effect gives this upper-level, warm air the characteristic spiral pattern.

DIF: B   OBJ: 3-1

13. What problems face people who do not evacuate early from low-lying areas during hurricanes?

   ANS: If people do not leave early, many low-lying areas can be flooded and cut off. Bridges and roads may be washed out, trapping people. Power lines, gas lines, and water supplies are often cut, leaving areas without vital service, shelters, and food for several days. Emergency workers may also have to risk their lives to rescue those who refuse to evacuate.

   DIF: A   OBJ: 3-7

14. How do hurricanes damage undersea areas?

   ANS: Changes in salinity or mineral content upset marine ecosystems; wind and waves can kill marine organisms, even coral, in shallow-water reef areas.

   DIF: A   OBJ: 3-6

15. What types of damage can floods cause?

   ANS: bridges washed out, erosion of levees and roads, buildings destroyed, crops lost, human deaths

   DIF: A   OBJ: 3-4

16. Why would you be in more danger of a flash flood in a mountain valley than on a plain?

   ANS: In the steep terrain with little soil, rain runs quickly into streams and then downhill into valleys.

   DIF: A   OBJ: 3-4

17. Why is a storm surge more destructive in a narrow bay than on a flat coast?

   ANS: In a bay, the surge is directed into a confined area and vents all its force there.

   DIF: A   OBJ: 3-4

18. What threat does a hurricane pose to areas far inland?

   ANS: Smaller storms, such as tornadoes, can spin off and cause considerable damage.

   DIF: A   OBJ: 3-4

19. A wall of water slams into the coast during a hurricane, causing many casualties. Identify this event and explain why it occurs.

   ANS: This is a storm surge. It occurs when the high wind in a hurricane creates a mound of water. In shallow water, the water mound grows higher as it approaches shore.

   DIF: A   OBJ: 3-4

OTHER

If the underscored word or phrase makes the sentence true, write "true" in the space provided. If the underscored word or phrase makes the sentence false, write the correct term or phrase in the space provided.

1. Hurricane winds in the northern hemisphere spiral in a counterclockwise direction.

   ANS: true   DIF: B   OBJ: 3-3

2. Hurricane winds in the southern hemisphere spiral in a counterclockwise direction.

   ANS: clockwise   DIF: B   OBJ: 3-3

3. Tornadoes are the largest and most destructive storms on Earth.

   ANS: Hurricanes   DIF: B   OBJ: 3-1

4. A tsunami forms as winds push water toward the center of a hurricane.

   ANS: storm surge   DIF: B   OBJ: 3-1

5. Lightning can melt metal and start forest fires with temperatures of up to 30 000°C.

   ANS: true   DIF: B   OBJ: 3-4

6. When not started by careless people, forest fires are most commonly started by earthquakes.

   ANS: lightning   DIF: B   OBJ: 3-4

7. Coral reefs grow in deep ocean waters.

   ANS: shallow   DIF: B   OBJ: 3-6

8. Storm surges that push seawater into river systems can damage delicate ecosystems by decreasing salinity.

   ANS: increasing   DIF: B   OBJ: 3-6

9. Typhoons are hurricanes that originate in the Pacific Ocean.

   ANS: true   DIF: B   OBJ: 3-1

10. Most Atlantic hurricanes originate in the warm tropical ocean west of Africa.

   ANS: true   DIF: A   OBJ: 3-1

CHAPTER 4—BIOTIC AND ABIOTIC FACTORS

MULTIPLE CHOICE

1. Dust and water vapor in the upper atmosphere tend to _____.
   a. absorb radiant energy from the sun
   b. reflect radiant energy back into the upper atmosphere
   c. absorb harmful ultraviolet portions
   d. form ozone

   ANS: B   DIF: A   OBJ: 4-3

2. Harmful ultraviolet radiation is prevented from reaching Earth when it is _____.
   a. reflected off of clouds
   b. absorbed by water vapor
   c. reflected back into space
   d. absorbed by ozone

   ANS: D   DIF: A   OBJ: 4-3

3. Landmasses tend to _____.
   a. only absorb the sun's energy
   b. only radiate the sun's energy
   c. absorb and radiate the sun's energy
   d. reflect 90 percent of the sun's energy back into space

   ANS: C   DIF: B   OBJ: 4-3

4. The range of temperatures on Earth helps to determine _____.
   a. which species will be able to survive in which area
   b. the direction light from the sun will take
   c. whether sunlight is reflected or absorbed
   d. and control all other abiotic factors

   ANS: A   DIF: A   OBJ: 4-3

5. Radiant energy that reaches Earth's atmosphere _____.
   a. is converted into ozone or water vapor
   b. is totally absorbed by ocean water
   c. may be changed into ultraviolet radiation
   d. may be reflected, transmitted, or absorbed

   ANS: D   DIF: B   OBJ: 4-3

6. Water can be described as _____.
   a. a molecule that releases heat quickly
   b. having a high thermal capacity
   c. being a poor solvent
   d. consisting of only two negatively charged ions

   ANS: B   DIF: A   OBJ: 4-4

7. A pond ecosystem is in the process of drying up. Its species diversity would most likely _____.
   a. increase due to rapid reproduction of those species left
   b. increase due to new species arriving from nearby ponds
   c. decrease due to increasing life spans for those species left
   d. decrease due to a lack of resources

   ANS: D   DIF: B   OBJ: 4-1

8. A chemical is placed in water and does not dissolve. One explanation is that _____.
   a. too much water was used
   b. the water may have been too acidic or basic
   c. the water was polluted
   d. the chemical was not an ionic compound

   ANS: D   DIF: A   OBJ: 4-4

9. The grouping that best shows the organization of an ecosystem would be _____.
   a. different populations form a species—different species form an ecosystem
   b. a species forms one population—different populations form an ecosystem
   c. similar species form different populations—different species form ecosystems
   d. similar species form different populations—similar populations form an ecosystem

   ANS: B   DIF: A   OBJ: 4-2

10. The statement that best describes a correct relationship in "species diversity" when comparing the number of different items in a shoe store to the number in a department store would be _____.
    a. "species diversity" in both stores is equal
    b. "species diversity" in a shoe store is higher than in a department store
    c. "species diversity" in a shoe store is lower than in a department store
    d. "species diversity" depends on the number of salespeople in each store

    ANS: C   DIF: A   OBJ: 4-2

11. Populations present in a forest ecosystem compared to those in a coral-reef ecosystem are _____.
    a. very similar
    b. very different
    c. somewhat alike
    d. identical

    ANS: B   DIF: B   OBJ: 4-2

12. The major population responsible for forming a coral reef would be _____.
    a. one-celled animals
    b. many-celled plants
    c. plant polyps
    d. animal polyps

    ANS: D   DIF: B   OBJ: 4-2

Table 4-1
pH of 5 Liquids

Liquid	pH Value
V	2
W	7
X	9
Y	3
Z	11

13. A sidewalk crack is an example of an urban ecosystem having _____
   a. a low species diversity
   b. no species
   c. more species than a forest
   d. more species than a coral reef

   ANS: A   DIF: B   OBJ: 4-2

14. Which of the following does NOT represent a biotic factor?
   a. animals
   b. bacteria
   c. rocks
   d. mushrooms

   ANS: C   DIF: B   OBJ: 4-1

15. Which of the following does NOT represent an abiotic factor?
   a. acid rain
   b. seaweed
   c. humidity
   d. floods

   ANS: B   DIF: B   OBJ: 4-3

16. A lake's water has a pH of five. This means that in the water there are _____
   a. more hydrogen ions than hydroxide ions
   b. more hydroxide ions than hydrogen ions
   c. equal numbers of hydrogen and hydroxide ions
   d. no hydrogen or hydroxide ions

   ANS: B   DIF: B   OBJ: 4-3

17. All of the goldfish in an aquarium tank represent a(n) _____
   a. ecosystem
   b. abiotic factor
   c. community
   d. population

   ANS: A   DIF: B   OBJ: 4-3

18. Why is the temperature at the equator greater than the temperature at the poles?
   a. The polar regions receive more energy from the sun than the equatorial territory does.
   b. The equator receives more energy from the sun than the polar regions do.
   c. The poles are always tilted away from the sun.
   d. The amount of sunlight reaching Earth at the equator varies greatly through the seasons.

   ANS: B   DIF: A   OBJ: 4-3

19. Liquid W in Table 4-1 would contain _____
   a. more hydrogen than hydroxide ions
   b. more hydroxide than hydrogen ions
   c. equal numbers of hydrogen and hydroxide ions
   d. no hydrogen or hydroxide ions

   ANS: C   DIF: B   OBJ: 4-4

20. Those liquids in Table 4-1 containing hydrogen and hydroxide ions would be _____
   a. X and Z only
   b. V and Y only
   c. W only
   d. V, W, X, Y, and Z

   ANS: D   DIF: B   OBJ: 4-4

21. Those liquids in Table 4-1 containing more hydroxide than hydrogen ions would be _____
   a. V and W
   b. V and Y
   c. X and Z
   d. W, X, and Z

   ANS: C   DIF: B   OBJ: 4-4

22. Those liquids in Table 4-1 that are acidic would be _____
   a. V and W
   b. V and Y
   c. W
   d. X and Z

   ANS: B   DIF: B   OBJ: 4-4

4-3

4-4

23. Those liquids in Table 4-1 that are basic would be _____.
   a. V, W, and X
   b. V and W
   c. Y and Z
   d. X and Z

   ANS: D   DIF: B   OBJ: 4-4

24. The liquid in Table 4-1 having the greatest number of hydrogen and fewest hydroxide ions would be _____.
   a. V
   b. W
   c. X
   d. Y

   ANS: A   DIF: B   OBJ: 4-4

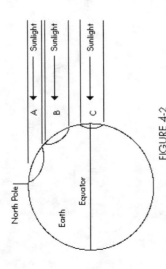

FIGURE 4-2

25. In Figure 4-2, those rays that are oblique as they strike Earth's surface would be _____.
   a. A only
   b. C only
   c. A and B
   d. A, B, and C

   ANS: C   DIF: B   OBJ: 4-3

26. In Figure 4-2, those rays that provide the most intense sunlight on Earth's surface would be _____.
   a. A only
   b. B only
   c. C only
   d. both A and C

   ANS: C   DIF: B   OBJ: 4-3

27. In Figure 4-2, those rays that provide the least radiant energy to Earth's surface would be _____.
   a. A
   b. A and C
   c. B and C
   d. C

   ANS: A   DIF: B   OBJ: 4-3

28. In Figure 4-2, those rays that would be spread over the smallest area on Earth's surface would be _____.
   a. A only
   b. B only
   c. A and B
   d. C only

   ANS: D   DIF: B   OBJ: 4-3

29. In Figure 4-2, the correct order for those rays delivering most to least heat to Earth's surface is _____.
   a. A, C, B
   b. A, B, C
   c. C, B, A
   d. C, A, B

   ANS: C   DIF: A   OBJ: 4-3

COMPLETION

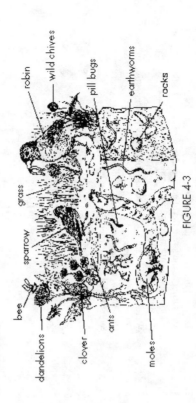

FIGURE 4-3

1. The interactions of the organisms shown in Figure 4-3 with the soil, sunlight, temperature, and water make this meadow an example of a(n) _____.

   ANS: ecosystem   DIF: B   OBJ: 4-1

2. All of the organisms pictured in Figure 4-3 represent the _____ in this meadow ecosystem.

ANS: biotic factors   DIF: B   OBJ: 4-2

3. The numbers of different species of birds, insects, plants, and worms in Figure 4-3 show that this meadow has a high _____.

ANS: species diversity   DIF: B   OBJ: 4-2

4. The earthworms in Figure 4-3 belong to the same _____ because they can mate and produce fertile offspring.

ANS: species   DIF: B   OBJ: 4-2

5. All the dandelions living in the meadow shown in Figure 4-3 make up a(n) _____ of dandelions.

ANS: population   DIF: B   OBJ: 4-2

6. Clover, grass, and wild chives represent the plant _____ of the meadow shown in Figure 4-3.

ANS: community   DIF: B   OBJ: 4-2

7. Coniferous trees get their name from the fact that they bear _____.

ANS: cones   DIF: B   OBJ: 4-2

8. Coniferous forests show a species diversity that is _____.

ANS: high   DIF: A   OBJ: 4-2

9. A group of populations in an area that interact with one another form the basis for a(n) _____.

ANS: ecosystem   DIF: B   OBJ: 4-2

10. Biotic factors in an ecosystem are always made up of _____.

ANS: living things   DIF: B   OBJ: 4-1

11. Abiotic factors in an ecosystem are always made up of _____.

ANS: nonliving things   DIF: B   OBJ: 4-3

12. Pond lilies providing a sheltered nursery for young fish is an example of population _____.

ANS: interaction   DIF: B   OBJ: 4-2

13. An example of a coniferous tree would be _____.

ANS: pine, spruce, fir, or juniper   DIF: B   OBJ: 4-2

MATCHING

Match each item with the correct statement below. Write the answer in the space provided.

a. species
b. pH scale
c. base
d. solvent
e. solute

f. acid
g. population
h. ecosystem
i. polar
j. community

1. _____ A coral reef is an example of a(n) _____.
2. _____ All humans belong to the same _____.
3. _____ Tomato juice is considered a(n) _____.
4. _____ Measuring of the strengths of acids and bases is done on the _____.
5. _____ All of the students in your school represent a(n) _____.
6. _____ A solution with a pH of 9 is a(n) _____.
7. _____ Water molecules are _____ because they carry both negative and positive charges.
8. _____ Water is the universal _____.
9. _____ Clown fish, sea anemones, and coral form a(n) _____ on a reef.
10. _____ Sugar is the _____ when it is dissolved in coffee.

1. ANS: h   DIF: B   OBJ: 4-1
2. ANS: a   DIF: B   OBJ: 4-2
3. ANS: f   DIF: A   OBJ: 4-3
4. ANS: b   DIF: B   OBJ: 4-3
5. ANS: g   DIF: B   OBJ: 4-2
6. ANS: c   DIF: B   OBJ: 4-3
7. ANS: i   DIF: B   OBJ: 4-4
8. ANS: d   DIF: B   OBJ: 4-4
9. ANS: j   DIF: B   OBJ: 4-2
10. ANS: e   DIF: B   OBJ: 4-4

SHORT ANSWER

1. On a cold day, you decide to make hot chocolate. You measure the cocoa mix into a mug, heat the water, then add it to the mug and stir. What substances represent the solution, solute, and solvent in your mug?

ANS: The solution is the cocoa; the solute is the cocoa mix, and the solvent is the hot water.

DIF: B   OBJ: 4-4

2. What do tropical rain forests and coral reefs have in common?

ANS: Both are examples of ecosystems that have high species diversity.

DIF: A   OBJ: 4-1

3. A group of sea gulls lives on the New Jersey coast. Another group lives on the coast of Florida. The sea gulls are the same species, but they do not interact. Do these two groups make up a population of sea gulls? Why?

ANS: No. A population is defined as a group of organisms of the same species living in a specific area.

DIF: B   OBJ: 4-2

4. Why should you not leave a dog or cat inside a parked car with the windows up in the summertime?

ANS: Sunlight entering through the closed glass windows will be trapped inside, generating intense heat. Soon the temperature inside the car will rise to dangerous levels. Because dogs and cats cannot get out of the car themselves, they could suffer, or even die, from the heat.

DIF: A   OBJ: 4-3

5. Tightly closed cones hold the seeds of the jack pine (*Pinus banksiana*). After a forest fire, however, the first seedlings to appear are those of the jack pine. What one abiotic factor might release the jack pine seeds during a forest fire?

ANS: The jack pine cones respond to the high temperatures the forest fire generates by opening to release their seeds.

DIF: B   OBJ: 4-3

6. What happens to the sun's radiant energy when it strikes Earth?

ANS: Part is reflected back into space by clouds, land, and water; some is absorbed by clouds, land, and oceans; the ozone layer absorbs ultraviolet radiation.

DIF: A   OBJ: 4-3

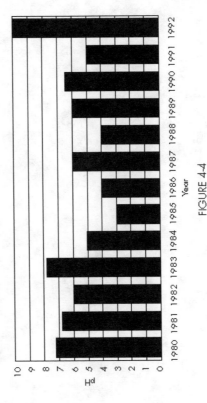

FIGURE 4-5

7. Which ecosystem in Figure 4-5 shows the lowest number of species?

ANS: B   DIF: B   OBJ: 4-1

8. Which ecosystem in Figure 4-5 shows the highest number of species?

ANS: A   DIF: B   OBJ: 4-1

9. Which ecosystem in Figure 4-5 might represent species diversity in a farmer's field?

ANS: B   DIF: A   OBJ: 4-1

10. Which ecosystem in Figure 4-5 might represent species diversity typical of a small area?

ANS: B   DIF: A   OBJ: 4-1

11. Which ecosystem in Figure 4-5 might represent species diversity of a large area?

ANS: A   DIF: A   OBJ: 4-1

12. Which ecosystem in Figure 4-5 might represent an area having few resources?

ANS: B   DIF: A   OBJ: 4-1

13. Which ecosystem in Figure 4-5 might represent an area having many resources?

ANS: A   DIF: A   OBJ: 4-1

14. Which ecosystem in Figure 4-5 might represent species diversity in a tropical rain forest?

ANS: A   DIF: B   OBJ: 4-1

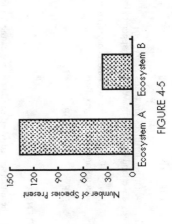

FIGURE 4-4

15. Figure 4-4 shows the pH of one pond at a fish farm. In what years do you think a lot of the fish died? Explain your answer.

ANS: Fish probably died in 1985, 1986, 1988, and 1992. They do not survive at either very high or very low pH levels.

DIF: A   OBJ: 4-3

16. Deciduous hardwood forests are common in Vermont, whereas grasslands are more often found in Iowa. Why are the ecosystems different in these two places?

ANS: If abiotic factors are different, such as less rainfall in the grasslands or richer soil in the hardwood forests, then the species supported by those factors will also be different. In the same way, biotic factors such as bison on the prairie or white-tailed deer in the forest can influence the survival of organisms.

DIF: A   OBJ: 4-3

17. A farmer fertilizes his fields every spring. Whenever it rains, the runoff from his fields goes into a wetland on his farm. What will happen to the wetland if this continues indefinitely? Why?

ANS: Eventually the wetland ecosystem will be changed, because fertilizer will inhibit some species and encourage others.

DIF: A   OBJ: 4-4

OTHER

If the underscored word or phrase makes the sentence true, write "true" in the space provided. If the underscored word or phrase makes the sentence false, write the correct term or phrase in the space provided.

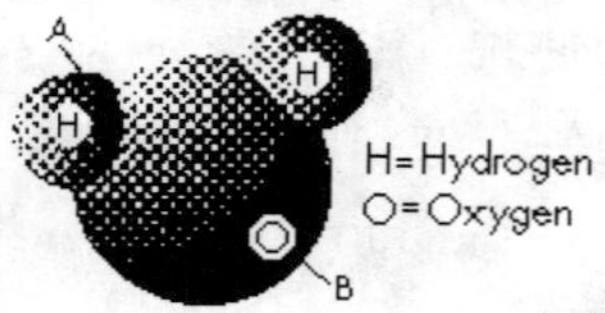

A Water Molecule

H=Hydrogen
O=Oxygen

FIGURE 4-1

1. The part of the molecule marked A in Figure 4-1 has a negative charge. _____

ANS: positive   DIF: B   OBJ: 4-4

2. The part of the molecule marked B in Figure 4-1 attracts all electrons, even those from hydrogen. _____

ANS: true   DIF: B   OBJ: 4-4

3. The part of the molecule marked B in Figure 4-1 has a negative charge. _____

ANS: true   DIF: B   OBJ: 4-4

4. The molecule in Figure 4-1 has a positive and negative end and is therefore called a nonpolar molecule. _____

ANS: polar   DIF: B   OBJ: 4-4

5. When table salt (Na^+Cl^-) is added to water, chloride ions are attracted to end A of Figure 4-1.

ANS: true   DIF: A   OBJ: 4-4

6. When table salt (Na^+Cl^-) is added to water, sodium ions are attracted to end B of Figure 4-1.

ANS: true   DIF: A   OBJ: 4-4

CHAPTER 5—CYCLING OF MATTER AND ENERGY

MULTIPLE CHOICE

1. Centipedes and earthworms may both be found in soil. They both share the same _____.
   a. niche
   b. population
   c. habitat
   d. trophic level

   ANS: C   DIF: B   OBJ: 5-1

2. While both share living in soil, earthworms feed on dead plant material while centipedes feed off of small insects. These animals have _____.
   a. different habitats
   b. different ecosystems
   c. similar amounts of biomass
   d. different niches

   ANS: D   DIF: B   OBJ: 5-1

3. Autotrophs may be grouped into two categories called _____.
   a. omnivores and herbivores
   b. producers and consumers
   c. chemo- and photoautotrophs
   d. marine and land autotrophs

   ANS: C   DIF: B   OBJ: 5-1

4. Bacteria, slime molds, and fungi are all examples of _____.
   a. decomposers
   b. producers
   c. omnivores
   d. autotrophs

   ANS: A   DIF: B   OBJ: 5-1

5. A classmate always borrows paper from you and never replaces it. This type of action illustrates _____.
   a. commensalism
   b. mutualism
   c. parasitism
   d. how an ecosystem is formed

   ANS: C   DIF: A   OBJ: 5-2

6. Plants carry out respiration during _____.
   a. the day only
   b. the night only
   c. night and day
   d. periods of drought

   ANS: C   DIF: B   OBJ: 5-4

7. Plants carry out photosynthesis when _____.
   a. light is available
   b. no light is available
   c. respiration is not occurring
   d. unable to carry out transpiration

   ANS: A   DIF: B   OBJ: 5-4

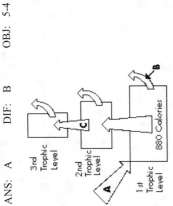

FIGURE 5-1

8. In Figure 5-1, the number of Calories passed to the second trophic level would be about _____.
   a. 880
   b. 440
   c. 1760
   d. 88

   ANS: D   DIF: A   OBJ: 5-2

9. In Figure 5-1, arrow B best represents energy _____.
   a. passed to the next trophic level
   b. lost from the food chain as heat
   c. passed back to the sun
   d. that is trapped inside all producers

   ANS: B   DIF: B   OBJ: 5-2

10. In Figure 5-1, arrow A best represents energy _____.
    a. used by organisms for growth
    b. trapped by consumers
    c. from the sun
    d. lost as heat

    ANS: C   DIF: B   OBJ: 5-2

11. If arrow A in Figure 5-1 could be assigned a number of Calories, it would be _____.
    a. greater than 880
    b. equal to 880
    c. less than 880
    d. about 10 percent of 880

    ANS: A   DIF: A   OBJ: 5-2

12. Arrow C in Figure 5-1 would represent energy flow when a(n) _____.
   a. herbivore eats a consumer
   b. producer carries out photosynthesis
   c. consumer eats a herbivore
   d. autotroph eats a heterotroph

   ANS: C   DIF: B   OBJ: 5-2

```
        4th
      Trophic
       Level
    ┌─────────┐
    │    D    │
    └─────────┘
         ↑
        3rd
      Trophic
       Level
    ┌─────────┐
    │    C    │
    └─────────┘
         ↑
        2nd
      Trophic
       Level
    ┌─────────┐
    │    B    │
    └─────────┘
         ↑
        1st
      Trophic
       Level
    ┌─────────┐
    │    A    │
    └─────────┘
```

FIGURE 5-2

13. In Figure 5-2, arrows leading from one trophic level to the next represent _____.
   a. movement of organisms through the food chain
   b. flow of energy
   c. a way of showing the number of species at each level
   d. both choices a and b

   ANS: B   DIF: B   OBJ: 5-3

14. In Figure 5-2, organisms at level A _____.
   a. are decomposers
   b. are autotrophs
   c. are producers
   d. both choices b and c are correct

   ANS: D   DIF: B   OBJ: 5-3

15. In Figure 5-2, organisms at level A _____.
   a. can trap sunlight energy
   b. carry out photosynthesis
   c. are plants or other photoautotrophs
   d. a, b, and c are all correct

   ANS: D   DIF: B   OBJ: 5-3

16. In Figure 5-2, decomposers are represented by _____.
   a. letter B
   b. letter C
   c. letter D
   d. no letter

   ANS: D   DIF: B   OBJ: 5-3

17. In Figure 5-2, organisms at level B _____.
   a. must be heterotrophs
   b. must be autotrophs
   c. must be carnivores
   d. both a and b are correct

   ANS: A   DIF: A   OBJ: 5-3

18. In Figure 5-2, organisms at level C _____.
   a. could be carnivores
   b. could be herbivores
   c. could be chemoautotrophs
   d. both a and b are correct

   ANS: A   DIF: A   OBJ: 5-3

19. In Figure 5-2, organisms at level B must be _____.
   a. omnivores
   b. autotrophs
   c. herbivores
   d. decomposers

   ANS: C   DIF: B   OBJ: 5-3

20. In Figure 5-2, organisms at levels B, C, and D are all _____.
   a. producers
   b. unable to carry out photosynthesis
   c. decomposers
   d. omnivores

   ANS: B   DIF: A   OBJ: 5-3

21. Figure 5-2 is a forest food chain. Squirrels and deer would be found at _____.
   a. levels A, B, C, and D
   b. level A
   c. levels C and D only
   d. level B

   ANS: D   DIF: A   OBJ: 5-3

22. Figure 5-2 is a forest food chain. Trees and ferns would be found at _____.
   a. level A
   b. level B
   c. levels C and D
   d. levels A and B

   ANS: A   DIF: A   OBJ: 5-3

23. If humans were included in Figure 5-2, they could appear at _____.
   a. only level A
   b. levels A and C
   c. levels B, C, and D
   d. only level D

   ANS: C   DIF: A   OBJ: 5-3

COMPLETION

1. Robins are adapted to a feeding _____ that includes feeding on the ground.

   ANS: niche   DIF: B   OBJ: 5-1

2. Plants recycle water to the atmosphere by the process of _____.

   ANS: transpiration   DIF: B   OBJ: 5-4

3. A partnership between two different species is called _____.

   ANS: symbiosis   DIF: A   OBJ: 5-2

4. Soil bacteria play an important part in nutrient cycling for the _____.

   ANS: nitrogen cycle   DIF: B   OBJ: 5-4

5. Decaying leaves provide a _____ for both earthworms and fungi.

   ANS: habitat   DIF: B   OBJ: 5-1

Table 5-1
A Table of Symbiotic Relationships

TYPE OF RELATIONSHIP	SPECIES 1	SPECIES 2
PARASITISM	HELPED	A
B	C	HELPED
COMMENSALISM	HELPED	D

6. Space **A** in Table 5-1 should contain the word _____

   ANS: harmed   DIF: A   OBJ: 5-1

7. Space **B** in Table 5-1 should contain the word _____

   ANS: mutualism   DIF: A   OBJ: 5-1

8. Space **C** in Table 5-1 should contain the word _____

   ANS: helped   DIF: A   OBJ: 5-1

9. Space **D** in Table 5-1 should contain the word or words _____

   ANS: not affected (or not harmed or helped)   DIF: A   OBJ: 5-1

MATCHING

Match each item with the correct statement below. Write the answer in the space provided.

a. omnivores   g. photosynthesis
b. bacteria   h. producers
c. decomposers   i. heterotrophs
d. food webs   j. food chain
e. trophic levels   k. herbivores
f. autotrophs

_____ 1. process by which autotrophs make their own food
_____ 2. organisms that feed on plants and animals
_____ 3. capable of making their own food
_____ 4. method for showing energy flow in an ecosystem
_____ 5. example of a decomposer
_____ 6. organisms that feed only on plants
_____ 7. cannot make their own food
_____ 8. recycle nutrients
_____ 9. obtain energy from sunlight
_____ 10. include organisms that obtain energy in similar ways
_____ 11. show all possible feeding relationships

1. ANS: g   DIF: B   OBJ: 5-2
2. ANS: a   DIF: B   OBJ: 5-2
3. ANS: h   DIF: B   OBJ: 5-2
4. ANS: j   DIF: B   OBJ: 5-2
5. ANS: b   DIF: B   OBJ: 5-2
6. ANS: k   DIF: B   OBJ: 5-3
7. ANS: i   DIF: B   OBJ: 5-2
8. ANS: c   DIF: B   OBJ: 5-2
9. ANS: f   DIF: B   OBJ: 5-3
10. ANS: e   DIF: B   OBJ: 5-3
11. ANS: d   DIF: B   OBJ: 5-2

SHORT ANSWER

1. Use the following terms in a sentence: photosynthesis, respiration, carbon dioxide, plants.

   ANS: Photosynthesis and respiration are two life processes in plants that involve carbon dioxide.

   DIF: A   OBJ: 5-2

2. When fossil fuels are burned, atmospheric carbon dioxide levels increase. What happens to the total amount of carbon? Explain.

   ANS: The amount of carbon remains constant because the carbon in fossil fuels is converted to atmospheric carbon dioxide. It will be recycled through living organisms.

   DIF: B   OBJ: 5-4

3. Explain why beak shape in birds is an adaptation to a niche.

ANS: The shape of a bird's beak allows it to eat seeds, fruit, or insects, or gather nectar. These methods of getting food are some of the defining characteristics of an organism's niche.

DIF: A   OBJ: 5-1

4. In what form do humans obtain nitrogen?

ANS: Nitrogen is eaten as plant or animal protein.

DIF: A   OBJ: 5-4

5. Explain how lichens illustrate symbiosis.

ANS: Lichens are a partnership between fungi and algae or cyanobacteria.

DIF: A   OBJ: 5-2

6. Why is less energy available at each trophic level?

ANS: Energy is lost through respiration, decay, and heat at each trophic level.

DIF: A   OBJ: 5-3

7. How can several species share the same habitat?

ANS: Different species can share the same habitat by occupying different niches.

DIF: A   OBJ: 5-1

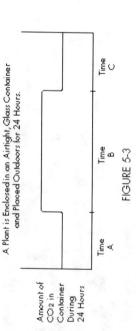

A Plant is Enclosed in an Airtight, Glass Container and Placed Outdoors for 24 Hours.

FIGURE 5-3

8. Which time period or periods in Figure 5-3 correspond(s) to daylight?

ANS: Periods A and C

DIF: A   OBJ: 5-4

---

9. Explain how you are able to tell from Figure 5-3 when daylight occurs.

ANS: Periods A and C show a decrease in the amount of carbon dioxide present. This decrease results from plants using the gas for photosynthesis.

DIF: A   OBJ: 5-4

10. Which time period or periods correspond(s) in Figure 5-3 to nighttime?

ANS: Period B

DIF: A   OBJ: 5-4

11. Explain how you are able to tell from Figure 5-3 when nighttime occurs.

ANS: Period B shows an increase in the amount of carbon dioxide present. This increase results from plants releasing the gas into the air during respiration.

DIF: A   OBJ: 5-4

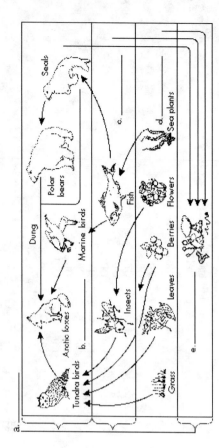

FIGURE 5-4

12. Label the lettered parts of Figure 5-4 to show the following features: producers, herbivores, heterotrophs, decomposers, omnivores.

ANS: a. heterotrophs, b. omnivores, c. herbivores, d. producers, e. decomposers

DIF: B   OBJ: 5-3

13. Which organisms in Figure 5-4 feed on more than one trophic level?

ANS: tundra birds, polar birds, decomposers

DIF: B   OBJ: 5-2

14. How do decomposers recycle nutrients?

ANS: Decomposers break down organic material into reusable nutrients. As organisms decay, they release carbon to the atmosphere in the form of carbon dioxide. This is recycled when plants undergo photosynthesis. Decomposers also recycle nitrogen present in wastes and organic remains. Some is converted to gaseous nitrogen and is eventually returned to plants after being fixed by soil bacteria.

DIF: A   OBJ: 5-2

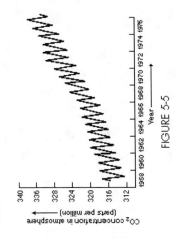

FIGURE 5-5

15. According to Figure 5-5, what happened to the amount of carbon dioxide in the atmosphere in the 20-year period from 1958 to 1978? What is the average change in carbon dioxide per year?

ANS: The amount of carbon dioxide in the atmosphere increased. It increased about 20 ppm over 20 years, or 1 ppm per year.

DIF: A   OBJ: 5-4

16. Could the increase in carbon dioxide shown in Figure 5-5 between 1958 and 1978 relate to burning fossil fuels or clear-cutting forests? Explain.

ANS: Yes, burning fossil fuels results in more atmospheric carbon dioxide. Clear-cutting of forests can add to the carbon dioxide in the atmosphere in two ways. If trees are burned, carbon dioxide is released. Also, fewer trees are available to use the carbon dioxide for photosynthesis. Carbon dioxide levels in the atmosphere might increase.

DIF: A   OBJ: 5-4

17. Infer what would cause the annual peaks and troughs seen in Figure 5-5.

ANS: The peaks appear to come each year and could be seasonal, due to increases in the amount of respiration and decreases in photosynthesis in the winter months. In the summer, an increase in photosynthesis would use up more carbon dioxide, which would explain the troughs in the graph.

DIF: A   OBJ: 5-4

18. Carbon dioxide in the atmosphere reflects a large amount of infrared radiation back to Earth and thus acts as a heat blanket. What might be a long-term effect of continued heavy burning of fossil fuels?

ANS: Fossil fuels release carbon dioxide when they burn. If the level of atmospheric CO_2 increases, surface temperatures could rise, causing global warming. Sea levels could rise if the polar ice caps melted.

DIF: B   OBJ: 5-4

19. How could increased levels of carbon dioxide be a good thing?

ANS: If the carbon dioxide could increase photosynthetic activity, primary production would receive a boost and might be able to support more biomass at the upper trophic levels. This would be a good thing from the standpoint of having to feed a growing population.

DIF: B   OBJ: 5-4

20. Use the pyramid of energy to explain why polar bears have no predators, excluding the minor effect of humans.

ANS: Polar bears are at the top of a food chain. An animal large enough to capture polar bears would have to use up a lot of energy and cover a lot of ground to be a successful predator. At this level, the transfer of energy is inefficient and not great enough to support another trophic level.

DIF: B   OBJ: 5-4

21. Some rain falling on the land surfaces eventually becomes groundwater. What happens to rain that doesn't get into the groundwater?

ANS: Some water evaporates, some runs off the land into streams, and some is taken up by plant roots and transpired back into the atmosphere.

DIF: B   OBJ: 5-4

22. A successful parasite doesn't kill its host. In fact, there has been an evolutionary tendency toward less-negative interactions. Explain.

ANS: Over time, most successful parasites would be those that do less harm because a parasite that kills its host will die as well. If this happens before it reproduces, the parasite will not pass on its genes. Also, hosts may have become more resistant to parasites over the years.

DIF: A   OBJ: 5-2

23. Scientists have been concerned that excessive ultraviolet radiation in the Antarctic may threaten populations of minute photosynthetic organisms called phytoplankton, which live in the ocean. Why is this a concern?

ANS: Phytoplankton are primary producers and are at the very bottom of the ocean food web. If they are significantly reduced in number, there will be less energy to support consumers at each successive trophic level.

DIF: A   OBJ: 5-2

24. Examination of a heterotroph's teeth can reveal information about its diet. Is this always true for humans? Explain.

ANS: No, a person's teeth would not yield information indicating whether he or she were a vegetarian. Humans are omnivores, so their teeth are adapted for processing both plants and animals.

DIF: A   OBJ: 5-1

OTHER

If the underscored word or phrase makes the sentence true, write "true" in the space provided. If the underscored word or phrase makes the sentence false, write the correct term or phrase in the space provided.

1. The burning of fossil fuels releases <u>oxygen</u> into the atmosphere. _____

ANS: carbon dioxide   DIF: B   OBJ: 5-4

2. Carbon dioxide is composed of atoms of carbon and <u>nitrogen</u>. _____

ANS: oxygen   DIF: B   OBJ: 5-4

3. <u>Autotrophs</u> remove carbon dioxide from the atmosphere during photosynthesis.
_____

ANS: true   DIF: B   OBJ: 5-4

4. Water <u>evaporates</u> from Earth's oceans into the atmosphere. _____

ANS: true   DIF: B   OBJ: 5-4

5. When water vapor condenses, it may change into a <u>gas</u>.

ANS: liquid (or solid)   DIF: B   OBJ: 5-4

6. DNA and protein both require the essential element <u>nitrogen</u>. _____

ANS: true   DIF: A   OBJ: 5-4

7. Living organisms <u>can</u> use nitrogen in its gaseous form. _____

ANS: cannot   DIF: A   OBJ: 5-4

8. The decay of organisms by decomposers adds <u>nitrogen</u> gas to the atmosphere.
_____

ANS: carbon dioxide   DIF: B   OBJ: 5-4

CHAPTER 6—CHANGES IN ECOSYSTEMS

MULTIPLE CHOICE

1. The one event that does NOT aid in disturbing ecosystems would be _____
   a. logging of forests
   b. increased use of automobiles
   c. improved mass-transportation systems
   d. burning of fossil fuels

ANS: C   DIF: B   OBJ: 6-5

2. Asbestos, a dangerous air pollutant, has damaging effects on our _____
   a. lungs
   b. skin
   c. digestive system
   d. vision

ANS: A   DIF: B   OBJ: 6-5

3. An effect of acid precipitation would be _____
   a. lowering of pH in lakes
   b. removing minerals from the soil
   c. increasing levels of DDT
   d. both a and b

ANS: D   DIF: B   OBJ: 6-5

4. Animals may stop reproducing when _____
   a. their population increases exponentially
   b. they experience crowding
   c. the predator population increases
   d. their population declines

ANS: B   DIF: B   OBJ: 6-2

5. Pioneer species _____
   a. are typically found in a climax community
   b. tend to be shade-tolerant
   c. are generally hardy
   d. crowd out ferns and grasses

ANS: B   DIF: B   OBJ: 6-4

6. Diversity increases when _____
   a. species compete for space
   b. there is biological magnification
   c. organisms first colonize a new site
   d. organisms change the environment during the process of succession

ANS: D   DIF: A   OBJ: 6-4

7. DDT causes thin eggshells for top carnivore birds because _____.
   a. birds are more susceptible than fish to DDT toxicity
   b. DDT levels became increasingly concentrated at each trophic level
   c. birds are predators whose prey DDT decimates
   d. all of the above

   ANS: B   DIF: A   OBJ: 6-5

8. Efficient burning of fossil fuels results in _____.
   a. carbon dioxide and water
   b. sulfur dioxide
   c. nitrogen, sulfur, and particulates
   d. carbon monoxide

   ANS: A   DIF: B   OBJ: 6-5

9. The aftermath of the fires at Yellowstone provided an example of _____.
   a. primary succession
   b. eliminating predator-prey interactions
   c. burning fossil fuels
   d. secondary succession

   ANS: D   DIF: B   OBJ: 6-4

10. Pollution in lakes, rivers, and underground wells causes a serious problem because _____.
    a. humans and other organisms depend on water from these sources
    b. it easily enters the food chain through aquatic organisms
    c. aquatic organisms tend to concentrate pollutants that cannot be broken down
    d. all of the above

    ANS: D   DIF: B   OBJ: 6-5

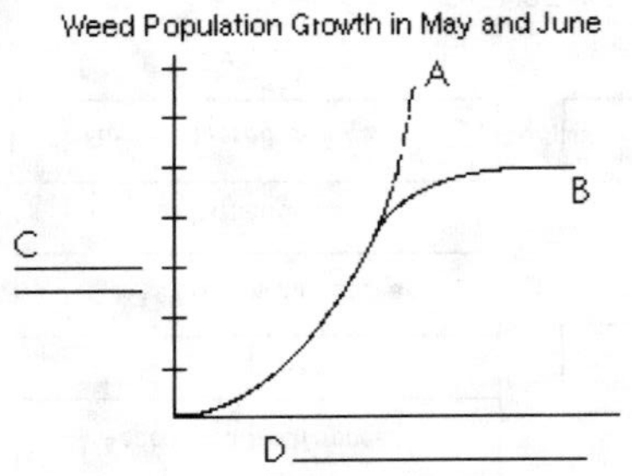

Weed Population Growth in May and June

FIGURE 6-2

11. When completing the graph in Figure 6-2, the best label for line A would be _____.
    a. July growth
    b. number of weeds
    c. biotic potential
    d. carrying capacity reached

    ANS: C   DIF: B   OBJ: 6-2

12. When completing the graph in Figure 6-2, the best label for line B would be _____.
    a. biotic potential
    b. linear growth
    c. carrying capacity reached
    d. 1000 weeds present

    ANS: C   DIF: B   OBJ: 6-2

13. When completing the graph in Figure 6-2, the best label for area C would be _____.
    a. time and temperature
    b. number of weeds
    c. May, June
    d. exponential growth

    ANS: B   DIF: B   OBJ: 6-2

14. When completing the graph in Figure 6-2, the best label for area D would be _____.
    a. number of weeds
    b. limiting factors
    c. average weed size
    d. time

    ANS: B   DIF: B   OBJ: 6-2

15. When completing the graph in Figure 6-2, the best units for label C would be _____.
    a. numbers
    b. months
    c. years
    d. days

    ANS: D   DIF: B   OBJ: 6-2

16. When completing the graph in Figure 6-2, the best units for label D would be _____.
    a. years
    b. months
    c. numbers
    d. grams of weed mass

    ANS: A   DIF: B   OBJ: 6-2

17. Weed growth may have appeared as line A instead of line B in Figure 6-2 if it were not for possible _____.
    a. decreasing amounts of water in the environment
    b. increasing amounts of light in the environment
    c. increasing amounts of water in the environment
    d. decreasing amounts of oxygen in the environment

    ANS: A   DIF: A   OBJ: 6-2

18. Weed growth may have appeared as line A instead of line B in Figure 6-2 if it were not for possible ___
   a. changes in linear growth
   b. limiting factors
   c. changes in exponential growth
   d. slow growth phases taking too long

   ANS: B   DIF: A   OBJ: 6-2

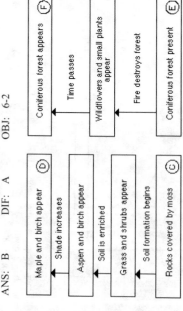

FIGURE 6-3

19. Both Examples A and B in Figure 6-3 illustrate the process of ___
   a. pioneer communities
   b. succession
   c. climax communities
   d. decomposition

   ANS: B   DIF: A   OBJ: 6-4

20. Example A in Figure 6-3 illustrates the process of ___
   a. pollution
   b. secondary succession
   c. primary succession
   d. no change in habitat

   ANS: C   DIF: A   OBJ: 6-4

21. Example B in Figure 6-3 illustrates the process of ___
   a. primary succession
   b. secondary succession
   c. soil enrichment
   d. natural events out of control

   ANS: B   DIF: B   OBJ: 6-4

22. In Figure 6-3, if Example A takes 500 years to complete, then Example B should take ___
   a. 500 years to complete
   b. 1000 years to complete
   c. less than 500 years to complete
   d. 1–2 years to complete

   ANS: C   DIF: B   OBJ: 6-4

23. A climax community disrupted by a natural disturbance is best shown in Figure 6-3 with Example ___
   a. A
   b. B
   c. both A and B
   d. neither A nor B

   ANS: B   DIF: B   OBJ: 6-4

24. The letters in Figure 6-3 that best represent climax communities would be ___
   a. C and D
   b. C and E
   c. C and F
   d. D, E, and F

   ANS: B   DIF: B   OBJ: 6-4

25. The letter(s) in Figure 6-3 that best show(s) pioneer species would be ___
   a. C
   b. D
   c. E
   d. E and F

   ANS: D   DIF: B   OBJ: 6-4

26. The plants in Figure 6-3 that best illustrate hardy species would be ___
   a. aspen and birch
   b. small plants
   c. mosses
   d. grasses and shrubs

   ANS: A   DIF: B   OBJ: 6-4

27. Example A in Figure 6-3 shows ___
   a. a decrease in species diversity from C to D
   b. a buildup of ash-covered soils
   c. a decrease in the role of decomposers
   d. an increase in species diversity from C to D

   ANS: D   DIF: A   OBJ: 6-4

28. The Example in Figure 6-3 similar to events that might occur if flooding of a prairie took place
would be _____.
   a. A
   b. B
   c. both A and B
   d. neither A nor B

ANS: B   DIF: A   OBJ: 6-4

COMPLETION

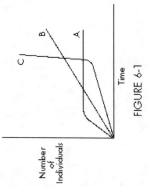

FIGURE 6-1

1. The graph line in Figure 6-1 that shows a rapid population increase would be _____.

ANS: C   DIF: B   OBJ: 6-1

2. The graph line in Figure 6-1 that shows exponential growth would be _____.

ANS: C   DIF: A   OBJ: 6-1

3. The graph line in Figure 6-1 that shows a steady rate of growth would be _____.

ANS: B   DIF: B   OBJ: 6-1

4. The graph line in Figure 6-1 that shows a potential for explosive growth would be _____.

ANS: C   DIF: A   OBJ: 6-1

5. The graph line in Figure 6-1 that shows linear growth would be _____.

ANS: B   DIF: B   OBJ: 6-1

6. The graph line in Figure 6-1 that shows a population that has reached its carrying capacity would be _____.

ANS: A   DIF: A   OBJ: 6-2

7. The graph line in Figure 6-1 that shows how a living population of flies could NOT grow would be _____.

ANS: B   DIF: A   OBJ: 6-1

MATCHING

Match each item with the correct statement below. Write the answer in the space provided.

   a. biotic potential
   b. carrying capacity
   c. pollution
   d. acid rain
   e. climax community
   f. succession

_____ 1.   environmental contamination by excess waste
_____ 2.   a gradual change in the structure of an ecological community
_____ 3.   the highest rate of reproduction under ideal conditions
_____ 4.   forms when nitrogen and sulfur oxides dissolve in water vapor
_____ 5.   the largest number of individuals an environment can support
_____ 6.   a stable, mature community

1. ANS: c   DIF: B   OBJ: 6-2
2. ANS: f   DIF: B   OBJ: 6-4
3. ANS: a   DIF: B   OBJ: 6-3
4. ANS: d   DIF: B   OBJ: 6-5
5. ANS: b   DIF: B   OBJ: 6-2
6. ANS: e   DIF: B   OBJ: 6-4

SHORT ANSWER

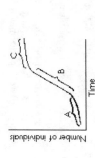

FIGURE 6-4

1. Explain why the slope of the line is steeper in region B in Figure 6-4 than in region A.

ANS: There are fewer individuals reproducing in A than in B.

DIF: A   OBJ: 6-3

2. What happens in region C in Figure 6-4?

ANS: The population reaches the carrying capacity of the environment; the reproduction rate declines, and as many individuals die as are born.

DIF: A   OBJ: 6-2

3. In Figure 6-4, is stress on the population most likely to occur at region A, B, or C?

ANS: region C

DIF: A   OBJ: 6-2

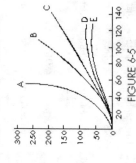

FIGURE 6-5

4. Compare the yeast population growth represented by line A in Figure 6-5 with that of line E.

ANS: The population is still growing exponentially in A and has leveled off in E.

DIF: B   OBJ: 6-1

5. Infer the cause of the yeast population change in line E in Figure 6-5.

ANS: The population has leveled off, because the carrying capacity of the environment has been reached.

DIF: A   OBJ: 6-1

6. Is the carrying capacity shown in Figure 6-5 constant? Explain.

ANS: No, carrying capacity changes as conditions in the environment change.

DIF: A   OBJ: 6-1

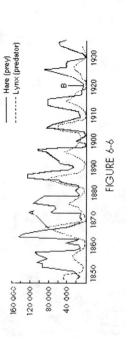

FIGURE 6-6

7. Explain why the predator population increased at point A in Figure 6-6.

ANS: As prey population grows, predators have more food and their density increases after a reproductive lag.

DIF: A   OBJ: 6-3

8. Why does the predator population decrease at point B in Figure 6-6?

ANS: The predator population becomes so dense that the prey are eaten faster than they reproduce. As the prey population declines, the predators starve.

DIF: A   OBJ: 6-3

9. When a volcano erupts, causing molten lava to cover parts of a mature forest, what type of ecological succession follows the hardened lava? Explain.

ANS: Although the preexisting community is disrupted, secondary succession does not occur because the ground is rock. The formation of soil has to begin with primary succession.

DIF: B   OBJ: 6-4

10. Why is acid rain harmful? How can it be decreased?

ANS: By changing the pH in ponds and lakes, acid rain kills aquatic organisms. It also leaches minerals from soils and damages buildings. It can be controlled by using low-sulfur coals and scrubbers, by burning efficiently, or by using less fossil fuel.

DIF: B   OBJ: 6-5

11. How can species share resources and avoid interspecific competition?

ANS: Territorial behavior is one way organisms can protect the resources in a given area. Another is to have structural adaptations, such as long roots that obtain nutrients at different levels. Different species may feed at different levels of the same tree.

DIF: B   OBJ: 6-3

12. Why is the removal of asbestos insulation from school buildings hazardous?

ANS: Removal dislodges asbestos fibers, which float in the air and may be inhaled. Both workers and building occupants risk lung damage.

DIF: B   OBJ: 6-5

13. Can a population reach its biotic potential? Explain.

ANS: Probably not. There would have to be unlimited space, unlimited nutrient resources, no competitors, and no disease. Even in a laboratory, conditions are never ideal.

DIF: A   OBJ: 6-2

OTHER

If the underscored word or phrase makes the sentence true, write "true" in the space provided. If the underscored word or phrase makes the sentence false, write the correct term or phrase in the space provided.

1. A predator-prey feeding relationship affects the population size of only the predator.

ANS: both predator and prey   DIF: B   OBJ: 6-3

2. In a predator-prey feeding relationship between lynx and hare, the hare is the predator.

ANS: prey   DIF: B   OBJ: 6-3

3. A decrease in prey population will result in an increase in predator population.

ANS: decrease   DIF: B   OBJ: 6-3

4. An increase in predator population follows an increase in prey population.

ANS: true   DIF: A   OBJ: 6-3

5. Factors such as disease and competition are examples of density-independent factors.

ANS: density-dependent factors   DIF: A   OBJ: 6-3

6. Density-dependent factors have an increasing effect as a population grows.

ANS: true   DIF: A   OBJ: 6-3

7. Density-independent factors are usually biotic.

ANS: abiotic   DIF: A   OBJ: 6-3

8. Being nonterritorial helps an animal avoid competing with other species for food and shelter.

ANS: territorial   DIF: B   OBJ: 6-3

9. Crowding of animals may result in death of older and weaker individuals.

ANS: true   DIF: B   OBJ: 6-3

10. Competition, predation, and crowding are limiting factors that control population size.

ANS: true   DIF: B   OBJ: 6-3

11. New communities or organisms form as a result of primary succession.

ANS: true   DIF: A   OBJ: 6-4

12. Interspecific competition occurs when members of the same species compete for resources, such as food or space.

ANS: different   DIF: A   OBJ: 6-3

13. Population doubling that occurs every 24 hours in a bacterial culture is an example of exponential growth.

ANS: true   DIF: B   OBJ: 6-1

14. Carbon dioxide resulting from the burning of fossil fuels can damage respiratory organs.

ANS: Particulates   DIF: B   OBJ: 6-5

Refer to Table 6-1. If the underscored word or phrase makes the sentence true, write "true" in the space provided. If the underscored word or phrase makes the sentence false, write the correct term or phrase in the space provided.

Table 6-1
Levels of DDT Reported in a Lake Ecosystem

WATER/ORGANISM	AMOUNTS OF DDT PRESENT
water	.000003 ppm*
organism A	.39 ppm
organism B	.04 ppm
organism C	.00004 ppm
organism D	.003 ppm

* = parts per million

15. The concentration of DDT present in all organisms is the same.

ANS: differs   DIF: B   OBJ: 6-5

16. Organism A has the highest concentration of DDT in its tissues.

ANS: true   DIF: B   OBJ: 6-5

17. Organism A must be a(n) autotroph.

ANS: heterotroph   DIF: A   OBJ: 6-5

18. Organism A would be the <u>first</u> trophic level in a food chain.

ANS: fourth   DIF: A   OBJ: 6-5

19. Organism C could be <u>algae.</u>

ANS: true   DIF: B   OBJ: 6-5

20. Organism D could be <u>small fish</u> that feed on algae.

ANS: true   DIF: B   OBJ: 6-5

21. The correct sequence for trophic levels would be <u>D, C, A, B.</u>

ANS: C, D, B, A   DIF: A   OBJ: 6-5

CHAPTER 7—BIOCHEMISTRY

MULTIPLE CHOICE

1. Which one of the following can be classified as saturated or unsaturated?
   a. lipids
   b. carbohydrates
   c. proteins
   d. starch

   ANS: A   DIF: B   OBJ: 7-4

2. Which one of the following can store the most energy per mass?
   a. lipids
   b. carbohydrates
   c. proteins
   d. starch

   ANS: A   DIF: B   OBJ: 7-4

3. Which one of the following is NOT classified as an element?
   a. cobalt
   b. nitrogen
   c. starch
   d. iodine

   ANS: C   DIF: B   OBJ: 7-1

4. The amount of energy needed to change the temperature of 1 g of water by 1°C is defined as a
   ___
   a. kilocalorie
   b. calorie
   c. Calorie
   d. joule

   ANS: B   DIF: B   OBJ: 7-2

5. Which one of the following elements is NOT found naturally in the human body?
   a. oxygen
   b. carbon
   c. calcium
   d. plutonium

   ANS: D   DIF: B   OBJ: 7-1

6. Which one of the following would NOT be considered a polymer?
   a. starch
   b. cellulose
   c. lipid
   d. glycine

   ANS: D   DIF: A   OBJ: 7-3

7. Which one of the following does NOT agree with how enzymes work?
   a. The current model of enzyme action is known as the lock-and-key model.
   b. Individual enzymes are versatile and work with many types of substrates.
   c. Enzymes are biological catalysts.
   d. Enzymes speed up chemical reactions by lowering the energy needed to break chemical bonds.

   ANS: B   DIF: A   OBJ: 7-5

8. Which one of the following is NOT a way of breaking long polymer chains into smaller parts?
   a. hydrolysis
   b. amylase breaking down carbohydrates
   c. protease breaking down fats into amino acids
   d. lipase breaking down fats into glycerol and fatty acids

   ANS: C   DIF: A   OBJ: 7-8

9. From where does your body get the energy it needs to function?
   a. individual atoms of oxygen, hydrogen, and carbon
   b. evaporation of sweat
   c. directly from the condensation of water on the skin
   d. the breaking of chemical bonds during chemical reactions in the body

   ANS: D   DIF: A   OBJ: 7-2

10. Which one of the following provides the main source of energy for most organisms?
    a. glucose
    b. cellulose
    c. glycerol
    d. alanine

    ANS: A   DIF: A   OBJ: 7-3

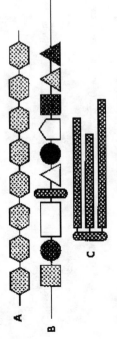

FIGURE 7-4

11. The enzyme lipase works on _____ in Figure 7-4.
    a. A, B, and C
    b. A and B, but not C
    c. A only
    d. C only

    ANS: D   DIF: B   OBJ: 7-5

12. Which diagram in Figure 7-4 represents the substances digested in the stomach?
    a. A, B, and C
    b. A and B, but not C
    c. A only
    d. C only

    ANS: B   DIF: B   OBJ: 7-8

13. On a gram-to-gram basis, which substance in Figure 7-4 contains more Calories?
    a. A
    b. B
    c. C
    d. All provide the same Calories per gram.

    ANS: C   DIF: B   OBJ: 7-2

14. Which statement about digestion of the substances shown in Figure 7-4 is true?
    a. The digestion of compounds A, B, and C yields glucose molecules, amino acids, and glycerol and fatty acids, respectively.
    b. Molecules like compound C can yield saturated and unsaturated amino acids and glycerol.
    c. All amino acids are identical once protein has been digested.
    d. Only the digestion of compound A involves hydrolysis.

    ANS: A   DIF: B   OBJ: 7-9

COMPLETION

1. Fats are types of _____ that are generally solid at room temperature.

   ANS: lipids   DIF: B   OBJ: 7-3

2. A(n) _____ is a specific molecule that an enzyme chemically recognizes and reacts with.

   ANS: substrate   DIF: B   OBJ: 7-5

3. A chemical reaction can produce a new substance from substrates, but the enzyme involved is _____.

   ANS: unchanged   DIF: B   OBJ: 7-6

4. An inhibitor can prevent an enzyme from functioning by changing the shape of the _____ of the enzyme.

   ANS: active site   DIF: B   OBJ: 7-7

5. The element _____ is in every amino acid molecule but not in carbohydrate or fat molecules.

   ANS: nitrogen   DIF: A   OBJ: 7-4

6. Most of the chemical bonds formed by organisms involve the carbon atom. Carbon atoms form _____ bonds.

ANS: covalent   DIF: B   OBJ: 7-4

7. Because fats are not soluble in water, the absence of _____ produced by the liver will interfere with the digestion of fats.

ANS: bile salts   DIF: A   OBJ: 7-8

8. The action of an enzyme can be blocked if a(n) _____ binds to the enzyme before the enzyme can interact with the substrate.

ANS: inhibitor   DIF: B   OBJ: 7-7

9. Alteration of the enzyme's _____ is one way enzyme action is inhibited.

ANS: active site   DIF: A   OBJ: 7-7

10. A slice of bread with 100 Calories contains _____ calories of energy.

ANS: 100 000   DIF: B   OBJ: 7-2

11. Digestion involves the addition of the ions of a water molecule across bonds in carbohydrates, fats, and proteins in a chemical process called _____.

ANS: hydrolysis   DIF: A   OBJ: 7-8

12. Fats and oils are both _____.

ANS: lipids   DIF: B   OBJ: 7-3

13. Digestion of the starch in a cracker begins in the mouth with the enzyme _____.

ANS: amylase   DIF: B   OBJ: 7-8

14. Of the three food categories, _____ are the most concentrated form of energy.

ANS: fats   DIF: A   OBJ: 7-2

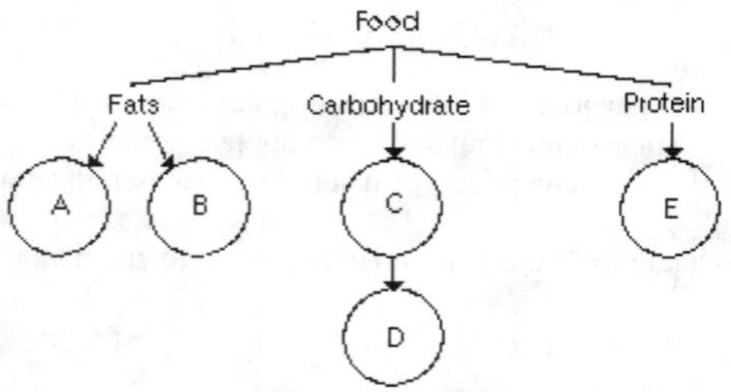

FIGURE 7-1

15. The name of the overall process represented by Figure 7-1 is _____.

ANS: digestion   DIF: B   OBJ: 7-8

16. In Figure 7-1, the products represented by A and B are _____ and _____.

ANS: glycerol, fatty acids   DIF: B   OBJ: 7-9

17. In Figure 7-1, the products represented by C and D are _____ and _____.

ANS: complex sugars, glucose   DIF: B   OBJ: 7-9

18. In Figure 7-1, the product represented by E is _____.

ANS: amino acids   DIF: B   OBJ: 7-9

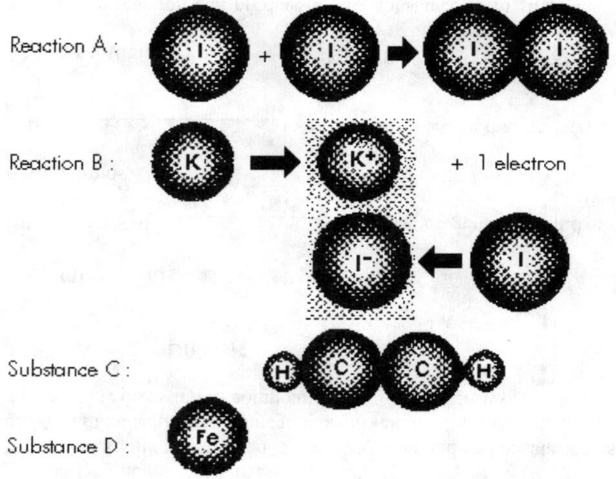

FIGURE 7-2

19. In Figure 7-2, the product of Reaction A is bonded together by a(n) _____ bond.

ANS: covalent   DIF: B   OBJ: 7-1

20. In Figure 7-2, the products of Reaction B are bonded together by a(n) _____ bond.

ANS: ionic   DIF: B   OBJ: 7-1

21. In Figure 7-2, Substance C is classified as a(n) _____.

ANS: compound   DIF: A   OBJ: 7-1

22. In Figure 7-2, Substance D is classified as a(n) _____.

ANS: element   DIF: A   OBJ: 7-1

Table 7-1
Food Information for Peanuts (per serving)

Food Substance	Mass	Calories
Fat	14 g	126
Carbohydrate	6 g	36
Protein	7 g	28

23. In Table 7-1, the total number of kilocalories in one serving of peanuts is _____.

ANS: 190   DIF: B   OBJ: 7-2

24. In Table 7-1, the total number of calories in one serving of peanuts is _____.

ANS: 190 000   DIF: B   OBJ: 7-2

25. In Table 7-1, the number of Calories in 1 g of fat is _____ Calories.

ANS: 126 Calories/14 g = 9 Calories/g   DIF: A   OBJ: 7-2

26. In Table 7-1, the number of Calories in 1 g of protein is _____.

ANS: 28 Calories/7 g = 4 Calories/g   DIF: A   OBJ: 7-2

MATCHING

Match each item with the correct statement below. Write the answer in the space provided.

a. amino acids
b. digestion
c. chemical reactions
d. lock-and-key
e. amylase
f. oxygen
g. lipids
h. substrate
i. enzymes
j. inhibitor
k. carbohydrates
l. calories
m. hydrolysis
n. proteins

1. ____ Carbohydrates, lipids, and proteins contain the elements carbon, hydrogen, and _____.
2. ____ Chemicals that can be thought of as "chemical motivators" in your body are called _____.
3. ____ The rate of _____ in the body can be controlled by enzymes.
4. ____ Enzymes can be controlled by other molecules known as _____ molecules.
5. ____ The process of breaking down food into smaller molecules that the body can absorb is _____.

---

6. ____ Starch is broken down in the mouth by the enzyme _____.
7. ____ the building blocks of proteins
8. ____ a model for enzyme reactions
9. ____ the main source of energy in foods
10. ____ fats belong to this category of foods
11. ____ polymeric chains of amino acids linked together
12. ____ the specific molecule that an enzyme reacts with
13. ____ the splitting apart of molecules by the addition of water
14. ____ measure of the chemical reaction in which the temperature of 1 g of water is raised 1°C

1. ANS: f   DIF: B   OBJ: 7-3
2. ANS: i   DIF: B   OBJ: 7-5
3. ANS: c   DIF: B   OBJ: 7-6
4. ANS: j   DIF: B   OBJ: 7-7
5. ANS: b   DIF: B   OBJ: 7-8
6. ANS: e   DIF: B   OBJ: 7-9
7. ANS: a   DIF: B   OBJ: 7-4
8. ANS: d   DIF: B   OBJ: 7-5
9. ANS: k   DIF: B   OBJ: 7-2
10. ANS: g   DIF: B   OBJ: 7-4
11. ANS: n   DIF: B   OBJ: 7-4
12. ANS: h   DIF: A   OBJ: 7-6
13. ANS: m   DIF: A   OBJ: 7-9
14. ANS: l   DIF: B   OBJ: 7-2

SHORT ANSWER

1. What are some common characteristics among all enzymes?

ANS: Enzymes speed up reactions, not make new reactions occur. They are not permanently changed during reactions and are reusable. Each individual enzyme works on one particular set of substrates.

DIF: A   OBJ: 7-5

2. What is the purpose of hydrolysis in the digestion of food?

ANS: Hydrolysis occurs when enzymes split polymers into smaller molecules, and hydrogen and hydroxide ions from water reattach to the molecules.

DIF: A   OBJ: 7-8

3. Why is it important to eat a well-balanced diet in terms of protein?

ANS: Our bodies can make 12 amino acids. The other eight must be obtained from protein from other sources.

DIF: A   OBJ: 7-4

4. Why is it hard for our bodies to digest fat?

ANS: Fats are not soluble in water. It is more difficult for fats to undergo hydrolysis.

DIF: A   OBJ: 7-9

FIGURE 7-3

5. Using Figure 7-3, explain how the enzyme can catalyze the reaction A + B → AB.

ANS: Substrates A and B can fit into the active site of the enzyme and come together to produce AB at a lower energy level than if the enzyme were not present.

DIF: A   OBJ: 7-6

6. Using Figure 7-3, is it possible for the enzyme to act as a catalyst in the reaction of C + D → CD? Explain.

ANS: No. The shape of the active site on the enzyme can allow substrate C to fit but does not allow a fit, and therefore an energy advantage, for substrate D.

DIF: A   OBJ: 7-6

7. In Figure 7-3, how can substrates C and/or D act as inhibitors in the reaction of A + B → AB?

ANS: Substrates C and D can fit into the active site of the enzyme, preventing substrate B from fitting into the active site of the enzyme along with substrate A.

DIF: A   OBJ: 7-7

8. How can body temperature affect the activity of the substrates and the enzyme found in Figure 7-3?

ANS: Fluctuations in body temperature can change the shape of the active site on the enzyme and prevent vital chemical reactions from occurring.

DIF: A   OBJ: 7-7

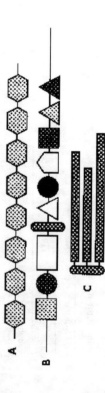

FIGURE 7-4

9. The diagrams in Figure 7-4 represent molecules of fat, protein, and carbohydrate. Identify each and explain your choice.

ANS: A represents a straight-chain polymer of identical smaller molecules. This is a carbohydrate, specifically starch; starch is a straight-chain molecule of glucose. B is also a straight-chain polymer, but the smaller molecules are not identical. Protein fits this representation because it is a polymer of up to 20 different amino acids. C represents a fat molecule. The vertical rectangle represents glycerol; the three horizontal rectangles represent three fatty acid molecules.

DIF: A   OBJ: 7-4

10. In what ways can individual atoms become more stable?

ANS: Atoms can become more stable by reacting with other atoms to form chemical bonds. Some atoms lose or gain electrons to form ions. The electrostatic attraction between ions forms ionic bonds. Other atoms share electrons. This process leads to covalent bonds.

DIF: A   OBJ: 7-1

11. Why is it important to distinguish between saturated and unsaturated fats when considering a healthy diet?

ANS: An unsaturated fat has one or more double bonds between the carbon atoms in its fatty acid chain. The chain is not holding as much hydrogen as it could. In a saturated fat, only single bonds are found between the carbon atoms in its fatty acid chain. It is holding as many hydrogen atoms as it can. Saturated fats tend to cause more health problems than unsaturated fats. It is, however, best to avoid both fats in our diets.

DIF: A   OBJ: 7-4

12. How can the body control the rate of chemical reactions to maintain a healthy balance in the body?

ANS: The rate of chemical reactions can be controlled by enzymes. One way is for the body to adjust the production of enzymes to control the actual number of enzymes present. Another way is to adjust the body environment, such as temperature, to allow enzymes to operate at optimum conditions. Another way is to slow down the rate of chemical reactions by the use of inhibitors so that enzymes do not catalyze reactions.

DIF: A   OBJ: 7-7

13. What are some of the enzymes involved in the digestion of carbohydrates, proteins, and fats? Where are each of these enzymes found?

ANS: Amylase found in saliva breaks down starch into complex sugars. Pepsin found in the stomach breaks down protein polymers into smaller chains of amino acids. Lipase found in the small intestine breaks fats into glycerol and fatty acids with the help of bile salts from the liver.

DIF: A   OBJ: 7-9

MULTIPLE CHOICE

1. In a chemical equation, such as $2H_2 + O_2 \rightarrow 2H_2O$, the numbers in front of the letters are called _____.
   a. coefficients
   b. yields
   c. reactants
   d. products

   ANS: A   DIF: B   OBJ: 8-1

2. Nitrogen gas must be converted to _____ to be useful to plants.
   a. ammonia
   b. ammonium
   c. nitrous oxide
   d. nitrites

   ANS: B   DIF: B   OBJ: 8-4

3. Phosphorus is usually found in the form of calcium phosphate in _____.
   a. the air
   b. plant roots
   c. streams
   d. rocks

   ANS: D   DIF: A   OBJ: 8-4

4. In the _____ of photosynthesis, water is split into hydrogen and oxygen.
   a. Calvin cycle
   b. carbon cycle
   c. light reactions
   d. Haber process

   ANS: C   DIF: A   OBJ: 8-5

5. Cellular respiration is an example of a(n) _____.
   a. catabolic reaction
   b. anabolic reaction
   c. light reactions
   d. nitrogen cycle

   ANS: A   DIF: B   OBJ: 8-6

6. During hot summer days, water evaporates from the ocean's surface. Late in each day, there is probably a short rainfall. What does this example illustrate?
   a. law of conservation of energy
   b. law of conservation of matter
   c. Haber process
   d. Calvin cycle

   ANS: B   DIF: A   OBJ: 8-1

---

14. What are amino acids? Why are they important to our bodies?

    ANS: Amino acids are the parts that make up the protein polymer. They contain a carbon atom that is covalently bonded with a hydrogen atom, an amino group, a carboxyl group, and an R group that varies with the amino acid. Some proteins are enzymes, so the arrangement of amino acid sequence in a protein is important.

    DIF: A   OBJ: 7-4

15. Explain the relationship between protein eaten in a person's diet and the protein present in that person's muscle tissue.

    ANS: Protein consumed in a diet is composed of amino acids assembled into protein by plants or animals. When a person eats a protein food, digestion of the protein, which begins in the stomach and is completed in the small intestine, releases amino acids. These amino acids are absorbed, and some of them are incorporated into muscle tissue. Although they may have the same molecules, the sequence of amino acids will now be different because human protein is forming.

    DIF: A   OBJ: 7-9

16. All enzymes are proteins. What happens to any enzymes present in food?

    ANS: Enzymes are digested in the same way that other proteins would be digested. Pepsin begins the digestion in the stomach, producing amino acid chains. Proteases in the small intestine further digest the amino acid chains, yielding individual amino acids that are available for absorption and incorporation into protein.

    DIF: A   OBJ: 7-9

17. Explain the difference between an ionic bond and a covalent bond.

    ANS: An ionic bond forms between two charged ions, one positive and the other negative. One atom gives up electrons, forming a positive ion. A second atom takes the electrons and forms a negative ion. In contrast, covalent bonds involve the sharing of electrons between atoms.

    DIF: B   OBJ: 7-4

18. What is the relationship between digestion and hydrolysis?

    ANS: Digestion is the process of breaking down food into smaller molecules that the body can absorb. Many of the individual reactions in the digestion of carbohydrates, fats, and proteins involve hydrolysis. Hydrolysis occurs when a large molecule is split into smaller molecules and the H+ and OH- from water attach to the smaller molecules.

    DIF: B   OBJ: 7-9

19. Sir Hans Adolf Krebs made a discovery in 1937. What was it, and why was it so important?

    ANS: Krebs discovered exactly how cells use chemicals to convert carbohydrates into energy. It was important because he introduced new techniques into the study of metabolism, led others to new discoveries, and enabled us to understand how the body converts food into energy.

    DIF: A   OBJ: 7-8

7. Carbon is cycled in ecosystems through _____
   a. photosynthesis in green plants
   b. decomposition of dead organisms
   c. combustion of fossil fuels
   d. all of the above

   ANS: D   DIF: A   OBJ: 8-4

8. The wavelengths of light that chlorophyll absorbs include _____
   a. X rays
   b. green light
   c. red and blue light
   d. radio waves

   ANS: C   DIF: A   OBJ: 8-5

9. Why was the Calvin cycle once referred to as the "dark reactions" of photosynthesis?
   a. because these reactions do not depend upon sunlight to occur
   b. because these reactions must take place at night
   c. because these reactions require dark shades of visible light
   d. none of the above

   ANS: A   DIF: B   OBJ: 8-5

10. Which of the following is produced as a result of photosynthesis?
    a. carbon dioxide
    b. water
    c. sugar
    d. all of the above

    ANS: C   DIF: B   OBJ: 8-5

A   B   C
$S + O_2 \rightarrow SO_3$

FIGURE 8-1

11. Reactants in Figure 8-1 are shown by _____
    a. A and C
    b. A and B
    c. A only
    d. C only

    ANS: B   DIF: A   OBJ: 8-1

12. Products in Figure 8-1 are shown by _____
    a. A
    b. B
    c. A and B
    d. C

    ANS: D   DIF: A   OBJ: 8-1

13. For the balancing of the equation in Figure 8-1, molecule A will have a coefficient of _____
    a. 1
    b. 2
    c. 3
    d. 4

    ANS: B   DIF: A   OBJ: 8-1

14. For the balancing of the equation in Figure 8-1, molecule B will have a coefficient of _____
    a. 1
    b. 2
    c. 3
    d. 4

    ANS: C   DIF: A   OBJ: 8-1

15. When correctly balanced, the equation shown in Figure 8-1 should _____
    a. have 2 times the number of atoms to the left compared to the right of the arrow
    b. have 2 times the number of atoms to the right compared to the left of the arrow
    c. have equal numbers of atoms on both sides of the arrow
    d. have no atoms to the left or right of the arrow

    ANS: C   DIF: B   OBJ: 8-1

The Nitrogen Cycle

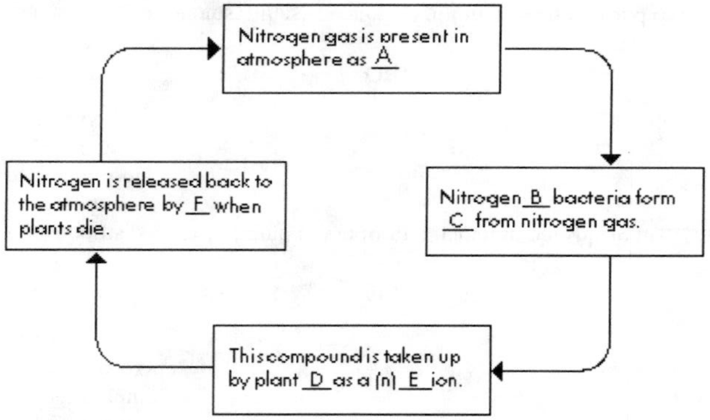

Nitrogen gas is present in atmosphere as _A_

Nitrogen _B_ bacteria form _C_ from nitrogen gas.

This compound is taken up by plant _D_ as a(n) _E_ ion.

Nitrogen is released back to the atmosphere by _F_ when plants die.

FIGURE 8-2

16. The choice that best completes space A in Figure 8-2 would be _____
    a. NH_4^+
    b. NH_3
    c. N_2
    d. NO_3

    ANS: C   DIF: A   OBJ: 8-4

17. The choice that best completes space B in Figure 8-2 would be ___
   a. decomposing
   b. demanding
   c. deficient
   d. fixing

ANS: D   DIF: B   OBJ: 8-4

18. The choice that best completes space C in Figure 8-2 would be ___
   a. N_2
   b. NH_3
   c. PO_4^{3-}
   d. NO_3^-

ANS: B   DIF: B   OBJ: 8-4

19. The choice that best completes space D in Figure 8-2 would be ___
   a. roots
   b. seeds
   c. flowers
   d. leaves

ANS: A   DIF: B   OBJ: 8-4

20. The choice that best completes space E in Figure 8-2 would be ___
   a. NH_3
   b. unchanged
   c. NH_4^+
   d. N_2

ANS: C   DIF: B   OBJ: 8-4

21. The choice that best completes space F in Figure 8-2 would be ___
   a. animals
   b. weathering
   c. lightning
   d. decomposers

ANS: D   DIF: B   OBJ: 8-4

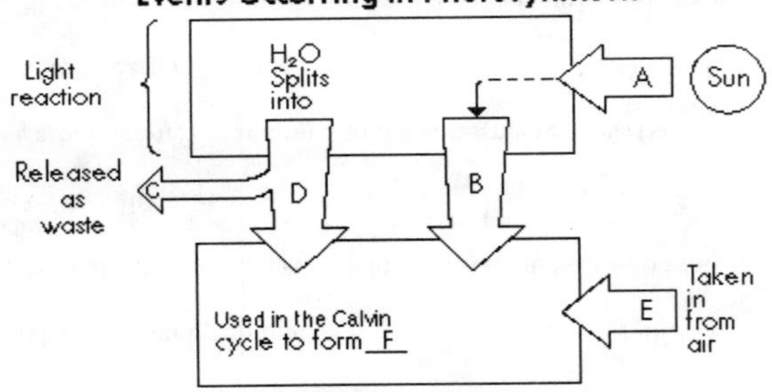

Events Occurring in Photosynthesis

FIGURE 8-3

22. The choice that correctly explains arrow A in Figure 8-3 would be ___
   a. chemical energy
   b. light energy
   c. water
   d. green light

ANS: B   DIF: A   OBJ: 8-5

23. The choice that correctly explains arrow B in Figure 8-3 would be ___
   a. light energy
   b. chlorophyll
   c. energy-storing molecules
   d. water

ANS: C   DIF: A   OBJ: 8-5

24. The choice that correctly explains arrow C in Figure 8-3 would be ___
   a. hydrogen ions
   b. oxygen
   c. chlorophyll
   d. glucose

ANS: B   DIF: A   OBJ: 8-5

25. The choice that correctly explains arrow D in Figure 8-3 would be ___
   a. glucose
   b. two 3-carbon molecules
   c. oxygen
   d. hydrogen ions

ANS: D   DIF: A   OBJ: 8-5

26. The choice that correctly explains arrow E in Figure 8-3 would be ___
   a. carbon dioxide
   b. water
   c. oxygen
   d. chlorophyll

ANS: A   DIF: B   OBJ: 8-5

27. The choice that correctly completes box F in Figure 8-3 would be ___
   a. water
   b. carbon dioxide
   c. two 3-carbon molecules
   d. oxygen

ANS: C   DIF: B   OBJ: 8-5

COMPLETION

1. Carbon atoms in starch and cellulose become part of the food supply in an ecosystem when they are _____.

ANS: eaten by animals   DIF: B   OBJ: 8-2

2. Animals that can digest cellulose convert it back into molecules of _____.

ANS: glucose   DIF: A   OBJ: 8-2

3. Carbon atoms are returned to the atmosphere as part of the gas _____.

ANS: carbon dioxide   DIF: B   OBJ: 8-2

4. Plants may use glucose to form another carbohydrate called _____, which animals do not form.

ANS: cellulose   DIF: A   OBJ: 8-2

5. Bacteria and fungi release carbon dioxide into the air as they break down dead organisms during _____.

ANS: decomposition   DIF: B   OBJ: 8-2

6. Carbon dioxide is released into the air during the burning of _____.

ANS: fossil fuels, wood, or organic debris   DIF: B   OBJ: 8-2

7. The chemical bond between two nitrogen atoms is so strong that this gas usually does not _____.

ANS: easily react with other atoms   DIF: B   OBJ: 8-4

8. Nitrogen fixation occurs naturally in the atmosphere when storms produce _____.

ANS: lightning   DIF: B   OBJ: 8-4

9. Weathering of rocks will release phosphorus into the _____.

ANS: soil   DIF: B   OBJ: 8-4

10. A person's _____ consists of all the chemical reactions within his or her body.

ANS: metabolism   DIF: B   OBJ: 8-2

11. Plant cell walls have a rigid structure because glucose molecules in _____ are strongly bonded together.

ANS: cellulose   DIF: B   OBJ: 8-3

12. _____ is the process in plants in which water and carbon dioxide are used to make glucose.

ANS: Photosynthesis   DIF: B   OBJ: 8-5

13. The _____ states that atoms are neither created nor destroyed during chemical reactions.

ANS: law of conservation of matter   DIF: B   OBJ: 8-1

14. The pigment in green plants that absorbs red and blue light is _____.

ANS: chlorophyll   DIF: B   OBJ: 8-5

15. Stored energy in glucose is converted to usable energy in a series of chemical reactions called _____.

ANS: cellular respiration   DIF: B   OBJ: 8-7

16. Bacteria in nodules on plant roots change atmospheric nitrogen to other forms in the process of _____.

ANS: nitrogen fixation   DIF: B   OBJ: 8-4

17. As chlorophyll absorbs energy from the sun, electrons are released in a series of reactions known as _____.

ANS: light reactions   DIF: A   OBJ: 8-5

18. Hydrogen and carbon dioxide are used to produce simple sugars in the part of photosynthesis known as the _____.

ANS: Calvin cycle   DIF: A   OBJ: 8-5

19. The type of chemical process that uses energy to produce and build up complex molecules such as starch is known as a(n) _____ reaction.

ANS: anabolic   DIF: B   OBJ: 8-6

SHORT ANSWER

1. Why are nitrogen and phosphorus so important to plants?

ANS: Nitrogen and phosphorus are components of amino acids, which plant cells use to make proteins.

DIF: B   OBJ: 8-3

2. Does cellular respiration occur at night? Explain your answer.

ANS: Yes. Cellular respiration is the process in which stored energy in glucose is converted to usable energy whenever it is needed by cells.

DIF: A   OBJ: 8-7

3. The Calvin cycle occurs without sunlight, yet it is dependent upon the light reactions of photosynthesis. Explain.

ANS: In the Calvin cycle, energy from energy-storing molecules and hydrogen are used to produce the three-carbon sugars that eventually form sugar, starch, and cellulose, a process possible only as long as the products from photosynthesis are available.

DIF: A   OBJ: 8-5

4. Is a fidgety, thin person who cannot gain weight more likely to have a high or a low metabolism? Why?

ANS: probably a high metabolism: a high cellular respiration rate always breaking down glucose to provide the energy for the restless activity; such people also use the energy released by digestion right away without storing any in fat cells

DIF: A   OBJ: 8-6

5. Why would a successful effort to introduce nitrogen-fixing bacteria into the roots of wheat, corn, and rice be important?

ANS: It would make these vital crops self-fertilizing, increase their yield, and therefore better feed Earth's growing population.

DIF: A   OBJ: 8-3

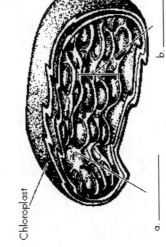

Chloroplast

a. _____   b. _____

FIGURE 8-6

6. Label Figure 8-6, a diagram of a chloroplast.   DIF: A   OBJ: 8-5

ANS: A. stroma, B. grana

$$X \left\{ \begin{array}{c} \overset{A}{}\ \overset{B}{}\ \overset{C}{}\ \overset{D}{} \\ CO_2 + H_2O \rightarrow C_6H_{12}O_6 + O_2 \end{array} \right.$$

$$Y \left\{ \begin{array}{c} \overset{E}{}\ \overset{F}{}\ \overset{G}{}\ \overset{H}{} \\ C_6H_{12}O_6 + O_2 \rightarrow CO_2 + H_2O \end{array} \right.$$

FIGURE 8-4

7. Which letter, X or Y, in Figure 8-4 shows the equation for photosynthesis?

ANS: X   DIF: B   OBJ: 8-7

8. Which letter, X or Y, in Figure 8-4 shows the equation for cellular respiration?

ANS: Y   DIF: B   OBJ: 8-7

9. Which letters in Figure 8-4 show the products of photosynthesis?

ANS: C and D   DIF: B   OBJ: 8-7

10. Which letters in Figure 8-4 show the reactants for photosynthesis?

ANS: A and B   DIF: B   OBJ: 8-7

11. Which letters in Figure 8-4 show the products of cellular respiration?

ANS: G and H   DIF: B   OBJ: 8-7

12. Which letters in Figure 8-4 show the reactants of cellular respiration?

ANS: E and F   DIF: B   OBJ: 8-7

13. Which letter, X or Y, in Figure 8-4 shows a reaction that converts stored energy in glucose to usable energy?

ANS: Y   DIF: A   OBJ: 8-7

14. Which letter, X or Y, in Figure 8-4 shows a catabolic reaction?

ANS: Y   DIF: A   OBJ: 8-7

15. If carbon going from the atmosphere to green plants to animals and back to the atmosphere is an example of short-term cycling, what is an example of the long-term carbon cycling process?

ANS: Carbon atoms in fossil fuels, held captive for millions of years, are not released into the cycle until the fuels are burned.

DIF: B   OBJ: 8-5

16. Other than growing green plants to eat or look at, what possible health benefit could green plants provide?

ANS: All green plants release oxygen. All organisms need oxygen for cellular respiration.

DIF: A   OBJ: 8-5

17. Why is phosphorus important to humans?

ANS: DNA contains it; it forms bones and teeth; it transfers energy within cells.

DIF: B   OBJ: 8-3

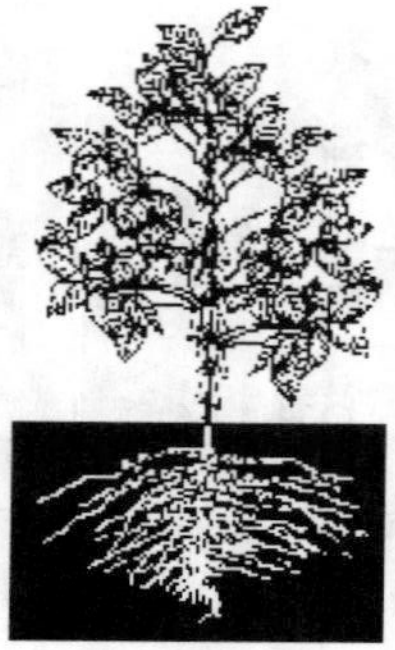

6. Protein, a compound that forms muscle and skin, contains the element phosphorus. _____

ANS: nitrogen   DIF: A   OBJ: 8-3

7. Energy is released during a catabolic reaction. _____

ANS: true   DIF: B   OBJ: 8-6

8. Complex molecules are broken down during anabolic reactions. _____

ANS: catabolic   DIF: B   OBJ: 8-6

9. Complex molecules are built up during catabolic reactions. _____

ANS: broken down   DIF: B   OBJ: 8-6

10. Cellular respiration is a type of catabolic reaction. _____

ANS: true   DIF: A   OBJ: 8-6

11. Molecules such as starch are formed during anabolic reactions. _____

ANS: true   DIF: B   OBJ: 8-6

Soybean
FIGURE 8-5

18. Explain how the plant in Figure 8-5 is a part of the nitrogen cycle.

ANS: Nodules on the roots contain bacteria that convert atmospheric nitrogen to ammonium and nitrate ions for plant use. After the plant becomes a waste product, either directly or processed by animals, decomposing bacteria will eventually restore nitrogen to the atmosphere. _____

DIF: B   OBJ: 8-5

OTHER

If the underscored word or phrase makes the sentence true, write "true" in the space provided. If the underscored word or phrase makes the sentence false, write the correct term or phrase in the space provided.

1. The NH_4^+ ion is a valuable source of phosphorus for plants. _____

ANS: nitrogen   DIF: B   OBJ: 8-3

2. Amino acids must contain nitrogen. _____

ANS: true   DIF: B   OBJ: 8-3

3. The element phosphorus plays an important role in energy transfer within cells. _____

ANS: true   DIF: B   OBJ: 8-3

4. Each basic unit that forms DNA contains nitrogen in the form of a phosphate group. _____

ANS: phosphorus   DIF: B   OBJ: 8-3

5. PO_4- ions, used by plants, may eventually end up in your bones or teeth. _____

ANS: true   DIF: A   OBJ: 8-3

CHAPTER 9—SOIL FORMATION

MULTIPLE CHOICE

1. Nonpolluting rainwater is slightly acidic with a pH of _____.
   a. 10–11
   b. 7.0
   c. 5.6–5.7
   d. 1.0

   ANS: C   DIF: A   OBJ: 9-3

2. Physical weathering is caused by _____.
   a. wind
   b. water
   c. ice
   d. all of the above

   ANS: D   DIF: B   OBJ: 9-3

3. Earthworms contribute to soil formation by _____.
   a. aerating the surface sediment
   b. secreting organic acids
   c. mixing organic material into the soil
   d. both a and c

   ANS: D   DIF: A   OBJ: 9-4

4. Soils in desert areas are _____.
   a. thick and well developed
   b. thin and poorly developed
   c. rich in organic matter
   d. formed rapidly

   ANS: B   DIF: A   OBJ: 9-1

5. The C horizon in a soil profile _____.
   a. consists of partly weathered parent material
   b. consists of unweathered parent material
   c. contains a large amount of organic material
   d. consists of plant roots and animal burrows

   ANS: A   DIF: B   OBJ: 9-5

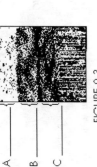

A ⎫
B ⎬
C ⎭

FIGURE 9-3

6. In Figure 9-3, the A horizon is a layer _____.
   a. of unaltered parent material
   b. that has gained material from leaching
   c. that has lost material from leaching
   d. of partly weathered parent material

   ANS: C   DIF: B   OBJ: 9-5

7. A thick layer of organic matter is present in the _____ of Figure 9-3.
   a. B horizon of soils in arid climates
   b. A horizon of soils in humid forests
   c. B horizon of rainforests
   d. C horizon of soils in moist, warm climates

   ANS: C   DIF: A   OBJ: 9-5

8. The layer that is vulnerable to erosion is _____ of Figure 9-3.
   a. the A horizon
   b. the B horizon
   c. the C horizon
   d. all of the above

   ANS: B   DIF: B   OBJ: 9-5

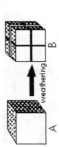

A → weathering → B

FIGURE 9-4

9. Assume that the cube shown in Figure 9-4 is a rock. Which of the following is true?
   a. Chemical weathering is more effective on the cube labeled A because there is more surface area.
   b. Physical weathering occurs after chemical weathering.
   c. Physical weathering results in more soil particles and a smaller total surface area.
   d. Physical weathering breaks the rock into smaller pieces and exposes more surface area for chemical weathering.

   ANS: D   DIF: A   OBJ: 9-3

10. Microorganisms contribute to soil formation by _____.
    a. increasing water penetration
    b. increasing the nitrogen content
    c. burrowing through the parent material
    d. preventing erosion

    ANS: A   DIF: B   OBJ: 9-4

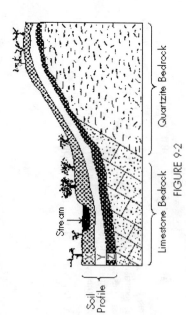

Stream

Soil Profile   X Y Z

Limestone Bedrock   Quartzite Bedrock

FIGURE 9-2

11. The lack of large trees at the top of the hill in Figure 9-2 is most likely due to _____.
    a. less oxygen at the higher elevation
    b. thin, poorly developed soil
    c. higher salinity
    d. all of the above

    ANS: B   DIF: A   OBJ: 9-5

12. In Figure 9-2, the limestone bedrock is _____.
    a. more resistant to chemical weathering
    b. found in the area of thin soils
    c. weathered rapidly by chemical means
    d. eroded to form highly acidic soils

    ANS: C   DIF: A   OBJ: 9-3

13. Soils in the valley shown in Figure 9-2 are _____.
    a. thicker
    b. more fertile
    c. thinner
    d. both a and b

    ANS: D   DIF: A   OBJ: 9-4

14. The horizon labeled X in Figure 9-2 is the _____.
    a. C horizon
    b. A horizon
    c. B horizon
    d. unaltered parent material

    ANS: B   DIF: B   OBJ: 9-5

15. In Figure 9-2, the most fertile soil for agriculture will be found _____.
    a. at the top of the hill
    b. on the steep slope
    c. in the valley near the stream
    d. in the layer labeled Z

    ANS: C   DIF: A   OBJ: 9-5

COMPLETION

1. _____ is the process by which rock and mineral matter are broken down into smaller pieces by physical and chemical reactions.

    ANS: Weathering   DIF: B   OBJ: 9-3

2. Relatively _____ mountains are steep and jagged with little vegetation.

    ANS: young   DIF: A   OBJ: 9-4

3. _____ soils can be thick with deeply weathered soil profiles.

    ANS: Tropical   DIF: A   OBJ: 9-1

4. The _____ horizon in a soil profile is thin and rich in organic matter.

    ANS: A   DIF: B   OBJ: 9-5

5. The _____ horizon in a soil profile consists of partly weathered parent material.

    ANS: C   DIF: B   OBJ: 9-5

6. Frost wedging is an example of _____.

    ANS: physical weathering   DIF: B   OBJ: 9-3

7. _____ occurs when water percolates through the upper layer of soil and washes minerals downward.

    ANS: Leaching   DIF: B   OBJ: 9-2

8. Litter and humus are _____.

    ANS: organic matter   DIF: B   OBJ: 9-1

MATCHING

Match each item with the correct statement below. Write the answer in the space provided.

a. hydroponics   i. topography
b. physical weathering   j. lime
c. erosion   k. texture
d. chemical weathering   l. silviculture
e. soil   m. minimum tillage
f. humus   n. litter
g. parent material   o. cotton
h. soil profile

_____ 1. breakdown of rock material without changing the chemical composition
_____ 2. source material (rock or sediment) altered to form a soil
_____ 3. configuration of the land surface
_____ 4. percentage of different sizes of particles in a soil
_____ 5. science of growing plants in a nutrient solution
_____ 6. a neutralizing agent
_____ 7. plant that is widely produced for fabric
_____ 8. the growing of trees
_____ 9. process that moves weathered rock from one place to another
_____ 10. practice of not plowing a field after the harvest
_____ 11. the action of weak acids on parent rock
_____ 12. the remains of decomposed litter
_____ 13. composed of weathered rock and organic matter
_____ 14. dead leaves, sticks, and plant parts
_____ 15. contains layers that give a record of the total environment in which soil formed

1. ANS: b   DIF: B   OBJ: 9-3
2. ANS: g   DIF: B   OBJ: 9-4
3. ANS: i   DIF: B   OBJ: 9-4
4. ANS: k   DIF: B   OBJ: 9-4
5. ANS: a   DIF: B   OBJ: 9-6
6. ANS: j   DIF: B   OBJ: 9-6
7. ANS: o   DIF: B   OBJ: 9-6
8. ANS: l   DIF: B   OBJ: 9-7
9. ANS: c   DIF: B   OBJ: 9-2
10. ANS: m   DIF: B   OBJ: 9-6
11. ANS: d   DIF: A   OBJ: 9-3
12. ANS: f   DIF: B   OBJ: 9-1
13. ANS: e   DIF: B   OBJ: 9-1
14. ANS: n   DIF: B   OBJ: 9-1
15. ANS: h   DIF: B   OBJ: 9-5

SHORT ANSWER

1. Why is soil an important resource?

ANS: Soils support terrestrial plant life and therefore all life on land. Agriculture is an important human industry that is based to a great extent on soil productivity.

DIF: B   OBJ: 9-8

9. Nutrients needed for plant growth can be added to depleted soils in the form of artificial or natural _____.

ANS: fertilizer   DIF: B   OBJ: 9-6

10. Soil accumulates over time as a result of the weathering of _____.

ANS: parent rock   DIF: B   OBJ: 9-2

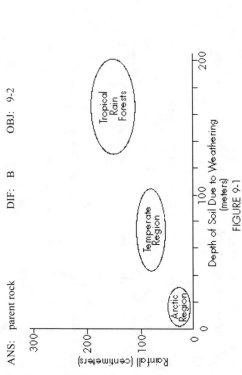

FIGURE 9-1

11. In Figure 9-1, the thickest soil profile would be found in the _____ region.

ANS: tropical rain forest   DIF: A   OBJ: 9-5

12. Desert regions would most resemble the _____ in Figure 9-1.

ANS: Arctic region   DIF: A   OBJ: 9-5

13. The other climatic variable not shown in Figure 9-1 that contributes to the depth of soil due to weathering is _____.

ANS: temperature   DIF: A   OBJ: 9-5

14. The _____ region in Figure 9-1 is where soils will be the most poorly developed.

ANS: Arctic   DIF: A   OBJ: 9-5

15. Based on Figure 9-1, chemical weathering is most important in the _____ region.

ANS: tropical rain forest   DIF: A   OBJ: 9-3

2. What farming techniques can be used to reduce soil erosion?

ANS: contour plowing, terracing, planting wind rows of trees or bushes, crop rotation, and minimum tillage

DIF: B   OBJ: 9-6

3. What are some of the advantages of organic farming over conventional farming methods?

ANS: Commercial fertilizers, pesticides, and herbicides are not used, thus saving money and preventing the possible pollution of food, air, and water.

DIF: A   OBJ: 9-6

4. What beneficial effects do earthworms have on the soil?

ANS: Burrowing aerates the soil and allows moisture to penetrate. Earthworms also add organic matter to the soil.

DIF: B   OBJ: 9-6

5. What affects the time needed to form a soil?

ANS: type of parent material, climate, biological activity, vegetation, and topography

DIF: B   OBJ: 9-4

6. Why is the weathering of rock by chemical action more intense in a tropical rain forest than in other areas?

ANS: As temperature increases, the rate of chemical reactions and decomposers increases. The additional moisture in rain forests increases the amount of water carrying acids to the parent rock.

DIF: A   OBJ: 9-4

7. What are the sources of acids involved in chemical weathering?

ANS: Carbon dioxide, sulfur dioxide, and nitrogen oxides in the atmosphere mix with water to make weak acids. Plants produce acids as they grow, and decomposers release acids. Water percolating through humus brings acids to the lower soil horizons.

DIF: A   OBJ: 9-4

8. Why does chemical weathering become more effective with the help of frost action?

ANS: Frost action increases the surface area that is exposed to weak acids.

DIF: A   OBJ: 9-2

9. Is frost wedging effective in polar areas?

ANS: Temperatures must range across water's freezing point, so frost wedging isn't effective in areas that are always frozen.

DIF: A   OBJ: 9-2

10. Why is terracing used in agriculture?

ANS: Terracing prevents soil and nutrient loss through water runoff. This method allows areas on hillsides to be farmed.

DIF: A   OBJ: 9-6

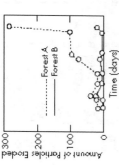

FIGURE 9-5

11. Which line in Figure 9-5, A or B, represents a forest that was clear-cut? Explain.

ANS: Line A shows more erosion occurring over time and represents a forest that was clear-cut.

DIF: B   OBJ: 9-7

12. Infer why there is a time lag before line A in Figure 9-5 begins to show an increase.

ANS: Roots are still in place, and litter and humus continue to hold soil in place until they are completely decomposed.

DIF: B   OBJ: 9-7

13. What happens to soil after trees are removed? Why?

ANS: Soil is no longer held in place by roots and can be carried away by rain or wind.

DIF: B   OBJ: 9-7

14. Infer what the effects of clear-cutting would be on the soil's temperature and nutrients.

ANS: Temperature would increase as there is less shade and less litter. Nutrients would be washed away instead of being recycled through the trees.

DIF: A   OBJ: 9-7

15. List the factors that influence soil formation and how each factor affects the resultant soil profile.

ANS:
Climate: areas with higher temperatures and rainfalls have higher rates of chemical weathering. The seasonality of the climate also affects the weathering rate. Areas with higher rates of chemical weathering have thicker soil profiles.
Parent Material: the composition of the parent material will influence the resulting soil composition.
Topography: soils formed on hilltops and steep slopes are more susceptible to erosion and are generally less well developed.
Time: depending on the other factors, some soils develop rapidly (tens-hundreds of years), while others can be millions of years old.

DIF: A   OBJ: 9-4

16. The horizons in a soil profile are defined by what characteristics?

ANS: The soil layers or horizons are distinguished by color, organic content, mineral and chemical composition, amount of moisture, and texture.

DIF: A   OBJ: 9-5

17. How could the type of vegetation affect the formation of soil in an area?

ANS: The type of vegetation will affect the depth of root penetration, root size, and root density, which will affect the soil horizons. Different types of plants use different minerals from the soil for their growth and will affect the biochemical reactions taking place in the soil. The type and density of plants affect erosion as well.

DIF: A   OBJ: 9-4

18. If you were hired to develop a soil classification, what characteristics would you base the classification system on?

ANS: climate the soil was developed in, vegetation type, soil texture, soil organic content, the presence of various distinctive minerals (such as clay, calcite, salts, etc.), soil color, degree and depth of weathering (degree of horizonation)

DIF: A   OBJ: 9-1

19. How does widespread deforestation affect the economy in the area?

ANS: Deforestation leads to air pollution, soil erosion, and loss of habitat. Soils in many areas are rapidly depleted of nutrients through single-crop agriculture, which, along with soil erosion, lowers productivity. Habitat loss can endanger economically valuable plants and animals. As the soil becomes depleted, either expensive fertilizers must be used to keep up productivity or areas are abandoned and more forests are cleared.

DIF: A   OBJ: 9-7

20. Recall from Chapter 5 that plants play an important part in the water cycle. What role does transpiration play in controlling runoff?

ANS: Much of the water in a forest is cycled through trees via the roots, some of it soaks into the ground, some of it evaporates, and the rest is released into the atmosphere via transpiration. Without trees, water runs off the ground into streams, carrying soil with it.

DIF: A   OBJ: 9-7

21. If you inherited an unproductive piece of land, what could you do to improve your chances for successful planting?

ANS: Test the soil for nutrients and organic matter content. Then add fertilizer, topsoil, and organic matter and plant cover crops to hold the soil. Crop rotation will keep the soil healthy and contour plowing will prevent erosion.

DIF: A   OBJ: 9-6

22. How could the use of pesticides affect soil formation?

ANS: Pesticides can kill microorganisms, such as earthworms, millipedes, and moles. These organisms aerate the soil, allow more water to enter, and change the soil chemically. These actions assist the weathering of parent material.

DIF: A   OBJ: 9-4

23. In temperate areas, tree rings show more growth occurring in summer than in winter. If this growth pattern is also true for roots, when would you expect to see more physical and chemical weathering?

ANS: In the summer, physical weathering would be greater due to the expansion of the roots. Chemical weathering due to acid secretion during growth would also be greater during summer.

DIF: A   OBJ: 9-2

24. Infer why soil is turned over before planting.

ANS: Any litter on the surface will decompose faster into humus after it is turned over. Nutrients will be mixed, and the added organic matter gives the soil better water-holding properties.

DIF: A   OBJ: 9-6

25. Why do people who live near rain forests clear-cut them even though this practice is destructive to the ecosystem?

ANS: These people need the land for food crops and the wood for fuel.

DIF: B   OBJ: 9-7

MULTIPLE CHOICE

1. Which one of the following would be used as a pesticide against mold and mildew?
   a. insecticide
   b. fungicide
   c. herbicide
   d. rodenticide

   ANS: B   DIF: B   OBJ: 10-1

2. Which of the following pesticides is unstable and acts for only a short time?
   a. DDT
   b. nicotine
   c. heptachlor
   d. both DDT and heptachlor

   ANS: B   DIF: B   OBJ: 10-2

3. Which one of the following would NOT be considered a biological control against pests?
   a. frogs
   b. marigolds
   c. heptachlor
   d. ladybird beetles

   ANS: C   DIF: B   OBJ: 10-3

4. Which one of the following is NOT used to maintain the freshness of food?
   a. canning
   b. freezing
   c. drying
   d. ladybird beetles

   ANS: D   DIF: B   OBJ: 10-4

5. Which of the following can be classified as an antioxidant?
   a. BHT and BHA
   b. UHT
   c. mold inhibitor
   d. rennin

   ANS: A   DIF: B   OBJ: 10-5

6. Which of the following is an effect of heat on food?
   a. change in color
   b. loss of water-soluble vitamins
   c. denaturing of protein
   d. all choices are correct

   ANS: D   DIF: B   OBJ: 10-6

OTHER

If the underscored word or phrase makes the sentence true, write "true" in the space provided. If the underscored word or phrase makes the sentence false, write the correct term or phrase in the space provided.

1. A solution with a pH of 7.0 is acidic. _____

   ANS: neutral   DIF: A   OBJ: 9-3

2. Regions with high average rainfalls and temperatures have lower rates of chemical weathering. _____

   ANS: higher   DIF: A   OBJ: 9-3

3. The burrowing activity of many animals causes weathering. _____

   ANS: true   DIF: A   OBJ: 9-2

4. The rock limestone is resistant to chemical weathering. _____

   ANS: quartzite   DIF: A   OBJ: 9-2

5. Shale parent rock commonly produces soils with high clay content. _____

   ANS: true   DIF: A   OBJ: 9-4

7. Which type of cooking takes advantage of the relationship among temperature, pressure, and volume?
   a. conventional cooking
   b. pressure cooking
   c. solar cooking
   d. microwave oven cooking

   ANS: B   DIF: B   OBJ: 10-7

8. DDT and heptachlor can be classified as what type of pesticide?
   a. insecticide
   b. herbicide
   c. fungicide
   d. rodenticide

   ANS: A   DIF: A   OBJ: 10-1

9. Which of the following statements about antioxidants is true?
   a. They all are on the "Generally Regarded as Safe" list.
   b. They are the only chemical that can be added to food according to the Delaney Clause.
   c. They are the only inhibitor that can be added to food.
   d. They are added to food to slow spoilage.

   ANS: D   DIF: A   OBJ: 10-6

10. Which of the following is NOT a pest control method?
    a. insecticide
    b. antioxidant
    c. biological control
    d. herbicide

    ANS: B   DIF: A   OBJ: 10-1

11. Which of the following is NOT a method of food preservation?
    a. freezing
    b. canning
    c. drying
    d. baking

    ANS: D   DIF: A   OBJ: 10-7

12. Which of the following is NOT a food additive?
    a. inhibitor
    b. antioxidant
    c. pasteurize
    d. preservative

    ANS: C   DIF: A   OBJ: 10-7

13. Which of these is NOT a desirable food component?
    a. nutrients
    b. vitamins
    c. mold
    d. protein

    ANS: C   DIF: A   OBJ: 10-7

COMPLETION

1. _____ are pesticides that control weeds.

   ANS: Herbicides   DIF: B   OBJ: 10-1

2. The pesticide heptachlor was found to contaminate the food product _____ in Oahu, Hawaii, in March 1982.

   ANS: milk   DIF: B   OBJ: 10-2

3. Modern pest management is called _____

   ANS: integrated pest control (IPC)   DIF: B   OBJ: 10-3

4. Conventional ovens transfer heat by _____

   ANS: conduction   DIF: B   OBJ: 10-7

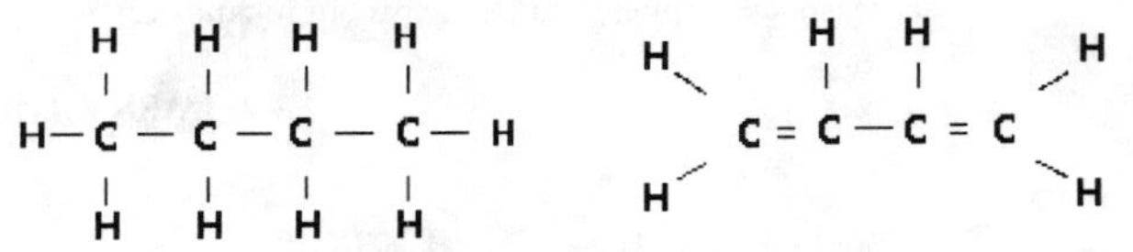

FIGURE 10-1

5. In Figure 10-1, the bonds in the compound on the left would best be described as _____

   ANS: single   DIF: B   OBJ: 10-2

6. In Figure 10-1, the bonds in the compound on the right would best be described as _____

   ANS: double   DIF: B   OBJ: 10-2

7. In Figure 10-1, the bonds in the compound on the left would most probably be found in a _____ pesticide.

   ANS: natural   DIF: B   OBJ: 10-3

5. _____ the product protected by a pesticide
6. _____ forbids using cancer-causing substances in food processing
7. _____ substance that slows down a chemical process
8. _____ a pesticide that is effective for a specific pest
9. _____ prevents or slows down reaction with oxygen
10. _____ chemical that repels or destroys a pest
11. _____ treatment with high temperature to retard spoilage
12. _____ uses a living organism or its products to control pests
13. _____ the pest a pesticide is designed to control

1. ANS: c   DIF: B   OBJ: 10-1
2. ANS: h   DIF: B   OBJ: 10-5
3. ANS: d   DIF: B   OBJ: 10-6
4. ANS: f   DIF: B   OBJ: 10-7
5. ANS: g   DIF: B   OBJ: 10-3
6. ANS: i   DIF: B   OBJ: 10-4
7. ANS: k   DIF: B   OBJ: 10-4
8. ANS: j   DIF: B   OBJ: 10-1
9. ANS: l   DIF: B   OBJ: 10-4
10. ANS: e   DIF: B   OBJ: 10-1
11. ANS: m   DIF: B   OBJ: 10-5
12. ANS: a   DIF: B   OBJ: 10-3
13. ANS: b   DIF: B   OBJ: 10-1

SHORT ANSWER

1. What are some of the ways that insecticides can affect insects?

   ANS: Some are stomach poisons, some affect the nervous system, some affect breathing, and some affect the formation of the outer protective layer of the insect.

   DIF: A   OBJ: 10-2

2. Why is integrated pest control important in growing food?

   ANS: because several different tactics are used to control pests, and pesticide use can be safer for people and the environment

   DIF: A   OBJ: 10-3

3. What is the main bad effect of oxygen on food?

   ANS: It can cause food to spoil.

   DIF: A   OBJ: 10-4

4. Why must you refrigerate milk even after it has been pasteurized?

   ANS: Pasteurization kills most bacteria, but it only retards spoilage. Refrigeration helps to prolong freshness.

   DIF: A   OBJ: 10-5

---

8. In Figure 10-1, the bonds in the compound on the right would most probably be found in a _____ pesticide.

   ANS: synthetic   DIF: B   OBJ: 10-3

Table 10-1

Milk Samples	pH
Sample 1	6.8
Sample 2	6.5
Sample 3	5.4

9. Milk Sample _____ in Table 10-1 is the most acidic.

   ANS: 3   DIF: B   OBJ: 10-4

10. Milk Sample _____ in Table 10-1 is the most basic.

    ANS: 1   DIF: B   OBJ: 10-4

11. Milk Sample _____ in Table 10-1 is the closest to neutral pH.

    ANS: 1   DIF: B   OBJ: 10-4

12. Milk Sample _____ in Table 10-1 is the most likely to be spoiled.

    ANS: 3   DIF: B   OBJ: 10-4

MATCHING

Match each item with the correct statement below. Write the answer in the space provided.

a. biological control   h. pasteurized
b. target   i. Delaney Clause
c. host   j. selective
d. denaturation   k. inhibitor
e. pesticide   l. antioxidant
f. vibrate   m. pasteurization
g. host

1. _____ If a pesticide is being used to protect plants from a certain insect, the insect is the _____ target and the plant is the _____.
2. _____ Milk that has been treated with high temperature to kill bacteria and viruses has been _____.
3. _____ The heating of amino acid chains that causes them to uncoil is known as _____.
4. _____ A microwave oven cooks food by causing water molecules in the food to _____.

5. What are some of the chemical and physical changes that can occur in food when it is heated?

ANS: changing appearance and color, losing water-soluble nutrients and vitamins, producing gases such as carbon dioxide, denaturing proteins, and changing texture

DIF: A   OBJ: 10-6

6. Compare and contrast Pasteur's method of pasteurization with the Ultra High Temperature process.

ANS: UHT uses a higher temperature for a shorter time than Pasteur's method, and it destroys more bacteria.

DIF: B   OBJ: 10-5

7. Why is controlling the temperature important while cooking food?

ANS: The temperature must be high enough to kill bacteria but not so high that the food breaks down and loses nutrients.

DIF: B   OBJ: 10-6

8. Compare the way a conventional oven cooks food with the way a microwave oven cooks.

ANS: A conventional oven uses heat, whereas a microwave oven uses microwaves as the source of energy. A conventional oven transfers heat by conduction to the surface of the food, while a microwave oven cooks from the inside out as the food's water molecules vibrate.

DIF: B   OBJ: 10-7

9. Why are antioxidants needed?

ANS: Oxygen is very reactive and causes food to spoil.

DIF: B   OBJ: 10-4

10. A cake requires baking soda for the release of carbon dioxide during baking. What would happen if this ingredient were omitted?

ANS: The cake would not rise; it would be flat and doughy.

DIF: B   OBJ: 10-6

11. What is the chemical difference between naturally occurring organic pesticides and many synthetic pesticides?

ANS: The chemical bonds in naturally occurring organic pesticides are not as stable as the chemical bonds in many synthetic pesticides.

DIF: B   OBJ: 10-3

12. How does the chemical difference between naturally occurring organic pesticides and many synthetic pesticides affect the use of these compounds as pesticides?

ANS: Naturally occurring pesticides easily break down in nature; therefore, they need frequent application. Many synthetic pesticides do not break down easily in nature; therefore, they accumulate in organisms and may be harmful as they move up the food chain.

DIF: A   OBJ: 10-3

13. Does pasteurization prevent milk from spoiling? Explain.

ANS: No. By killing bacteria, pasteurization retards spoilage but cannot prevent it.

DIF: A   OBJ: 10-5

14. Why is it better to steam vegetables than to boil them in water?

ANS: Steamed vegetables retain water-soluble vitamins whereas boiled vegetables do not.

DIF: B   OBJ: 10-7

15. Why is it important that foods be neither undercooked nor overcooked?

ANS: Undercooking can cause illness if bacteria are not killed. Overcooking can destroy nutrients or cause decomposition.

DIF: A   OBJ: 10-6

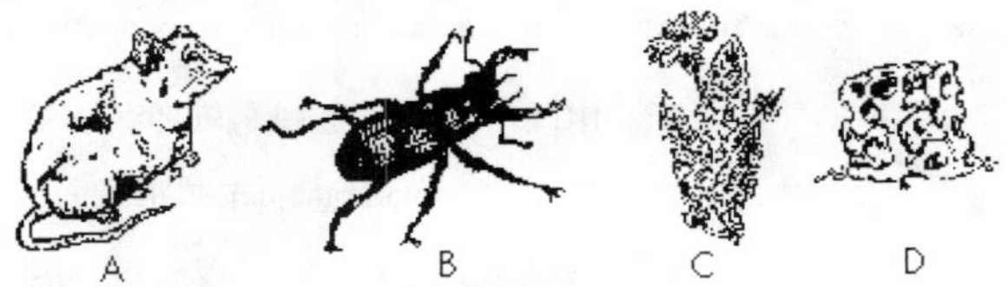

A   B   C   D

FIGURE 10-3

16. For each pest in Figure 10-3, identify the appropriate pesticide.

ANS: A. rodenticide; B. insecticide; C. herbicide; D. fungicide

DIF: A   OBJ: 10-1

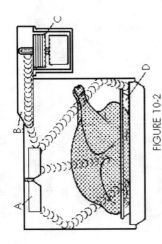

FIGURE 10-2

17. In the microwave oven in Figure 10-2, what is part A and what is its purpose?

ANS: It is the stirrer. It helps to lessen the effect of interference of microwaves, which causes hot and cold areas in the food.

DIF: A   OBJ: 10-7

18. In the microwave oven in Figure 10-2, what is part B and what is its purpose?

ANS: It is the waveguide. It guides the microwave from the magnetron into the oven.

DIF: B   OBJ: 10-7

19. In the microwave oven in Figure 10-2, what is part C and what is its purpose?

ANS: It is the magnetron. It produces microwaves.

DIF: B   OBJ: 10-7

20. In the microwave oven in Figure 10-2, why is part D, a turntable, often used?

ANS: Microwaves interfere with each other, causing waves with high amplitude in one area of the oven but canceling out waves in another. This causes hot and cold areas. A turntable helps even out the hot and cold areas in food.

DIF: A   OBJ: 10-7

21. Suppose you need to use a pesticide in your garden. What procedure would you follow to select the correct pesticide and use it safely?

ANS: First, identify the host and target. Identify pesticides that are selective for the target without affecting the host. Carefully read the pesticide's label. Follow the mixing and applying instructions that are given. Follow any safety information.

DIF: A   OBJ: 10-1

22. Why shouldn't pesticides be banned?

ANS: Pesticides are important because they allow us to grow lots of food with few people. Weeds take needed water and nutrients from food crops. Pests can eat food crops. The risks of using some types of pesticides may not be greater than the harm done by the pest on the food crop.

DIF: A   OBJ: 10-2

23. What are the advantages and disadvantages of using biological controls to reduce pests?

ANS: An advantage is that the plant or insect pests do not develop resistance to the pesticide when a biological control is used. A disadvantage is that the biological control may not have any natural predators and could become a pest itself.

DIF: A   OBJ: 10-3

24. What are some of the newer methods to keep foods fresh and prevent spoilage?

ANS: Newer methods include the use of refrigerators, safer and cleaner canning methods, safer antioxidants, and testing of food additives. Federal laws, such as the Delaney Clause, closely regulate the use of chemicals in food.

DIF: A   OBJ: 10-4

25. Describe the difference between the old style of pasteurization and the newer style known as Ultra High Temperature (UHT).

ANS: The older method heated milk to 62 degrees Celsius for 30 minutes. This would kill most of the bacteria and break down enzymes that react with milk fat. The newer method heats milk to 138 degrees Celsius for 1 second. This method kills more bacteria but does not cause milk to clump.

DIF: A   OBJ: 10-5

OTHER

If the underscored word or phrase makes the sentence true, write "true" in the space provided. If the underscored word or phrase makes the sentence false, write the correct term or phrase in the space provided.

1. DDT is an underscored unstable pesticide. _____

ANS: stable   DIF: B   OBJ: 10-2

2. Compounds that prevent or slow down reactions with oxygen are underscored antioxidants. _____

ANS: true   DIF: B   OBJ: 10-4

3. UHT is a new method of pasteurization. _____

ANS: true   DIF: B   OBJ: 10-5

4. Green food will lose its green color when underscored calcium from the plant's chlorophyll decomposes from overheating. _____

ANS: magnesium   DIF: B   OBJ: 10-6

5. Pressure-cooking is important in the processing of some underscored nonacidic, home-canned products. _____

ANS: true   DIF: B   OBJ: 10-7

CHAPTER 11—RESOURCES

MULTIPLE CHOICE

1. Which of the following is a renewable natural resource?
   a. gold
   b. oil
   c. limestone
   d. nitrogen

   ANS: D   DIF: B   OBJ: 11-1

2. Which of the following uses the lowest percentage of the energy presently consumed in the United States?
   a. transportation
   b. residential and commercial users
   c. industrial users
   d. none of the above

   ANS: A   DIF: B   OBJ: 11-3

3. Which of the following resources accounts for the greatest percentage of the waste stream in the United States?
   a. steel
   b. plastic
   c. glass
   d. paper

   ANS: D   DIF: B   OBJ: 11-4

4. The United States gets most of its energy from _____.
   a. solar sources
   b. nuclear sources
   c. oil and gas
   d. hydroelectric power plants

   ANS: C   DIF: B   OBJ: 11-4

5. Petroleum is formed _____.
   a. from the remains of marine organisms
   b. in a few hundred years
   c. by inorganic precipitation
   d. on the surface of the ocean

   ANS: A   DIF: B   OBJ: 11-1

6. Which of the following is nonrenewable?
   a. sunshine
   b. carbon
   c. nitrogen
   d. coal

   ANS: D   DIF: B   OBJ: 11-1

7. Which of the following is the most difficult resource to recycle?
   a. plastic
   b. glass
   c. paper
   d. aluminum

   ANS: A   DIF: A   OBJ: 11-3

8. The metal used to make the steel in a building is _____.
   a. renewable
   b. a fossil fuel
   c. a construction resource
   d. an energy resource

   ANS: C   DIF: B   OBJ: 11-1

9. Copper is _____.
   a. a renewable metal
   b. a nonrenewable, nonmetal mineral resource
   c. a metal used as fuel in nuclear reactors
   d. used to make pipes and electrical wires

   ANS: D   DIF: A   OBJ: 11-1

10. Of the following, the resource that is NOT an example of an energy resource is _____.
    a. phosphorus
    b. oil
    c. sunlight
    d. coal

    ANS: A   DIF: B   OBJ: 11-1

11. Of the following, the resource that is most recycled is _____.
    a. paper
    b. plastic
    c. aluminum
    d. glass

    ANS: C   DIF: B   OBJ: 11-3

12. The recycled material that is combined with asphalt and used to pave streets in some areas is _____.
    a. phosphorus
    b. glass
    c. aluminum
    d. plastic

    ANS: B   DIF: B   OBJ: 11-3

13. Of the following, the material that is NOT considered a renewable resource is _____.
a. oxygen
b. a tree
c. a forest
d. water

ANS: C   DIF: A   OBJ: 11-1

14. Of the following, the example that illustrates the reuse of a resource is _____.
a. making a swing from an old tire
b. using reprocessed aluminum cans to make a car engine
c. using a photovoltaic cell to produce electricity
d. using reprocessed glass as a material for making road pavement

ANS: A   DIF: B   OBJ: 11-1

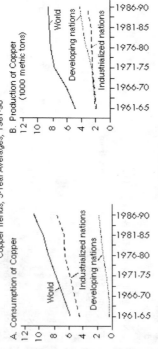

Copper Trends, 5-Year Averages, 1961-90

A. Consumption of Copper

B. Production of Copper (1000 metric tons)

FIGURE 11-2

15. Based on the graphs in Figure 11-2, the copper resources of the world are _____.
a. being produced faster than they are consumed
b. being consumed faster than they are produced
c. balanced between consumption and production
d. a renewable resource

ANS: B   DIF: A   OBJ: 11-1

16. Based on Graph A in Figure 11-2, the world's copper resources are _____.
a. being used more by developing nations
b. consumed equally by industrial and developing nations
c. being used more by industrial nations
d. being used less by industrial nations

ANS: C   DIF: A   OBJ: 11-1

17. Since 1971–1975, based on the Figure 11-2 graphs, the developing nations have _____.
a. produced significantly more of the world's copper resources
b. produced about the same amount of copper as the industrial nations
c. produced less copper than the industrial nations
d. consumed more copper than they produced

ANS: A   DIF: A   OBJ: 11-1

COMPLETION

1. To be classified as renewable, a natural resource must be replaced by natural processes in fewer than _____.

ANS: 100 years   DIF: B   OBJ: 11-2

2. _____ are estimated to be the home of one-half of the life-forms on Earth.

ANS: Rain forests   DIF: A   OBJ: 11-2

3. Oil and natural gas are forms of _____.

ANS: fossil fuel   DIF: B   OBJ: 11-1

4. Most metals and nonmetal mineral resources are _____.

ANS: nonrenewable   DIF: B   OBJ: 11-1

5. A barrel of petroleum equals _____ gallons.

ANS: 42   DIF: A   OBJ: 11-1

6. The decomposition of organic material under moist, warm, and well-aerated conditions forms _____.

ANS: compost   DIF: A   OBJ: 11-3

7. Fossil fuels and sunlight are two kinds of _____.

ANS: energy resources   DIF: B   OBJ: 11-1

8. A forest and topsoil are examples of _____.

ANS: nonrenewable resources   DIF: B   OBJ: 11-1

9. Sunlight, oxygen, and plants are examples of _____.

ANS: renewable resources   DIF: A   OBJ: 11-1

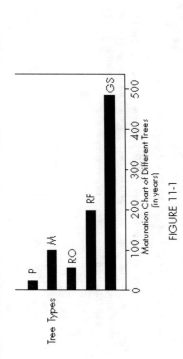

FIGURE 11-1

Tree Types: P, M, RO, RF, GS

Maturation Chart of Different Trees [in years]: 0 100 200 300 400 500

10. Based on the table in Figure 11-1, _____ and _____ type trees are nonrenewable resources.

ANS: RF, GS   DIF: A   OBJ: 11-1

11. The _____ type tree, represented in Figure 11-1, would be the best to harvest for firewood and paper pulp.

ANS: P   DIF: A   OBJ: 11-1

12. The slow-growing GS tree species represented in Figure 11-1 should not be harvested by the _____ logging method.

ANS: clear-cutting   DIF: A   OBJ: 11-1

13. An old-growth forest is _____.

ANS: nonrenewable   DIF: B   OBJ: 11-1

MATCHING

Match each item with the correct statement below. Write the answer in the space provided.

a. energy resource
b. petroleum resources
c. photovoltaic cells
d. reusable resource
e. solar energy
f. recyclable resource
g. ecotourism
h. hydroelectric plant
i. selective harvesting
j. nonrenewable resource
k. fossil fuel
l. renewable resource

1. _____ plastic milk jug and a gallon of motor oil
2. _____ vacations to photograph rare animals and plants
3. _____ harvesting of a small number of mature trees
4. _____ technology used to collect solar energy
5. _____ generates electricity by water-driven turbines
6. _____ resource that is not recycled or replaced by nature

---

7. _____ energy source formed from the remains of living things of long ago
8. _____ any material used to produce energy
9. _____ resource that is replaced or recycled naturally in less than 100 years
10. _____ energy in sunlight
11. _____ resource that can be used over and over again in its original form
12. _____ resource that can be reprocessed and used again rather than thrown away

1. ANS: b   DIF: A   OBJ: 11-1
2. ANS: g   DIF: A   OBJ: 11-1
3. ANS: i   DIF: A   OBJ: 11-1
4. ANS: c   DIF: B   OBJ: 11-2
5. ANS: h   DIF: B   OBJ: 11-2
6. ANS: j   DIF: B   OBJ: 11-1
7. ANS: k   DIF: B   OBJ: 11-2
8. ANS: a   DIF: B   OBJ: 11-1
9. ANS: l   DIF: B   OBJ: 11-1
10. ANS: e   DIF: B   OBJ: 11-2
11. ANS: d   DIF: B   OBJ: 11-1
12. ANS: f   DIF: B   OBJ: 11-3

SHORT ANSWER

1. What are the energy sources used in the United States?

ANS: oil, natural gas, nuclear energy, coal, the sun, water, and wind

DIF: B   OBJ: 11-2

2. Think of a short slogan (five words or less) that could be used in a neighborhood campaign to increase recycling.

ANS: Answers will vary; for example, "REnew, REuse, REcycle".

DIF: B   OBJ: 11-4

3. Why is only 2 percent of plastics recycled in the United States?

ANS: There are many different types of plastics, which makes it hard to sort and reprocess them. Also, there may be a contamination problem when recycled plastics are reused in food containers.

DIF: A   OBJ: 11-3

4. What is "glassphalt" and how is it used?

ANS: Glassphalt is a mixture of recycled glass and asphalt; it is used to pave streets.

DIF: B   OBJ: 11-3

5. What was the major goal of the 1987 Clean Water Act?

ANS: to provide safe, clean drinking water by building sewage- and wastewater-treatment plants

DIF: A   OBJ: 11-1

6. What recyclable items are used in automobiles?

ANS: steel, aluminum, glass, rubber, and plastic

DIF: B   OBJ: 11-3

7. What is an "earthship"?

ANS: a building constructed of recycled material that uses renewable energy sources and collects water from precipitation

DIF: A   OBJ: 11-3

8. Why are fossil fuels considered nonrenewable even though they are constantly being formed?

ANS: Humans consume fossil fuels much faster than they are being formed.

DIF: A   OBJ: 11-1

9. How do renewable resources differ from nonrenewable resources?

ANS: A natural process replaces renewable resources in a relatively short time, usually less than 100 years. Nonrenewable resources are not replaced by natural processes or are replaced at a rate that is much slower than the rate at which they are used.

DIF: A   OBJ: 11-1

10. How can the sun's energy be used to generate power?

ANS: Solar energy can be absorbed by a solar panel and used to heat water that can be used to provide hot water for a home; solar energy can be absorbed by a photovoltaic cell and used to produce electricity; solar energy drives the water cycle, which provides the water needed for a hydroelectric power plant to generate electricity.

DIF: B   OBJ: 11-2

11. Give two examples of ways you can reuse a natural resource.

ANS: Answers will vary but may include the following: clothing can be given to people who can use it; jars, cans, and cardboard boxes can be used for storage of materials instead of being thrown away; dishes, flatware, and cloth diapers could be used in place of materials that are intended to be used once and then thrown away.

DIF: B   OBJ: 11-3

12. Identify three materials you use daily that could be recycled rather than thrown away.

ANS: empty plastic, glass, or aluminum beverage containers; paper products such as magazines, newspapers, or notebook paper; packaging materials such as aluminum foil, plastic wrap, or corrugated cardboard

DIF: B   OBJ: 11-4

13. What are two benefits of recycling materials?

ANS: Recycling conserves natural resources by cutting back on the amounts of raw materials needed to make items; recycling often uses less energy than processing raw materials; recycling often produces less pollution than processing raw materials.

DIF: B   OBJ: 11-4

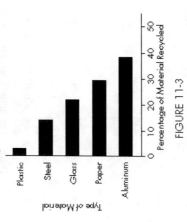

Recycling in the United States

FIGURE 11-3

14. According to Figure 11-3, what material is recycled in the United States in the largest amount?

ANS: aluminum   DIF: A   OBJ: 11-3

15. According to Figure 11-3, what material is recycled in the United States in the smallest amount?

ANS: plastic   DIF: A   OBJ: 11-3

16. According to Figure 11-3, what percentage of steel is recycled in the United States?

ANS: 15 percent   DIF: A   OBJ: 11-3

17. According to Figure 11-3, what percentage of the glass used in the United States is NOT recycled?

ANS: 80 percent   DIF: A   OBJ: 11-3

18. What do you think happens to the percentage of materials shown in Figure 11-3 that is not recycled?

ANS: Materials end up in landfills or are dumped illegally in various land and water areas.

DIF: A   OBJ: 11-4

19. If the sun provides limitless renewable energy, why is solar energy not used more?

ANS: Solar energy will not be more widely used until the cost is lower and it is more efficient. Also, research is needed into more efficient and powerful batteries to store energy for use during the night or on cloudy days. Many areas are not well suited for solar energy because of too many cloudy days, space problems for the collectors, or screening vegetation. It would be expensive to refit homes and industry to utilize solar energy.

DIF: A   OBJ: 11-2

20. How might a local city government encourage its citizens and businesses to recycle?

ANS: Various ideas could include pay by the pound or can to haul and dispose of trash, provide pickup services for recyclables, provide convenient recycling centers, or fund research into uses for recycled products.

DIF: B   OBJ: 11-4

21. Why is topsoil considered to be a nonrenewable resource?

ANS: To be renewable, a resource must be replaced by natural processes in 100 years or less. It can take 500 to 1000 years to form a few inches of topsoil from the decay of organic material and the breakdown of the parent material.

DIF: A   OBJ: 11-1

22. Why is it beneficial to recycle an aluminum can?

ANS: It costs less to recycle aluminum than to mine aluminum. Mining and processing the ore take more energy and may also pollute the air and water. Mining can damage or destroy animal and plant habitats. Recycling also saves space in landfills.

DIF: B   OBJ: 11-4

23. What are the basic steps in a water-treatment system? What does each step do?

ANS:
1) chlorination, which kills bacteria
2) formation of floc, which is a mixture of chemicals that combines with impurities to form a solid precipitate (floc)
3) settling basin, which allows the floc and other particles to settle out and be removed
4) filtration, in which water passes through a series of filters to further purify it

DIF: A   OBJ: 11-3

24. Individual trees are considered renewable resources, but entire forests are considered nonrenewable. Suggest how people might be provided with wood and other forest materials without destroying a forest.

ANS: Only some trees need be harvested in a given time period; replacement trees can be planted for each tree harvested.

DIF: A   OBJ: 11-3

25. A solar-powered car costs $2000 more than a gasoline-powered model. Why might the solar-powered car be considered a better investment over the life of the car?

ANS: The solar-powered car makes use of a nonpolluting, renewable energy resource, while the gasoline-powered car uses a nonrenewable resource that causes a great deal of pollution; also, money saved on gasoline may be much greater than $2000 over the life of the car.

DIF: A   OBJ: 11-2

26. Only 2 percent of the plastics used in this country is recycled. Suggest ways that people might be encouraged to recycle more of this material.

ANS: Make people more aware through advertising that plastics are recyclable; have the local government pass an ordinance requiring recycling of certain plastics.

DIF: A   OBJ: 11-4

27. A pair of jeans has a rip in the knee. Suggest three ways the jeans may be reused rather than thrown away.

ANS: Repair the tear in the jeans so they can be worn; cut them off above the tear so the jeans can be worn as shorts; cut the jeans apart and use the fabric as rags for cleaning and polishing or as material for some other article of clothing.

DIF: A   OBJ: 11-3

28. Do you think your family could use solar panels to meet your hot-water needs? Why or why not?

ANS: Responses will vary depending upon where students live. Accept all responses supported by logical reasoning.

DIF: A   OBJ: 11-2

OTHER

If the underscored word or phrase makes the sentence true, write "true" in the space provided. If the underscored word or phrase makes the sentence false, write the correct term or phrase in the space provided.

1. Solar energy is a nonrenewable resource. _____

ANS: renewable   DIF: B   OBJ: 11-1

2. More paper (by weight) is presently recycled in the United States than any other resource.

ANS: true   DIF: B   OBJ: 11-3

3. Water is a nonrenewable resource.

ANS: reusable (or renewable)   DIF: B   OBJ: 11-1

4. Fossil fuels are formed from the remains of plants and animals.

ANS: true   DIF: B   OBJ: 11-1

5. Solar energy provides more than 85 percent of the energy used in the United States.

ANS: Fossil fuels   DIF: A   OBJ: 11-2

CHAPTER 12—THE FORMATION OF RESOURCES

MULTIPLE CHOICE

1. In igneous rocks, the crystal size is affected by _____.
   a. the temperature of the magma
   b. the rate of cooling
   c. the pressure of metamorphism
   d. the presence of rare metals

   ANS: B   DIF: A   OBJ: 12-3

2. Layered intrusions have _____.
   a. alternating layers of sandstone and shale
   b. the same minerals throughout
   c. layers of different minerals
   d. been totally metamorphosed

   ANS: C   DIF: A   OBJ: 12-3

3. Bowen's reaction series shows _____.
   a. the order of mineral crystallization
   b. the mineral crystal sizes that are formed
   c. the mineral tetrahedra
   d. the origin of sedimentary rocks

   ANS: A   DIF: A   OBJ: 12-3

4. The silicon-oxygen tetrahedra in quartz forms a _____.
   a. single chain
   b. sheet structure
   c. double chain
   d. silicate framework

   ANS: D   DIF: A   OBJ: 12-3

5. The Bushveld Complex is an example of a _____.
   a. layered sedimentary unit
   b. contact metamorphic zone
   c. layered igneous intrusion
   d. diamond mine

   ANS: C   DIF: A   OBJ: 12-3

6. In Bowen's reaction series, the silicate mineral that forms at the lowest temperature is _____.
   a. quartz
   b. mica
   c. olivine
   d. feldspar

   ANS: A   DIF: A   OBJ: 12-1

7. Of the following, the resource most likely to be obtained from igneous rock is _____.
   a. ceramic
   b. graphite
   c. asbestos
   d. iron

   ANS: D   DIF: B   OBJ: 12-2

8. The minerals of Bowen's reaction series are mainly composed of _____ and oxygen atoms linked together by common elements of Earth's crust.
   a. feldspar
   b. silicon
   c. aluminum
   d. iron

   ANS: B   DIF: A   OBJ: 12-1

9. Of the following, the materials obtained from sedimentary rocks include _____.
   a. iron and fiberglass
   b. ceramic materials and graphite
   c. glass and iron
   d. ceramic materials and fiberglass

   ANS: D   DIF: B   OBJ: 12-2

10. Of the following processes, the one that most thoroughly illustrates the law of conservation of matter is _____.
    a. the rock cycle
    b. regional metamorphism
    c. contact metamorphism
    d. sedimentation

    ANS: A   DIF: A   OBJ: 12-7

11. The rock labeled Z in Figure 12-1 is _____.
    a. granite
    b. marble
    c. lava
    d. bauxite

    ANS: B   DIF: A   OBJ: 12-3

12. The feature labeled S in Figure 12-1 is _____.
    a. a layered intrusive
    b. the Bushveld Complex
    c. a volcano
    d. a limestone

    ANS: C   DIF: A   OBJ: 12-3

13. The rock layer labeled R in Figure 12-1 is burned, releasing sulfur dioxide and nitric oxide. The rock is _____.
    a. sandstone
    b. granite
    c. coal
    d. shale

    ANS: C   DIF: A   OBJ: 12-3

14. The molten rock at X in Figure 12-1 is called _____.
    a. magma
    b. lava
    c. metal ore
    d. pumice

    ANS: A   DIF: A   OBJ: 12-3

15. The rock at Zone A in Figure 12-1 has undergone _____.
    a. regional metamorphism
    b. sedimentation
    c. contact metamorphism
    d. erosion by water

    ANS: C   DIF: A   OBJ: 12-3

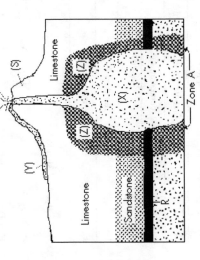

FIGURE 12-1

COMPLETION

Table 12-1

STARTING MATERIAL	PROCESS	RESULTING ROCK
A	contact metamorphism	marble
sand	cementation	**B**
shale	**C**	slate
lava	rapid cooling	**D**
E	slow cooling	granite

1. **A** in Table 12-1 should list _____.

   ANS: limestone   DIF: A   OBJ: 12-3

2. **B** in Table 12-1 should list _____.

   ANS: sandstone   DIF: A   OBJ: 12-3

3. **C** in Table 12-1 should list _____.

   ANS: regional metamorphism   DIF: A   OBJ: 12-3

4. **D** in Table 12-1 should list _____.

   ANS: obsidian   DIF: A   OBJ: 12-3

5. **E** in Table 12-1 should list _____.

   ANS: magma   DIF: A   OBJ: 12-3

6. Metals are commonly found in _____ rocks.

   ANS: igneous   DIF: A   OBJ: 12-3

7. Silicon from _____ is used to make glass.

   ANS: sandstones   DIF: A   OBJ: 12-3

8. Bauxite, a major ore of aluminum, is a _____ rock.

   ANS: sedimentary   DIF: A   OBJ: 12-3

9. Asbestos, a mineral found in _____ rocks, is used as a fireproof material.

   ANS: metamorphic   DIF: A   OBJ: 12-3

10. The _____ describes the processes that transform one rock type to another.

    ANS: rock cycle   DIF: A   OBJ: 12-3

11. Classify the following descriptions of rocks as igneous, sedimentary, or metamorphic: heat and pressure changed rock, _____; formed from magma, _____; minerals come out of solution, _____.

    ANS: metamorphic; igneous; sedimentary   DIF: B   OBJ: 12-7

12. Classify the following descriptions of rocks as igneous, sedimentary, or metamorphic: minerals join rock pieces, _____; form from lava, _____; oldest rocks of Earth's crust, _____.

    ANS: sedimentary; igneous; metamorphic   DIF: B   OBJ: 12-7

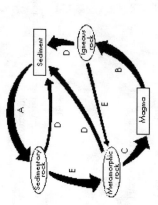

FIGURE 12-2

13. Compaction and cementation occur at point _____ in Figure 12-2.

    ANS: A   DIF: B   OBJ: 12-7

14. Melting occurs at point _____ in Figure 12-2.

    ANS: C   DIF: B   OBJ: 12-7

15. Erosion and deposition are shown at point _____ in Figure 12-2.

    ANS: D   DIF: B   OBJ: 12-7

16. Cooling and crystallization occur at _____ in Figure 12-2.

    ANS: B   DIF: B   OBJ: 12-7

17. Heat and pressure are present at _____ in Figure 12-2.

    ANS: E   DIF: B   OBJ: 12-7

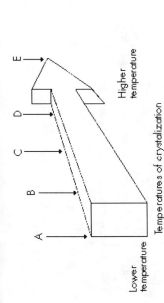

Lower temperature

Higher temperature

Temperatures of crystallization

FIGURE 12-3

18. _____ in Figure 12-3 shows the position of the hardest mineral in the series.

ANS: A   DIF: A   OBJ: 12-1

19. _____ in Figure 12-3 represents olivine.

ANS: E   DIF: A   OBJ: 12-1

20. _____ in Figure 12-3 represents the amphiboles.

ANS: C   DIF: A   OBJ: 12-1

MATCHING

Match each item with the correct statement below. Write the answer in the space provided.

a. marble
b. Bowen's reaction series
c. rock salt
d. lava
e. silicates

1. _____ order of mineral crystallization
2. _____ magma at Earth's surface
3. _____ minerals composed of silicon-oxygen tetrahedra
4. _____ metamorphosed limestone
5. _____ a chemical sedimentary rock

1. ANS: b   DIF: A   OBJ: 12-3
2. ANS: d   DIF: A   OBJ: 12-3
3. ANS: e   DIF: A   OBJ: 12-3
4. ANS: a   DIF: A   OBJ: 12-3
5. ANS: c   DIF: A   OBJ: 12-3

SHORT ANSWER

1. How is limestone used in manufacturing cars?

   ANS: Limestone is used as flux in steelmaking.

   DIF: A   OBJ: 12-3

2. What types of rock can be eroded to form sedimentary rocks?

   ANS: igneous, metamorphic, and preexisting sedimentary rocks

   DIF: A   OBJ: 12-3

3. In the Bushveld Complex in South Africa, what forms the layers?

   ANS: different types of minerals in a layered, igneous intrusion

   DIF: A   OBJ: 12-3

4. What atoms form a silicate tetrahedron?

   ANS: four oxygen atoms surrounding one silicon atom

   DIF: A   OBJ: 12-3

5. What do the origins of extrusive igneous rocks and sedimentary rocks have in common?

   ANS: They both form at or near Earth's surface.

   DIF: A   OBJ: 12-3

6. How does the Bowen's reaction series relate to the resistance of different minerals to weathering?

   ANS: The first minerals to form in the Bowen's reaction series form at high temperatures and pressures. These minerals are not stable at the low temperatures and pressures of the weathering environment at Earth's surface. The Bowen's reaction series, if flipped upside down, can be used as a weathering stability diagram.

   DIF: A   OBJ: 12-3

7. What allows the rock pumice to float? Relate your answer to the origin of the rock.

   ANS: When a lava that is rich in gas rises to the surface, the gas bubbles increase in size. The density of pumice is so low because of the numerous, large holes formed by the gas bubbles that it floats.

   DIF: A   OBJ: 12-3

8. How do the layered mineral layers form in a layered igneous intrusion?

   ANS: As the first minerals form from the cooling magma, they sink to the bottom of the magma chamber. As the cooling continues, the mineral composition changes as elements are used up by the crystallizing minerals. As new minerals form, they also sink to the bottom, forming layers of different composition.

   DIF: A   OBJ: 12-3

If the underscored word or phrase makes the sentence true, write "true" in the space provided. If the underscored word or phrase makes the sentence false, write the correct term or phrase in the space provided.

1. One of the most weather-resistant minerals at surface conditions is <u>olivine</u>.

   ANS: quartz   DIF: A   OBJ: 12-3

2. Minerals that form at high temperatures and pressures are <u>unstable</u> at Earth's surface.

   ANS: true   DIF: A   OBJ: 12-3

3. <u>Lava</u> is molten rock deep within Earth.

   ANS: Magma   DIF: A   OBJ: 12-3

4. Magma comes to the surface at <u>volcanoes</u>.

   ANS: true   DIF: A   OBJ: 12-3

5. The early crust of Earth was formed by <u>sedimentary</u> rocks.

   ANS: igneous   DIF: A   OBJ: 12-3

6. Earth's outermost layer of rock is called the <u>mantle</u>.

   ANS: crust   DIF: A   OBJ: 12-3

7. All extrusive igneous rocks have <u>large</u> mineral crystals.

   ANS: small   DIF: A   OBJ: 12-3

8. Sandstone is a type of <u>clastic</u> sedimentary rock.

   ANS: true   DIF: A   OBJ: 12-3

9. Bauxite is a major ore of <u>iron</u>.

   ANS: aluminum   DIF: A   OBJ: 12-3

10. <u>Regional</u> metamorphism occurs when an igneous intrusion heats up the surrounding rock.

    ANS: Contact   DIF: A   OBJ: 12-3

11. <u>Sedimentary</u> rocks form when hot melted material cools and becomes solid rock.

    ANS: Igneous   DIF: B   OBJ: 12-1

---

9. How are vein deposits formed?

   ANS: The remaining elements left after most of the magma has cooled and crystallized are often rare elements such as gold and silver. These rare leftovers are carried by hot, mineral-rich waters into cracks, fractures, and pores in the surrounding rock, where they crystallize.

   DIF: A   OBJ: 12-3

10. What important items that we use almost every day are from sediments or sedimentary rocks?

    ANS: Answers will vary. Some examples are rock salt, glass from sandstone or sand, rock gypsum made into drywall, gravel, clay to form ceramics, building stone, coal in power plants or fireplaces, silicon for computer chips, and others.

    DIF: A   OBJ: 12-3

11. Why does evaporation or a change in temperature cause the formation of chemical sedimentary rocks such as rock salt?

    ANS: Minerals dissolved in water come out of solution when water evaporates or temperature decreases. This precipitate forms chemical sedimentary rocks.

    DIF: A   OBJ: 12-3

12. Why are rocks composed of feldspar more prone to weathering than rocks rich in silicates such as quartz?

    ANS: Feldspars contain aluminum instead of silicon at the centers of their tetrahedra. As the amount of aluminum in the tetrahedra increases, the tetrahedra weakens, making it more prone to weathering.

    DIF: A   OBJ: 12-2

13. The stalagmites and stalactites of a cavern form as minerals settle out of solution and harden. Of what type of rock do you think these cave structures are made?

    ANS: chemical sedimentary rocks, because the rocks form from minerals that settle out of solution

    DIF: A   OBJ: 12-3

14. How might a metamorphic rock be changed to form a sedimentary rock?

    ANS: If the metamorphic rock is broken apart by weathering, the pieces of rock sediment may become cemented together as a sedimentary rock.

    DIF: A   OBJ: 12-3

15. What are two ways intrusive igneous rocks differ from extrusive igneous rocks?

    ANS: Intrusive rocks form deep in Earth, not on its surface, and have larger crystals than do extrusive igneous rocks.

    DIF: A   OBJ: 12-1

12. The type of rock formed when minerals settle out of solution and harden is clastic sedimentary rock. _____

ANS: chemical   DIF: B   OBJ: 12-3

13. In most contact metamorphism, rocks near an igneous intrusion are heated and changed by magma. _____

ANS: true   DIF: B   OBJ: 12-5

14. Slate, schist, and gneiss often form as a result of regional metamorphism.

ANS: true   DIF: B   OBJ: 12-5

15. The transformations from one type of rock to another make up Bowen's reaction series. _____

ANS: the rock cycle   DIF: B   OBJ: 12-7

16. Rocks that form from lava are classified as intrusive igneous rocks. _____

ANS: extrusive   DIF: B   OBJ: 12-1

17. The hot, melted material from which igneous rocks form deep inside Earth is called magma.

ANS: true   DIF: B   OBJ: 12-1

18. Conglomerate and sandstone are examples of chemical sedimentary rocks.

ANS: clastic   DIF: B   OBJ: 12-3

19. A rock that forms when heat and pressure change one type of rock to another is sedimentary rock.

ANS: metamorphic   DIF: B   OBJ: 12-5

20. Large crystals resulting from slow cooling are a characteristic of intrusive igneous rocks.

ANS: true   DIF: B   OBJ: 12-1

CHAPTER 13—PETROLEUM CHEMISTRY

MULTIPLE CHOICE

1. Which one of the following statements about the formation of petroleum is NOT correct?
   a. Petroleum is created in source rocks.
   b. The liquid portion of petroleum is called oil.
   c. The gas portion of petroleum is called natural gas.
   d. Organic matter does not have to be heated to form petroleum.

ANS: D   DIF: B   OBJ: 13-1

2. In which type of rock would you most likely find an oil reservoir?
   a. granite
   b. marble
   c. sandstone and limestone
   d. shale

ANS: C   DIF: B   OBJ: 13-3

3. Which one of the following techniques would NOT be used to explore and recover petroleum?
   a. combustion of petroleum
   b. seismic prospecting
   c. well logging
   d. geologic mapping

ANS: A   DIF: B   OBJ: 13-4

4. Which one of the following statements about hydrocarbons is NOT correct?
   a. Gasoline is made from hydrocarbons that are five to ten carbon atoms in length.
   b. The making of useful products from petroleum is called well logging.
   c. Natural gas is made from hydrocarbons with shorter chains of one to three carbon atoms.
   d. Some hydrocarbon compounds form ring structures.

ANS: B   DIF: B   OBJ: 13-5

5. Which petroleum refinery product would rise to the highest point in the fractionating tower?
   a. methane
   b. gasoline
   c. asphalt
   d. wax

ANS: A   DIF: B   OBJ: 13-6

6. Which one of the following is NOT a product of combustion of gasoline?
   a. carbon dioxide
   b. water
   c. carbon monoxide
   d. nylon

ANS: D   DIF: B   OBJ: 13-7

7. Lots of petroleum has been found in the northern part of Alaska. Which statement best describes the conditions that make the formation of oil possible in this area?
   a. Alaska has always been cold.
   b. Alaska was once a warmer, shallow sea area with abundant life.
   c. Alaska is a special place where heat was not needed to produce petroleum.
   d. Alaska has lots of granite, which stores lots of oil.
   ANS: B   DIF: A   OBJ: 13-1

8. Which sequence of geologic events would most likely form a petroleum deposit?
   a. heating of source rock, formation of porous trap, formation of nonporous seal, migration
   b. migration, heating of source rock, formation of nonporous seal, formation of porous trap
   c. heating of source rock, formation of nonporous seal, migration, formation of porous trap
   d. heating of source rock, formation of nonporous trap, formation of porous seal, migration
   ANS: A   DIF: A   OBJ: 13-2

9. Which one of the following is NOT used to search for petroleum deposits?
   a. Landsat satellite images
   b. structural cross-section maps of geological features
   c. seismographs
   d. Doppler radar
   ANS: D   DIF: A   OBJ: 13-3

COMPLETION

1. Microorganisms that died in ancient seas were covered by sediment that hardened into _____.
   ANS: source rocks   DIF: B   OBJ: 13-1

2. Organic matter must be _____ to produce hydrocarbons.
   ANS: heated   DIF: A   OBJ: 13-1

3. Toothlike fossils called conodonts help tell how hot rocks were because their _____ reflects the effects of heat on organic matter.
   ANS: color   DIF: A   OBJ: 13-1

4. The percentage of spaces between the grains of a rock account for its _____.
   ANS: porosity   DIF: A   OBJ: 13-2

5. Made of porous rock that is also permeable, a _____ also has a seal to trap petroleum.
   ANS: reservoir   DIF: B   OBJ: 13-2

6. Sound waves from small explosions on Earth's surface are reflected by different rock layers in a process called _____.
   ANS: seismic prospecting   DIF: B   OBJ: 13-4

7. A picture of the rock layers underground called a _____ is generated by a computer.
   ANS: seismic profile   DIF: B   OBJ: 13-4

8. Instruments lowered down a well hole measure properties of rocks and the _____ they contain.
   ANS: fluids   DIF: B   OBJ: 13-4

9. Hydrocarbons are made up of chains or _____ of carbon atoms that are chemically bonded to each other and to hydrogen.
   ANS: rings   DIF: B   OBJ: 13-5

10. Gasoline is made of hydrocarbons containing _____ of five to ten carbon atoms.
    ANS: chains   DIF: B   OBJ: 13-5

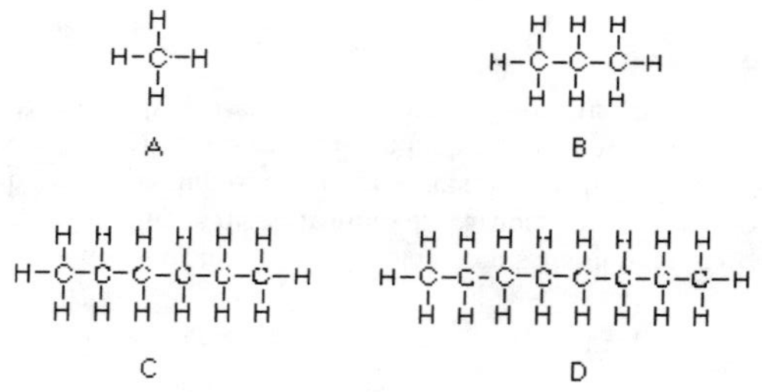

FIGURE 13-3

11. Propane contains three carbon atoms. Formula _____ in Figure 13-3 is the chemical structure of propane.
    ANS: B   DIF: B   OBJ: 13-7

12. Methane, the simplest hydrocarbon, is represented by letter _____ in Figure 13-3.
    ANS: A   DIF: B   OBJ: 13-7

13. Letter _____ in Figure 13-3 indicates the hydrocarbon hexane.
    ANS: C   DIF: B   OBJ: 13-7

14. Chemical structure _____ in Figure 13-3 is a hydrocarbon called octane.
    ANS: D   DIF: B   OBJ: 13-7

15. Letters _____ and _____ in Figure 13-3 represent hydrocarbons that could be components found in gasoline.
    ANS: C, D   DIF: B   OBJ: 13-7

20. In Figure 13-2, you would expect hydrocarbons of relatively _____ molecular mass to be collected at point A.

ANS: low   DIF: B   OBJ: 13-7

21. In Figure 13-2, you would expect hydrocarbons of intermediate molecular mass to be collected at point _____.

ANS: B or C   DIF: B   OBJ: 13-7

22. In Figure 13-2, high-molecular mass hydrocarbons such as paraffins, waxes, and asphalt would be collected at point _____.

ANS: D   DIF: B   OBJ: 13-7

23. In Figure 13-2, the sequence of material collection points D, C, B, A is in order of _____ hydrocarbon molecular mass.

ANS: decreasing   DIF: B   OBJ: 13-7

MATCHING

Match each item with the correct statement below. Write the answer in the space provided.

a. porosity
b. seismic prospecting
c. geophones
d. permeability
e. cracking
f. reservoir
g. combustion
h. migration
i. petroleum
j. conodont
k. source rocks

1. _____ method used to develop a picture of rocks below Earth's surface using an echo-sounding technique
2. _____ the detectors used to pick up reflected sound waves during seismic prospecting of oil deposits
3. _____ method used to split long-chain hydrocarbons into forms that can be used in gasoline
4. _____ process in which hydrocarbons are burned to release carbon dioxide, water, and energy
5. _____ when pores in rocks are connected, the rocks have this
6. _____ beginning as sediment, these become a source for oil and gas
7. _____ a complex mixture of hydrocarbons in the form of liquids and gases
8. _____ tiny fossils found in sedimentary rocks
9. _____ when oil moves from source rocks to a reservoir
10. _____ sandstone and limestone are rocks with lots of this
11. _____ this has features such as porous and permeable rocks, and a seal

1. ANS: b   DIF: B   OBJ: 13-3
2. ANS: c   DIF: B   OBJ: 13-4
3. ANS: e   DIF: B   OBJ: 13-6
4. ANS: g   DIF: B   OBJ: 13-7
5. ANS: d   DIF: B   OBJ: 13-2

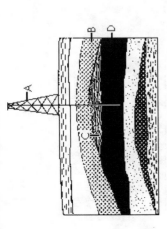

FIGURE 13-1

16. In Figure 13-1, A represents a(n) _____.

ANS: oil well platform, or rig   DIF: B   OBJ: 13-2

17. In Figure 13-1, B represents _____.

ANS: seal   DIF: B   OBJ: 13-2

18. In Figure 13-1, C represents _____.

ANS: natural gas   DIF: B   OBJ: 13-2

19. In Figure 13-1, D represents _____.

ANS: oil   DIF: B   OBJ: 13-2

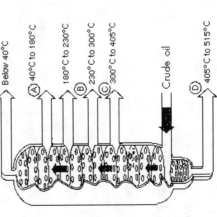

Below 40°C

A 40°C to 180°C

180°C to 230°C

B 230°C to 300°C

C 300°C to 405°C

Crude oil

D 405°C to 515°C

FIGURE 13-2

6. ANS: k   DIF: B   OBJ: 13-1
7. ANS: i   DIF: B   OBJ: 13-1
8. ANS: j   DIF: A   OBJ: 13-1
9. ANS: h   DIF: B   OBJ: 13-2
10. ANS: a   DIF: A   OBJ: 13-2
11. ANS: f   DIF: A   OBJ: 13-2

SHORT ANSWER

1. Why do refineries have tall towers?

ANS: The towers in a refinery are fractionating towers. They are where crude oil is heated and broken down into its components. These components separate out at various heights in the towers based on the material's boiling point.

DIF: A   OBJ: 13-6

2. What are some examples of products refined from petroleum?

ANS: Answers will vary. Some examples are gasoline, natural gas, asphalt, wax, solvents, lubricating oils, grease, and others.

DIF: A   OBJ: 13-7

3. What substances did petroleum form from?

ANS: It formed from the remains of once-living organic matter that lived in ancient seas. As the organisms died, they sank to the bottom of the sea. Many layers of organisms and sediments hardened and became petroleum source rock. Under heat and pressure, this organic material was turned into petroleum.

DIF: A   OBJ: 13-1

4. Explain how petroleum migrates from source rock to a trap.

ANS: Petroleum can migrate through rock if the rock is porous and permeable. Petroleum can travel most quickly through porous rock such as sandstone and limestone. Oil can be trapped by nonporous rock such as shale.

DIF: A   OBJ: 13-2

Table 13-1

Type of Rock/Soil	Porosity
Sandy soil	Porous
Clay soil	Porous
Sandstone	Porous
Shale	Nonporous

5. In Table 13-1, which type(s) of soil/rock has a large percentage of open space between particles?

ANS: sandy soil, clay soil, sandstone   DIF: B   OBJ: 13-2

6. In Table 13-1, which type(s) of soil/rock has the smallest percentage of open space between particles?

ANS: shale   DIF: B   OBJ: 13-2

7. In Table 13-1, which type(s) of soil/rock would most likely make a good seal for gas and oil deposits?

ANS: shale   DIF: B   OBJ: 13-2

8. In Table 13-1, which type of rock would have more pores in it?

ANS: sandstone   DIF: B   OBJ: 13-2

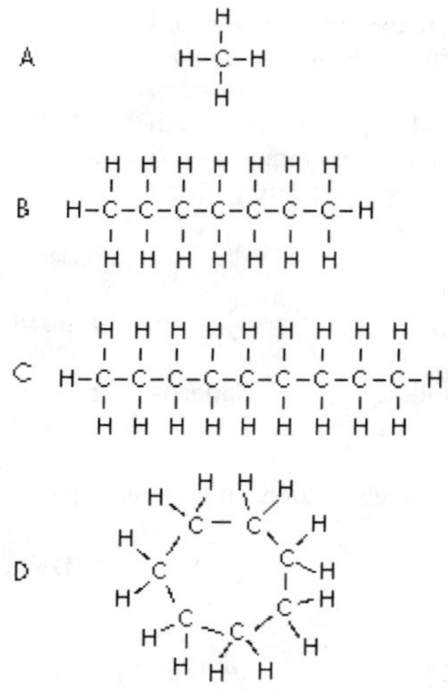

FIGURE 13-4

9. Identify hydrocarbon A in Figure 13-4, and tell where it might be found.

ANS: Methane; it would be found in natural gas.

DIF: B   OBJ: 13-5

10. Identify hydrocarbon B in Figure 13-4 and tell where it might be found.

ANS: Heptane; it would be found in gasoline.

DIF: B   OBJ: 13-5

11. Identify which of the compounds shown in Figure 13-4 would probably release the most energy when burned, and explain your answer.

ANS: C, nonane; it has the largest number of carbon atoms and the largest number of single bonds.

DIF: A   OBJ: 13-5

12. Look at Figure 13-4 and explain the relationship between hydrocarbon D and hydrocarbon B.

ANS: Both contain seven carbon atoms.

DIF: A   OBJ: 13-5

13. Describe several types of well logs that exist.

ANS: One type measures the electrical properties of rocks. Another type measures the level of natural radioactivity. Another type determines whether layers of rock are tilted or horizontal.

DIF: A   OBJ: 13-4

14. Suppose you think there is oil under some land that you own. What process would you use to see if there is enough oil to make an oil well economically feasible?

ANS: You could start by looking at a geological map of the type of rock that is under the land you own. If it has the correct type of rock for an oil trap to be present, you can then do seismic prospecting. If this proves to be promising, you can drill a well and log the well. This will give some information about whether the well is economically feasible.

DIF: A   OBJ: 13-3

15. Describe how seismic prospecting is much like using ultrasonic waves to make a picture of an unborn baby.

ANS: Both use the principle of reflection of sound waves. The reflected sound wave is detected by a receiver, a geophone in the seismic situation. If the distance between the detectors is known, and the time it takes for the sound wave to travel is known, then a computer can generate a picture of the rock or baby.

DIF: A   OBJ: 13-4

16. How does the number of carbon atoms in a hydrocarbon chain determine the use of that hydrocarbon?

ANS: The shorter carbon atom chains tend to be gases. As the length of the chain gets longer, it becomes a liquid. For example, a one-carbon molecule, methane, is a gas. The five to ten carbon atom chains are the liquids found in gasoline. The longer carbon atom chains are usually broken down into smaller chains by cracking.

DIF: A   OBJ: 13-5

17. What are some of the fractions that result from the refining of crude oil?

ANS: Answers may include bottled gases such as propane and butane, gasoline, kerosene, paint thinners, heating oil, diesel fuel, lubricating oils and greases, paraffin, waxes, and asphalt.

DIF: A   OBJ: 13-6

18. What are some uses for petrochemicals other than for gasoline?

ANS: Petrochemicals are used for synthetic fibers, synthetic polymers, paints, automobile bumpers, dashboards, and tires. They are used for packaging, and in the manufacture of drugs and communication equipment, among other things.

DIF: A   OBJ: 13-7

19. Explain why refining of crude oil is necessary.

ANS: Crude oil contains hundreds of different kinds of hydrocarbon compounds. Refining splits petroleum into its component parts so they can each be isolated and used separately.

DIF: A   OBJ: 13-6

20. Where does the energy that makes a car operate come from?

ANS: When hydrocarbons are burned, they react with oxygen to produce carbon dioxide, water, and energy that is produced when chemical bonds are broken. This is the source for the energy that makes a car's engine run.

DIF: B   OBJ: 13-7

21. Suppose you live in an area where there are a lot of limestone caves and caverns underground. Would this be a good place to look for oil? Explain your answer.

ANS: Yes, because oil is found in reservoirs in areas where rocks are both porous and permeable. Limestone can be both. The presence of underground caves suggests the possibility of deeper reservoirs of oil.

DIF: A   OBJ: 13-1

22. Materials thrown away in sanitary landfills sometimes contain toxic substances such as lead. Use this fact to explain why geologists are always consulted before a site is chosen for a new sanitary landfill.

ANS: Geologists do tests to find out what kind of rocks lie underground. A landfill should not be located where porous and permeable rocks are found because materials such as lead could migrate from the landfill through such rocks to underground and surface water sources.

DIF: A   OBJ: 13-2

23. Plastics, explosives, nylon, and polyester all are products made from petroleum. Explain why so many products can be made from petroleum.

ANS: Crude oil comes out of the ground as a mixture of liquids and gases. This mixture contains hundreds of different kinds of hydrocarbon compounds. Each compound has a chemical structure that determines its possible uses. Oil has so many uses because of all these different compounds.

DIF: A   OBJ: 13-7

OTHER

If the underscored word or phrase makes the sentence true, write "true" in the space provided. If the underscored word or phrase makes the sentence false, write the correct term or phrase in the space provided.

1. A critical factor in the formation of oil and gas in a source rock is <u>heat</u>. _____

ANS: true   DIF: B   OBJ: 13-1

2. Seismic prospecting is used during oil <u>refining</u>. _____

ANS: exploration   DIF: B   OBJ: 13-3

3. Finding out what is in a well hole after it has been drilled is called <u>cracking</u> the well. _____

ANS: logging   DIF: B   OBJ: 13-4

4. Crude oil is broken down into different petroleum products using a <u>fractionating tower</u>. _____

ANS: true   DIF: B   OBJ: 13-6

5. Many products produced today contain <u>synthetic</u> materials made from petroleum. _____

ANS: true   DIF: B   OBJ: 13-7

CHAPTER 14—RECYCLING

MULTIPLE CHOICE

1. Which of the following are considered hazardous wastes in groundwater?
   a. mercury
   b. lead
   c. cadmium
   d. all of the above

   ANS: D   DIF: A   OBJ: 14-5

2. Which of the following is not a step in the recycling process?
   a. collection
   b. sorting
   c. mining
   d. cleaning

   ANS: C   DIF: B   OBJ: 14-6

3. Which of the following are problems associated with low recycling rates?
   a. lack of space to store recyclables
   b. few recycling centers
   c. high transportation costs
   d. all of the above

   ANS: D   DIF: B   OBJ: 14-6

4. An example of an alloy is _____.
   a. plywood
   b. steel
   c. copper
   d. a car

   ANS: B   DIF: A   OBJ: 14-4

5. To reprocess glass bottles, they are _____.
   a. crushed
   b. magnetized
   c. melted
   d. both a and c

   ANS: B   DIF: A   OBJ: 14-4

6. Most municipal solid waste is _____.
   a. disposed of in landfills
   b. burned in incinerators
   c. recycled
   d. reused

   ANS: A   DIF: B   OBJ: 14-1

5. _____ incinerators are more efficient because the waste is sorted prior to burning.

ANS: Refuse-driven fuel   DIF: A   OBJ: 14-1

6. _____ are used in incinerators to neutralize acidic gases in the stacks.

ANS: Scrubbers   DIF: B   OBJ: 14-1

7. Recycling saves energy and _____.

ANS: resources   DIF: B   OBJ: 14-6

8. _____ occurs when the burning of fossil fuels releases sulfur dioxide, nitrogen oxide, or other by-products into the atmosphere.

ANS: Acid deposition or Acid rain   DIF: A   OBJ: 14-1

9. Sanitary landfills are constructed with liners of _____ or plastic.

ANS: clay   DIF: B   OBJ: 14-1

10. Incinerators produce a lightweight waste called _____, which can contain toxic dioxin and heavy metals.

ANS: fly ash   DIF: A   OBJ: 14-1

11. As many as _____ states have comprehensive recycling programs.

ANS: forty   DIF: A   OBJ: 14-6

12. Electrostatic precipitators reduce air pollution from incinerators by causing particles in _____ to become positively charged.

ANS: fly ash   DIF: B   OBJ: 14-1

13. Steel cans can be separated from other solid wastes easily because they contain _____, which is magnetic.

ANS: iron   DIF: B   OBJ: 14-4

14. Car batteries must be disposed of properly to prevent contamination of groundwater from _____.

ANS: lead   DIF: A   OBJ: 14-5

15. Grass clippings, piles of leaves, twigs, and weeds from the garden can be turned into nutrient-rich soil as a result of _____.

ANS: composting   DIF: B   OBJ: 14-7

---

7. Burning of solid wastes may result in _____.
   a. release of sulfur dioxide
   b. release of oxygen
   c. production of compost
   d. none of the above

ANS: A   DIF: B   OBJ: 14-1

8. Air pollution as a result of burning solid wastes can be reduced by the use of _____.
   a. scrubbers
   b. electrostatic precipitators
   c. large magnets
   d. both a and b

ANS: D   DIF: B   OBJ: 14-1

9. Making aluminum cans from recycled aluminum requires _____ less energy than making cans from bauxite ore.
   a. 50 percent
   b. 75 percent
   c. 95 percent
   d. 10 percent

ANS: C   DIF: B   OBJ: 14-5

10. Of the following, which is NOT a tool to manage solid wastes?
   a. composting organic matter
   b. dumping sewage in the ocean
   c. recycling plastic milk jugs
   d. burning tires in an incinerator

ANS: B   DIF: B   OBJ: 14-6

COMPLETION

1. Improper disposal of car batteries can result in lead and _____ contaminating groundwater.

ANS: hydrochloric acid   DIF: A   OBJ: 14-5

2. The first major step in the recycling process is to _____ the material.

ANS: collect   DIF: B   OBJ: 14-6

3. To conserve landfill space, yard and food wastes can be _____.

ANS: composted   DIF: A   OBJ: 14-1

4. _____ incinerators burn solid waste without presorting.

ANS: Mass-burn   DIF: A   OBJ: 14-1

MATCHING

Match each item with the correct statement below. Write the answer in the space provided.

a. cullet
b. methane
c. leachate
d. sanitary landfill
e. incinerator
f. alloy
g. composting
h. clay

i. glass
j. fly ash
k. steel
l. fluff
m. source reduction
n. recycling
o. lead

1. _____ contaminated liquid from a landfill
2. _____ flammable gas produced by decomposition of organic matter
3. _____ used as a cap and liner for landfills
4. _____ pieces of ground glass
5. _____ toxic metal found in car batteries
6. _____ a process of collecting, sorting, and processing waste materials to produce new materials or products
7. _____ place where solid wastes are dumped, compressed, and covered by a layer of dirt
8. _____ a process in which the amount of solid waste generated is reduced
9. _____ place where solid wastes are burned to produce electricity
10. _____ a process in which organic matter is decomposed by microorganisms
11. _____ a mixture of two or more elements in which one element is a metal
12. _____ a mixture of silica, limestone, and soda ash
13. _____ an alloy of iron and a small amount of carbon
14. _____ a mixture of carpet, fabric, plastics, glass, and dirt
15. _____ a mixture of light ash containing toxic materials such as dioxin

1.	ANS:	c	DIF:	B	OBJ:	14-1
2.	ANS:	b	DIF:	B	OBJ:	14-1
3.	ANS:	h	DIF:	B	OBJ:	14-1
4.	ANS:	a	DIF:	B	OBJ:	14-2
5.	ANS:	o	DIF:	B	OBJ:	14-3
6.	ANS:	n	DIF:	B	OBJ:	14-6
7.	ANS:	d	DIF:	B	OBJ:	14-1
8.	ANS:	m	DIF:	B	OBJ:	14-6
9.	ANS:	e	DIF:	B	OBJ:	14-1
10.	ANS:	g	DIF:	B	OBJ:	14-7
11.	ANS:	f	DIF:	A	OBJ:	14-4
12.	ANS:	i	DIF:	B	OBJ:	14-4
13.	ANS:	k	DIF:	B	OBJ:	14-4
14.	ANS:	l	DIF:	B	OBJ:	14-3
15.	ANS:	j	DIF:	A	OBJ:	14-1

SHORT ANSWER

1. You are in charge of research into new uses for recycled plastics at a manufacturing firm. List some of your new products and explain how they are related to recycled materials.

   ANS: Answers will vary. Examples include plastic tables, benches, chairs, trash bags, grocery bags, bird feeders, curbs, trash cans, shoes, gutters, storage sheds, and others. These items are made from recycled plastics.

   DIF: B   OBJ: 14-4

2. Why can't window glass, lightbulbs, or drinking glasses be recycled with glass jars and bottles?

   ANS: They are not made of the same kind of glass.

   DIF: B   OBJ: 14-4

3. Name two environmental problems associated with sanitary landfills.

   ANS: Rain and groundwater can dissolve or carry away toxic materials from landfills, causing water pollution. Flammable methane gas is produced as microorganisms decompose organic matter.

   DIF: A   OBJ: 14-1

4. Garbage researchers have found 30-year-old hot dogs intact in landfills. Why haven't these hot dogs decomposed?

   ANS: Garbage in landfills is buried under layers of dirt or plastic. Without sunlight and oxygen, buried materials do not break down efficiently.

   DIF: A   OBJ: 14-1

5. What do the terms "reduce, reuse, recycle" mean?

   ANS: Ways to manage solid wastes: reduce by throwing less trash away; reuse by keeping used items so that they can be used again; recycle by collecting, sorting, and processing items into new materials.

   DIF: B   OBJ: 14-6

6. Of the following, identify which items are easy to recycle and which items are difficult to recycle: glass jars, minerals in electronic devices, carpet fibers, plastic soda bottles, plastic soda bottle caps, aluminum cans, steel cans, copper, cardboard pizza boxes, car windshields, car tires, fabrics, milk jugs, newspaper, used motor oil.

   ANS: Easy to recycle: glass jars, plastic soda bottles, aluminum cans, steel cans, copper, cardboard pizza boxes, milk jugs, newspaper, used motor oil. Hard to recycle: minerals in electronic devices, carpet fibers, plastic soda bottle caps, car windshields, car tires, fabrics.

   DIF: A   OBJ: 14-5

7. Solid waste management methods include source reduction, recycling, composting, waste-to-energy combustion, and disposal in landfills. Which of these methods can you use directly so that less garbage is deposited in sanitary landfills?

ANS: Reduce the total amount of garbage that is thrown away; separate and collect recyclable items such as cans, newspapers, glass and plastic bottles and jars; make compost piles of all vegetable matter from yards or kitchens.

DIF: A   OBJ: 14-6

8. Why don't biodegradable things like newspaper and food decompose in a sanitary landfill?

ANS: They are buried and are not in contact with sunlight, oxygen, or bacteria requiring oxygen, which are the primary decomposers.

DIF: A   OBJ: 14-1

9. List at least three areas that would not be good landfill sites and give reasons.

ANS: Answers will vary. The following are examples.
1) near a river or lake; the landfill could leak and pollute the water
2) on a steep mountain slope; it would be hard to excavate the hole and find soil to cover the trash
3) over a fault; an earthquake could break the landfill liner and cause it to leak
4) in a residential neighborhood; problems such as traffic, noise, rodents, and odor would detract from the neighborhood

DIF: B   OBJ: 14-1

10. What problems are often associated with old, abandoned dumps?

ANS: Before laws controlled the dumping of hazardous wastes, anything and everything was disposed of in these sites. Also, they were not constructed with liners, or with gas and leachate collection systems.

DIF: A   OBJ: 14-1

11. List five disposable items you use at home and the reusable items you could buy instead.

ANS:
Disposable items: paper cups, paper napkins, paper grocery bags, regular batteries, cardboard juice boxes.
Reusable items: plastic cups/water bottles, cloth napkins, cloth grocery bags, rechargeable batteries, glass/plastic juice bottles.

DIF: B   OBJ: 14-6

12. What are the major steps in glass recycling?

ANS: 1) Separate glass by color. 2) Grind glass into uniform-sized pieces (cullet). 3) Melt the cullet. 4) Form the melted glass into new items.

DIF: B   OBJ: 14-4

13. What other items could you revitalize or repair to start a community program such as the one that recycled bicycles in Portland, Oregon? Explain how you would run your program.

ANS: Answers will vary. Examples are repair toys, wagons, or playground equipment and distribute them.
Or, collect yard waste/food waste from restaurants and start a community composting station and garden. Then distribute surplus produce to food pantries and shelters.

DIF: A   OBJ: 14-6

14. What parts of an automobile are commonly recycled?

ANS: the steel, aluminum, copper, zinc, and chromium in bodies and frames; lead and acid in batteries; tires are also recycled; parts such as radiators, etc. can be reused; oil and various fluids

DIF: B   OBJ: 14-3

15. How can you buy "recycle-smart" at the grocery and reduce waste?

ANS: Buy bulk foods, which reduces packaging. Don't buy single-serving or overpackaged items. Buy things in easily recyclable containers. Reuse plastic or paper grocery bags or use cloth bags.

DIF: B   OBJ: 14-7

16. Explain why consumption is the biggest obstacle to the recycling process.

ANS: If there is no market for recycled goods, there will be no demand for recycled materials. Until people start buying recycled goods deliberately, few companies will see the benefit of using recycled materials to manufacture new products.

DIF: A   OBJ: 14-2

17. Explain how recycling of natural resources could result in a decrease in acid rain.

ANS: Energy usually comes from the burning of fossil fuels, a process that can result in acid rain. Recycling products requires less energy than taking natural resources out of the ground, so recycling could result in a decrease in acid rain.

DIF: A   OBJ: 14-1

18. Your community just passed an ordinance that forbids disposal of yard wastes in landfills. As a result, your father bought a new lawnmower that cuts the grass into tiny pieces. Why?

ANS: The tiny grass pieces can be left on the lawn, where they will eventually decompose and provide nutrients.

DIF: B   OBJ: 14-6

19. You are thinking about going hiking at a newly built park. But then you find out that the park has been built on top of a 20-year-old sanitary landfill. Should you go there for a vacation? Explain your answer.

ANS: If this landfill was sited and built properly, there should be no problem in taking a vacation there. As long as there is proper drainage from the landfill so that toxic materials do not enter the groundwater, and the methane gas that builds up is vented or burned, the landfill will not decay for a long time.

DIF: A   OBJ: 14-1

20. Explain why incinerators and sanitary landfills are usually located close to cities and smaller towns even though no one wants such facilities in their own back yards.

ANS: It costs a lot of money to transport garbage. Trucks and sanitation workers who collect the trash must make several trips each day to the landfill or incinerator; if the facility were far away, the costs for fuel and workers' salaries would increase to a point that would make garbage collection too expensive for most people.

DIF: A   OBJ: 14-1

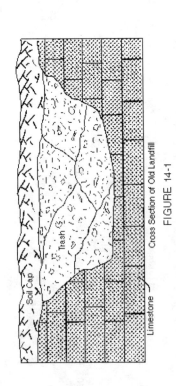

Cross Section of Old Landfill

FIGURE 14-1

21. The old landfill shown in Figure 14-1 was located in an abandoned limestone quarry. Contaminates from the landfill have been found in nearby water wells and streams. What should have been done to prevent this?

ANS: Plastic or clay liners should have been put in the bottom of the quarry and along the sides.

DIF: A   OBJ: 14-1

22. What possible problems could occur in the landfill shown in Figure 14-1 because of decomposing organic material?

ANS: Methane from decomposition could catch fire, the material could produce foul odors, and leachate could pollute groundwater.

DIF: B   OBJ: 14-1

---

23. What could be done to prevent problems from escaping gas in the landfill shown in Figure 14-1?

ANS: install a gas collection system

DIF: A   OBJ: 14-1

24. What is contaminated liquid from a landfill called, and how does water get into the landfill shown in Figure 14-1?

ANS: Leachate is the contaminated liquid. Water gets into a landfill as rain or groundwater.

DIF: A   OBJ: 14-1

25. What should have been installed in the landfill shown in Figure 14-1 to prevent leachate from polluting groundwater and nearby streams?

ANS: a leachate collection system of drains and pipes

DIF: A   OBJ: 14-1

OTHER

If the underscored word or phrase makes the sentence true, write "true" in the space provided. If the underscored word or phrase makes the sentence false, write the correct term or phrase in the space provided.

1. Plastic forms the largest percentage of municipal solid waste. _____

ANS: Paper   DIF: A   OBJ: 14-1

2. A(n) scrubber is a large furnace used to burn solid waste. _____

ANS: incinerator   DIF: A   OBJ: 14-1

3. A(n) sanitary landfill is a pit lined with clay or plastic where trash is dumped and then covered with soil. _____

ANS: true   DIF: A   OBJ: 14-1

4. Noncombustible trash is sorted out and shredded to be burned in an incinerator. _____

ANS: Combustible   DIF: A   OBJ: 14-1

5. Most of the solid waste generated by cities is recyclable. _____

ANS: true   DIF: B   OBJ: 14-2

6. A mixture of two or more elements using at least one metal is a(n) compound. _____

ANS: alloy   DIF: A   OBJ: 14-4

7. <u>Fluff</u> is crushed glass that is then remelted as part of the recycling process.

ANS: Cullet   DIF: B   OBJ: 14-4

8. Yard wastes such as grass clippings and leaves can be <u>composted</u>, which saves landfill space.

ANS: true   DIF: A   OBJ: 14-6

9. <u>Commercial</u> waste is dangerous material and requires special handling and disposal.

ANS: Hazardous   DIF: A   OBJ: 14-6

10. Steel is easy to separate from aluminum because steel is <u>lighter</u>.

ANS: magnetic   DIF: B   OBJ: 14-6

CHAPTER 15—EARTH'S CRUST IN MOTION

MULTIPLE CHOICE

1. The strongest recorded earthquake in the United States occurred in ____.
   a. San Diego, California
   b. Anchorage, Alaska
   c. New Madrid, Missouri
   d. Ventura, California

   ANS: C   DIF: A   OBJ: 15-6

2. Soil creep on a slope can be caused by ____.
   a. freezing and thawing
   b. rock talus
   c. limestone bedrock
   d. dry weather

   ANS: A   DIF: B   OBJ: 15-1

3. Mudflows can be caused by ____.
   a. fire-cleared slopes and heavy rains
   b. melting snow
   c. slopes covered in volcanic ash
   d. all of the above

   ANS: D   DIF: A   OBJ: 15-2

4. Landslides are ____.
   a. slow, flowing movements of soil
   b. only caused by heavy rains
   c. the rapid downhill movement of soil and rock
   d. caused by the collapse of limestone bedrock

   ANS: C   DIF: B   OBJ: 15-2

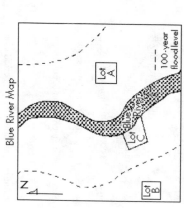

FIGURE 15-2

5. In Figure 15-2, the Blue River flows south. The west bank of the river near Lot C will _____.
   a. be eroded
   b. have sediment deposition
   c. have slower-moving water
   d. have higher tides
   ANS: A   DIF: B   OBJ: 15-4

6. The best use of the land for sale at Lot C in Figure 15-2 would be a _____.
   a. hospital
   b. sewage-treatment plant
   c. park
   d. housing development
   ANS: C   DIF: A   OBJ: 15-4

7. Lot A and Lot B in Figure 15-2 are both for sale. You want to buy a lot to build your dream house. Lot A is priced at $10 000 and Lot B at $25 000. Why might you buy the more-expensive Lot B?
   a. It is larger.
   b. It is safer from floods.
   c. You should buy the cheaper lot.
   d. It is closer to the river.
   ANS: B   DIF: A   OBJ: 15-4

8. The flat, low-lying area below the 100-year flood level is a _____.
   a. floodplain
   b. plateau
   c. mudflat
   d. coastline
   ANS: A   DIF: A   OBJ: 15-4

9. The Blue River flows into the Missouri River, which is _____.
   a. part of the Columbia River Drainage
   b. part of the Ohio River
   c. part of the Mississippi River Drainage
   d. west of the Rocky Mountains
   ANS: C   DIF: A   OBJ: 15-3

10. If the Blue River is part of the Mississippi River Drainage, then the waters of the Blue River should eventually flow into _____.
    a. the Gulf of Mexico
    b. the Pacific Ocean
    c. Hudson Bay
    d. Lake Erie
    ANS: A   DIF: A   OBJ: 15-3

COMPLETION

1. Rapid erosion typically occurs on the _____ bank of stream curves.
   ANS: outside   DIF: B   OBJ: 15-4

2. A _____ is a rapidly flowing mixture of soil and water.
   ANS: mudflow   DIF: B   OBJ: 15-2

3. Mudflows commonly follow _____, and can travel rapidly.
   ANS: heavy rains or melting snow   DIF: A   OBJ: 15-2

4. Sinkholes are a common occurrence in the state of _____.
   ANS: Florida   DIF: A   OBJ: 15-1

5. Continual rain over a long period can _____ the soil, causing flooding.
   ANS: saturate   DIF: B   OBJ: 15-3

6. The breaking apart of rock caused by the freezing of water within its cracks is an example of _____.
   ANS: physical weathering   DIF: B   OBJ: 15-1

7. An example of chemical weathering is the creation of a _____.
   ANS: sinkhole   DIF: B   OBJ: 15-1

8. The surface waves created by an earthquake are strongest near the earthquake's _____.
   ANS: epicenter   DIF: A   OBJ: 15-6

9. Ground that is soft and broken up by plant roots _____ and holds water well.
   ANS: absorbs   DIF: A   OBJ: 15-3

10. The more water the soil in a drainage basin can hold, the less often its streams or rivers will _____.
    ANS: flood   DIF: A   OBJ: 15-3

11. A practical step you might take to lessen the destructive effects of a(n) _____ is to use special building methods.
    ANS: earthquake   DIF: B   OBJ: 15-7

12. The least erosion occurs in the land on the _____ curves of rivers.
    ANS: inside   DIF: B   OBJ: 15-4

13. In most parts of the country, _____ are the least obvious risk to buildings and other structures.

ANS: earthquakes   DIF: B   OBJ: 15-6

14. _____ is a type of mass wasting occurring if the foundation of your house splits and part of the house slowly begins to move down the hillside.

ANS: Creep   DIF: B   OBJ: 15-2

15. Sinkholes often occur in areas with underlying _____.

ANS: limestone   DIF: A   OBJ: 15-1

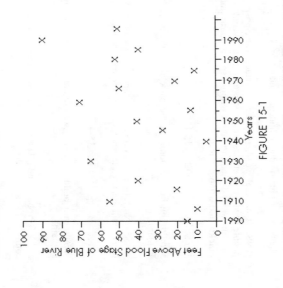

FIGURE 15-1

16. According to Figure 15-1, the worst flood on record caused by the Blue River occurred in _____.

ANS: 1990   DIF: B   OBJ: 15-3

17. The 100-year flood occurs when the Blue River is more than 60 feet above flood stage. Figure 15-1 shows that there have been _____ 100-year floods since 1900 on the Blue River.

ANS: three   DIF: A   OBJ: 15-3

18. Based on Figure 15-1, the 100-year flood level has occurred about every _____ years on the Blue River since 1900.

ANS: 30   DIF: B   OBJ: 15-3

19. The data in Figure 15-1 show that in the years _____ and _____, the Blue River did not exceed flood stage.

ANS: 1925, 1935   DIF: B   OBJ: 15-3

20. If the Blue River described in Figure 15-1 is located in Missouri, it is part of the _____ Drainage Basin.

ANS: Mississippi River   DIF: A   OBJ: 15-3

MATCHING

Match each item with the correct statement below. Write the answer in the space provided.

a. limestone   k. runoff
b. erosion   l. drainage basin
c. divide   m. physical weathering
d. unstable soils   n. flood plain
e. soil saturation   o. bedrock
f. landslide   p. chemical weathering
g. creep   q. mudflow
h. seismic waves   r. mass wasting
i. sinkhole   s. earthquake
j. fault   t. flood

____ 1. soils that move easily under the force of gravity
____ 2. rapid downhill movement of rock and soil
____ 3. helps cause floods
____ 4. slow, flowing soil movement
____ 5. collapsed limestone cave
____ 6. solid rock overlaid by unconsolidated material
____ 7. type of rock in which sinkholes most commonly form
____ 8. vibrations caused by earthquakes
____ 9. occurs on the outside of the bends in a river
____ 10. occurs when water interacts to break down rock material
____ 11. separating feature between two drainage basins
____ 12. mass wasting that rolls material down hillsides
____ 13. crack in Earth's crust
____ 14. term for mudflows, landslides, and creep
____ 15. produces waves in Earth's surface
____ 16. what happens when a stream overflows its banks
____ 17. what occurs when rain falls on saturated soil
____ 18. area surrounding a river that is covered by flood waters
____ 19. area from which streams and rivers collect runoff
____ 20. the mechanical breakdown of rock and soil

1. ANS: d   DIF: A   OBJ: 15-2
2. ANS: f   DIF: B   OBJ: 15-2
3. ANS: e   DIF: B   OBJ: 15-3
4. ANS: g   DIF: B   OBJ: 15-2
5. ANS: i   DIF: B   OBJ: 15-1

6. ANS: o DIF: B OBJ: 15-7
7. ANS: a DIF: B OBJ: 15-1
8. ANS: h DIF: B OBJ: 15-6
9. ANS: b DIF: B OBJ: 15-4
10. ANS: p DIF: B OBJ: 15-1
11. ANS: c DIF: A OBJ: 15-3
12. ANS: q DIF: B OBJ: 15-2
13. ANS: j DIF: B OBJ: 15-6
14. ANS: r DIF: B OBJ: 15-2
15. ANS: s DIF: B OBJ: 15-6
16. ANS: t DIF: B OBJ: 15-3
17. ANS: k DIF: B OBJ: 15-3
18. ANS: n DIF: B OBJ: 15-3
19. ANS: l DIF: B OBJ: 15-3
20. ANS: m DIF: B OBJ: 15-1

SHORT ANSWER

1. Which poses a greater risk to buildings and people—chemical weathering due to surface water or chemical weathering due to underground water? Explain.

ANS: Chemical weathering due to surface water poses much less of a threat to buildings and people because its effects are obvious and readily avoided. Weathering due to water underground, in contrast, is difficult to detect without special Earth-imaging equipment. Sinkholes often open quickly and without warning.

DIF: A   OBJ: 15-1

2. Would you build a home on the bank along the outer bend of a scenic, fast-flowing stream? Explain.

ANS: No. The banks on the outer bends of rivers or streams are subject to steady erosion. A house built at such a location would eventually be undercut.

DIF: B   OBJ: 15-4

3. Would you build on a flat, well-drained area with many limestone caverns beneath the soil? Explain.

ANS: Probably not. The limestone may be subject to chemical weathering. Such weathering could lead to a sinkhole.

DIF: B   OBJ: 15-1

4. Would a cliff overlooking the ocean be a good home site? Explain.

ANS: No. Wave action, especially that caused by storms, erodes cliffs and steep slopes on seashores. In time, the cliff would be undercut and slump into the sea.

DIF: B   OBJ: 15-5

5. Would you build a home on a level area on a floodplain that has not flooded in five years? Explain.

ANS: Probably not. All locations on a floodplain are subject to flood damage under the right conditions.

DIF: A   OBJ: 15-3

6. What factors can affect the damage caused by an earthquake?

ANS: Soil type can greatly affect damage. Buildings constructed on fill or unstable soil will receive more damage than similar structures constructed on bedrock. How buildings are constructed also affects damage; older masonry buildings receive more damage than braced wood frame buildings. Location is important as well; areas closer to the epicenter generally suffer greater damage. Houses near cliffs can be damaged by falling debris or landslides.

DIF: A   OBJ: 15-6

7. Where can you obtain information on the risk of earthquakes, landslides, and floods in a particular area?

ANS: from the U.S. Geological Survey, state geological surveys, university geology or civil engineering departments and libraries, and the Government Printing Office

DIF: A   OBJ: 15-6

8. What kinds of related disasters can be caused by earthquakes?

ANS: Fires and explosions due to broken gas lines are common related disasters. Loss of power and water from downed power lines and broken water mains can cause problems long after the quake. Tsunamis can occur if the epicenter is offshore. Landslides, mudflows, and soil creep can be triggered by quakes.

DIF: A   OBJ: 15-6

9. Why do landslides and mudflows often follow major fires?

ANS: Vegetation is destroyed by the fire. The bare slopes are then more vulnerable to erosion and therefore unstable.

DIF: A   OBJ: 15-6

10. What factors can contribute to soil creep?

ANS: Gravity is the major factor. Freezing and thawing, wetting and drying of the soil, plant roots, and burrowing animals can also affect slope stability.

DIF: A   OBJ: 15-2

11. Explain why the existence of underlying fault lines is not apparent on Earth's surface.

ANS: Faults can be many thousands of meters below the surface; even when evidence of fault movement appears, it may not last long because vegetation and weathering can quickly hide any evidence of fault movement.

DIF: A   OBJ: 15-6

12. Classify each of the following processes as either physical or chemical weathering and discuss the threat it poses to buildings and other structures: wave erosion, mass wasting, sinkholes.

ANS: Wave erosion is a type of physical weathering in which sediment carried by waves mechanically scours away the shoreline, gradually undercutting cliffs and washing away sand from pilings under buildings. Mass wasting (landslides, mudflows, falls, and creep) is a type of physical weathering in which gravity pulls down soil and rock. It can lead to cracked foundations, leaky roofs, and tilted and collapsed buildings. Sinkholes, a type of chemical weathering in which mildly acidic groundwater dissolves limestone, causes the surface to collapse and buildings to tilt, sink, or collapse.

DIF: A   OBJ: 15-7

13. Identify factors that influence the risk of flooding and give examples of each.

ANS: Flooding occurs when streams or rivers receive more runoff water than they can hold. Factors that lead to rapid runoff and increase the risk of flooding include soil type, vegetation, and slope. Soils that are hard and dense, such as clay, cannot absorb rainwater very quickly, so the water collects on the surface or runs off. Soils with little or no vegetation are also less absorbent and therefore prone to runoff. Water will run off steep slopes quickly with less chance for soaking into the ground.

DIF: A   OBJ: 15-3

14. Explain why mudflows and floods are more likely after certain other natural disasters have occurred.

ANS: Mudflows are more likely when volcanoes have erupted because areas covered with loose volcanic ash begin to move very easily when the ash mixes with water. Floods are more likely after forest fires. This is because soils denuded of vegetation are less absorbent and more likely to have runoff when it rains.

DIF: A   OBJ: 15-2

15. What evidence would indicate that mass wasting had occurred on a hillside? How could you tell which type of mass wasting had occurred?

ANS: Such evidence might include tilted utility poles, cracked road surfaces, rocks scattered at the bottom of the hill, or buildings with cracked foundations and uneven floors. You could tell which type of mass wasting occurred by considering the conditions that led to it and the way in which mass wasting had affected the hillside and any structures on it. A mudflow is likely to occur on a steeper, wetter hillside and might bury a building, whereas creep is more likely to occur on a dryer, gentler slope and to gradually shift a building off of its foundation. A fall may lead to a pile of rocks at the bottom of a very steep hill; a landslide will scatter rocks and soil down a more gradually sloping hillside.

DIF: A   OBJ: 15-2

OTHER

If the underscored word or phrase makes the sentence true, write "true" in the space provided. If the underscored word or phrase makes the sentence false, write the correct term or phrase in the space provided.

1. Unstable soils can move under the force of gravity.

ANS: true   DIF: B   OBJ: 15-2

2. The Leaning Tower of Pisa is tilted because of an earthquake.

ANS: unstable soil   DIF: A   OBJ: 15-2

3. Chemical weathering breaks rocks into smaller pieces from freezing and thawing.

ANS: Physical   DIF: A   OBJ: 15-1

4. Downhill movement of soil or rock material because of gravity is called mass wasting.

ANS: true   DIF: B   OBJ: 15-2

5. A landslide is the rapid downhill movement of rock.

ANS: true   DIF: B   OBJ: 15-2

6. Soil creep can occur on any slopes.

ANS: true   DIF: A   OBJ: 15-2

7. Sinkholes are formed by physical weathering in areas of limestone bedrock.

ANS: chemical   DIF: A   OBJ: 15-1

8. Sinkholes are formed by neutral groundwater dissolving limestone.

ANS: acidic   DIF: A   OBJ: 15-1

9. The Columbia River drains into the Atlantic Ocean.

ANS: Pacific   DIF: A   OBJ: 15-3

10. A wetland is the low-lying area near a stream that is covered with water during floods.

ANS: floodplain   DIF: A   OBJ: 15-3

CHAPTER 16—STRUCTURES AND MATERIALS

MULTIPLE CHOICE

1. In which one of the following is ceramic material NOT used?
   a. roofing tile
   b. grinding wheel
   c. metal coatings
   d. superconductors

   ANS: C   DIF: B   OBJ: 16-8

2. Which one of the following would be a natural building material?
   a. stone
   b. plastic
   c. polystyrene
   d. PVC

   ANS: A   DIF: B   OBJ: 16-3

3. Which one of the following is NOT an advantage of using stone as a building material?
   a. strong
   b. durable
   c. easy to cut and shape
   d. attractive covering over other types of building material

   ANS: C   DIF: B   OBJ: 16-4

4. Which one of the following is NOT a property that can be explained using the electron-sea model of metals?
   a. use of metals as insulators
   b. conductivity of heat and electricity
   c. ductility
   d. malleability

   ANS: A   DIF: B   OBJ: 16-5

5. Which of the following is an example of an alloy?
   a. steel
   b. iron
   c. plastic
   d. PVC

   ANS: A   DIF: B   OBJ: 16-6

6. Which one of the following statements about foundations for a large building is NOT correct?
   a. The type of soil and rock under the building needs to be known before the foundation is done.
   b. A raft foundation can be built directly on rock that is close to the surface.
   c. A raft foundation can be built on rock that is deep under the surface.
   d. A pier foundation can be built on rock that is deep under the surface.

   ANS: C   DIF: A   OBJ: 16-1

7. Which of the following statements about stress on buildings is correct?
   a. Each stress force must have a counterforce.
   b. Tensile stress results when forces that act on a building are uneven.
   c. Shear stress results when two forces are applied through a solid and push toward each other.
   d. Objects subjected to compression stress tend to twist apart.

   ANS: A   DIF: A   OBJ: 16-2

8. Which one of the following statements about wood is NOT correct?
   a. Softwood trees have cells that are larger and fewer in number because they grow quickly.
   b. Hardwood trees have cells that are smaller and have more cellulose fiber in the cell walls because they grow slowly.
   c. Xylem cells transport water through the tree.
   d. Wood does not rot easily and is relatively fireproof.

   ANS: D   DIF: A   OBJ: 16-3

9. Which of the following is NOT an advantage for using brick in a building?
   a. Bricks can withstand a large compression force.
   b. Bricks can be used in all climates, even warm, wet climates.
   c. Bricks are easy to make and lightweight.
   d. Bricks can be made into many different colors.

   ANS: B   DIF: A   OBJ: 16-4

10. Which of the following statements about the electron-sea model is correct?
    a. Both positive and negative charges are mobile.
    b. Only positive charges are mobile.
    c. Only negative charges are mobile.
    d. Neither negative nor positive charges are mobile.

    ANS: C   DIF: A   OBJ: 16-5

COMPLETION

1. The ability to be pulled into thin wires is the property of _____.

   ANS: ductility   DIF: B   OBJ: 16-5

2. The corrosion product that results from iron reacting with oxygen from the air is _____.

   ANS: rust or iron oxide   DIF: B   OBJ: 16-6

3. The type of plastic used in plumbing today is _____.

   ANS: PVC or polyvinyl chloride   DIF: B   OBJ: 16-7

4. The thermal insulating tiles on the outside surfaces of the space shuttle orbiter are made of _____

ANS: ceramics   DIF: B   OBJ: 16-8

5. Buckminster Fuller designed a unique, dome-shaped structure called a(n) _____

ANS: geodesic dome   DIF: B   OBJ: 16-2

6. _____ is made from water, sand, and small stones added to cement.

ANS: Concrete   DIF: B   OBJ: 16-3

MATCHING

Match each item with the correct statement below. Write the answer in the space provided.

a. electron-sea   f. softwood
b. brick   g. thin film
c. pier   h. cement
d. hardwood   i. brass
e. dome   j. insulator

1. _____ What type of foundation would be used for a building if no solid rock is found close to the surface?

2. _____ The shape of a _____ spreads out the load on a building so that gravity is evenly distributed down the sides of the building.

3. _____ Oak and maple are examples of _____ trees.

4. _____ is the building material that is a mixture of limestone and other materials that can be mixed with water and used as an adhesive.

5. _____ The properties of metals are explained with the _____ model.

6. _____ Copper and zinc are mixed together to form the alloy _____.

7. _____ A(n) _____ is a material through which heat and electricity cannot easily flow.

8. _____ A(n) _____ is a thin layer of metal applied to glass in warmer climates.

9. _____ Pine and fir are classified as _____ trees.

10. _____ is a ceramic made from moist clay that has been heat-treated to drive off moisture.

1. ANS: c   DIF: B   OBJ: 16-1
2. ANS: e   DIF: B   OBJ: 16-2
3. ANS: d   DIF: B   OBJ: 16-3
4. ANS: h   DIF: B   OBJ: 16-4
5. ANS: a   DIF: B   OBJ: 16-5
6. ANS: i   DIF: B   OBJ: 16-6
7. ANS: j   DIF: B   OBJ: 16-7
8. ANS: g   DIF: B   OBJ: 16-8
9. ANS: f   DIF: B   OBJ: 16-3
10. ANS: b   DIF: B   OBJ: 16-4

SHORT ANSWER

1. Why is steel stronger than iron?

ANS: As iron is heated, atoms from another element such as carbon replace some of the iron atoms or fit in between iron atoms. This resulting alloy has properties different from the original iron, resulting in a stronger material.

DIF: A   OBJ: 16-6

2. Why is PVC often used in place of metal pipes in plumbing?

ANS: PVC resists corrosion but is also strong and rigid.

DIF: A   OBJ: 16-7

3. Why are ceramics often used in place of metals?

ANS: Ceramics are strong and lightweight and can replace more costly metals in the manufacturing of airplanes, missiles, and spacecraft.

DIF: A   OBJ: 16-8

4. What are some examples of stress forces that a builder must consider when planning and constructing a new building?

ANS: Answers will vary. Examples of stress forces are soil movement; types of wind that the building might encounter such as hurricanes, thunderstorms, or tornadoes; and earthquake hazards. Location and type of bedrock is also important, as well as the weight and style of the building itself.

DIF: A   OBJ: 16-1

5. Why is a dome-shaped building particularly stable?

ANS: Domes can support their own weight because the load of each of the individual parts is spread out so that the compression force of gravity is evenly distributed down the sides of the dome. The forces on all of the parts are in equilibrium.

DIF: A   OBJ: 16-2

6. Assume that you are an architect planning a new home for a client. What advice would you give about the use of wood in your client's new home?

ANS: Wood can be carved into many shapes and can be nailed, glued, or tied together. If harvested properly, it is a renewable resource. However, wood can rot and is attacked by fungi, termites, and other insects, so it may be chemically treated to extend its life.

DIF: A   OBJ: 16-3

7. Why are soil and rock important factors in planning the foundation of a new building?

ANS: It is important to make sure the ground is stable enough to support the building. The foundation may need to be drilled into rock below the surface, so it is important to know how deep rock is. This is especially true for tall buildings.

DIF: A   OBJ: 16-2

8. Why are triangles used in building designs? Give an example of the use of triangles in a building design.

ANS: They spread the force over a wide area and make a structure more rigid. An example is the geodesic dome developed by Buckminster Fuller. Constructed of triangles made from rods that together form the dome, this lightweight structure is very strong.

DIF: A   OBJ: 16-2

9. What are the differences between the properties of hardwoods and softwoods? How can these differences be explained?

ANS: Hardwoods are more resistant to compression forces than softwoods are. Hardwood plant cells are smaller, more numerous, and contain more cellulose. Softwoods have larger and fewer cells and have less cellulose.

DIF: A   OBJ: 16-2

10. What are the advantages and disadvantages of using stone in constructing a building?

ANS: Stone is strong and durable; however, stone is very heavy and hard to cut into shapes.

DIF: B   OBJ: 16-8

11. What are the advantages and disadvantages of using wood to construct a building?

ANS: Wood is easy to cut into shapes, is easy to nail together, and is a renewable resource. However, wood can rot and is prone to attack from fungi and termites.

DIF: B   OBJ: 16-8

12. What are the advantages of using plastics to construct a building?

ANS: durability, nonflammability, good insulators of heat and electricity, resistance to corrosion

DIF: B   OBJ: 16-8

13. What are the advantages and disadvantages of using ceramics to construct a building?

ANS: Ceramics are hard, resistant to corrosion, and are able to withstand high temperatures without cracking. However, they can have structural defects such as microcracks that can cause them to fracture under stress.

DIF: B   OBJ: 16-8

14. What are the advantages of using thin films as a coating on the glass panels of buildings?

ANS: cooling-cost reduction, privacy for people inside the building

DIF: A   OBJ: 16-7

15. Why do some metals such as iron seem to corrode very easily while other metals such as aluminum and copper seem to resist corrosion when used in certain building applications?

ANS: Aluminum and copper can form protective oxide coatings that prevent further corrosion.

DIF: A   OBJ: 16-4

16. How are the two types of alloys formed? Give an example of each type.

ANS: The first occurs when atoms of the host metal are the same size as atoms of the additional element. The added atoms can replace some of the host atoms. Brass is an example; its zinc atoms and copper atoms are about the same size. The second type of alloy results when small atoms of an additional element fit between the spaces in the host atoms. Steel, whose smaller carbon atoms are added to iron, is an example.

DIF: B   OBJ: 16-6

17. Why is an eggshell strong?

ANS: Its dome shape spreads the compression force of gravity evenly down its sides.

DIF: A   OBJ: 16-2

18. What is an electron-sea model and what does it demonstrate?

ANS: a simple atomic model able to account for the properties of metal, such as malleability and lustrous appearance

DIF: B   OBJ: 16-5

19. What are an advantage and a disadvantage of using ceramics in car engines?

ANS: Ceramics make engines lighter and more heat resistant, but they also can shatter when something hard hits them.

DIF: B   OBJ: 16-8

20. What are some examples of hazardous building-material by-products that can be harmful to occupants?

ANS: glues in wood, formaldehyde, combustion of gases without proper ventilation, organic solvents, paints, toluene

DIF: A   OBJ: 16-8

24. In Figure 16-4, three companies have provided rough sketches of the types of roofs they would build for an indoor, multipurpose stadium. Which one of the proposals would you accept, and why, if money was not a concern?

ANS: The dome roof can support more stress and is more lightweight than other options.

DIF: A   OBJ: 16-2

25. Which one of the proposals shown in Figure 16-4 would you NOT accept under any situations?

ANS: The flat roof will collapse under too much stress.

DIF: A   OBJ: 16-2

26. Suppose your town can budget only $2.0 million for a roof. Under what environmental circumstances would Proposal B in Figure 16-4 be considered?

ANS: It might be considered in a warmer climate where snow and ice are not problems.

DIF: A   OBJ: 16-2

Table 16-1

Material	Conductor or Insulator	Use
plastic	A	plumbing, insulation
B	insulator	tiles, semiconductors
copper	conductor	C
D	insulator	pyramids, Washington Monument

27. In Table 16-1, what should replace the **A** to make the table correct?

ANS: insulator   DIF: B   OBJ: 16-7

28. In Table 16-1, what should replace the **B** to make the table correct?

ANS: ceramics   DIF: B   OBJ: 16-7

29. In Table 16-1, what should replace the **C** to make the table correct?

ANS: electric wire or cookware   DIF: B   OBJ: 16-7

30. In Table 16-1, what should replace the **D** to make the table correct?

ANS: stone   DIF: B   OBJ: 16-7

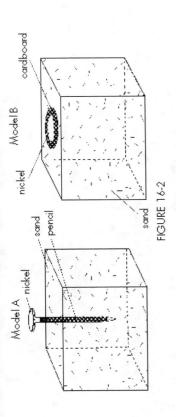

Model A   Model B

FIGURE 16-2

21. Which type of foundations do the models in Figure 16-2 represent?

ANS: Model A: pile foundation; Model B: mat or raft foundation

DIF: A   OBJ: 16-2

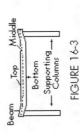

FIGURE 16-3

22. Suppose a beam starts to sag, as shown in Figure 16-3. What kind of stresses are occurring at the top, middle, and bottom of the beam, and in the supporting columns?

ANS: The top is undergoing greater compression stress; the bottom is undergoing greater tensile stress. The middle is undergoing shear stress. The supporting columns are undergoing compression stress.

DIF: A   OBJ: 16-1

23. If the beam in Figure 16-3 has to be made of concrete, what would be your recommendation for the type of concrete that should be used if the beam needs to be the strongest it possibly can be?

ANS: It should be made of prestressed concrete, which can support heavier loads than regular concrete or reinforced concrete can.

DIF: A   OBJ: 16-1

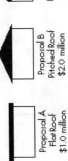

Proposal A
Flat Roof
$1.0 million

Proposal B
Pitched Roof
$2.0 million

Proposal C
Domed Roof
$3.0 million

FIGURE 16-4

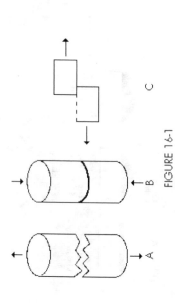

FIGURE 16-1

31. For Figure 16-1, describe the stress that is occurring on Object A.

ANS: It is tensile stress. This occurs when opposite forces are applied equally to lengthen or pull apart something.

DIF: B   OBJ: 16-1

32. For Figure 16-1, describe how Object A does not exhibit high tensile strength.

ANS: Tensile strength prevents an object from coming apart when it is subjected to tensile stress or tension. Because the object has come apart, it has low tensile strength.

DIF: B   OBJ: 16-2

33. For Figure 16-1, describe the stress that is occurring on Object B.

ANS: It is compression stress. It is the opposite of tensile stress. The objects are pushing against each other.

DIF: B   OBJ: 16-1

34. For Figure 16-1, describe the stress that is occurring on Object C.

ANS: It is shear stress. Lines of force are not directly across from each other.

DIF: B   OBJ: 16-1

35. What are the differences among cement, mortar, and concrete?

ANS: Cement is a building material that is a mixture of limestone and other materials that can be mixed with water and used as an adhesive. Mortar is a mixture of cement, sand, water, and lime and is used to hold bricks together. Concrete is made when water, sand, and small stones are added to cement. It can be poured into different shapes and is used for foundations, sidewalks, and driveways.

DIF: A   OBJ: 16-4

36. Describe the properties of metals. Why do metals have these properties?

ANS: Metals conduct heat and electricity. They are malleable, which means they can be hammered into sheets. They are ductile, which means they can be pulled into thin wire. These properties are explained by the electron-sea model. A regular arrangement of positively charged metal ions is found in a sea of electrons. Most of the electrons are confined to the metal ions, but the outer-level electrons can move freely from ion to ion. This mobility of electrons explains metallic properties.

DIF: A   OBJ: 16-5

37. What is corrosion? What are some ways that corrosion can be prevented?

ANS: Corrosion occurs when oxygen reacts with a metal to produce a new compound that is weaker than the original metal. Rust is an example of the product of a corrosion reaction between iron and oxygen. Alloys such as bronze, brass, and stainless steel are able to resist corrosion better than the individual metals they come from. Paint, enamel, or plastic can be applied to the surface of a metal to stop corrosion.

DIF: A   OBJ: 16-6

38. What are some examples of plastics used in today's buildings?

ANS: Answers will vary. Polyethylene is used in piping and electrical insulation. Polypropylene is used in carpet. Polystyrene is used in insulation. Polyvinyl chloride is used in plumbing, in siding, in floor tile, and as a substitute for rubber.

DIF: A   OBJ: 16-7

39. What are some advantages and disadvantages of using plastic instead of wood in a new building?

ANS: Plastics can be strong, lightweight, flexible, and durable. Color can be molded into plastic so that it does not need to be painted. Plastic will not rot and is resistant to water damage, fungi, and insects. However, plastic can be more expensive than wood and is not as easily nailed. Wood also has a more pleasing look.

DIF: A   OBJ: 16-8

OTHER

If the underscored word or phrase makes the sentence true, write "true" in the space provided. If the underscored word or phrase makes the sentence false, write the correct term or phrase in the space provided.

1. The electron-sea model is used to explain the properties of plastics. _____

ANS: metals   DIF: B   OBJ: 16-5

2. Inuit people build igloos as permanent residences. _____

ANS: temporary   DIF: B   OBJ: 16-4

CHAPTER 17—FORCES AND MACHINES

MULTIPLE CHOICE

1. A simple machine will do all of the following tasks EXCEPT _____ .
   a. change the direction of a force
   b. decrease the amount of required work
   c. transfer energy from one location to another
   d. decrease the time it takes to do work

   ANS: B   DIF: B   OBJ: 17-7

2. Two identical people run up a flight of stairs. The first person takes 10 seconds, while the second person takes 15 seconds. It is incorrect to state that _____ .
   a. each person is doing the same amount of work
   b. the weight of each person does not change
   c. the first person produces more power than the second person
   d. the second person produces more power than the first person

   ANS: D   DIF: B   OBJ: 17-5

3. A joule is equal to one _____ .
   a. newton-meter
   b. watt-meter
   c. newton/watt
   d. newton/meter

   ANS: A   DIF: B   OBJ: 17-5

4. In which of the following situations is work NOT being done on an object?
   a. A box of nails is lifted 2.0 m above the ground.
   b. A hammer is swung 1 meter to hit a nail.
   c. A person holds a pole while concrete is setting.
   d. A person climbs a distance of 10 m up a ladder.

   ANS: C   DIF: A   OBJ: 17-4

5. Which of the following machines is NOT a compound machine?
   a. drill
   b. maul
   c. wedge
   d. screwdriver

   ANS: C   DIF: A   OBJ: 17-8

6. A locomotive traveling at 55 mph requires a longer distance to stop completely than an automobile traveling at 55 mph does because _____ .
   a. automobiles have more efficient braking systems
   b. automobiles have more inertia
   c. locomotives have more inertia
   d. locomotives have no friction between their wheels and the tracks

   ANS: C   DIF: A   OBJ: 17-1

---

3. An object that is being twisted is undergoing shear stress. _____

   ANS: true   DIF: B   OBJ: 16-1

4. Reinforced concrete is used in places where compression stress is high. _____

   ANS: tensile stress   DIF: B   OBJ: 16-2

5. A tug-of-war game with a rope exerts tensile stress on the rope. _____

   ANS: true   DIF: B   OBJ: 16-1

6. The stress that is opposite to tensile stress is shear stress. _____

   ANS: compression stress   DIF: B   OBJ: 16-1

7. Examples of plastic are polyethylene, polypropylene, and PVC. _____

   ANS: true   DIF: B   OBJ: 16-7

8. Ceramics are dried sand materials. _____

   ANS: clay   DIF: B   OBJ: 16-4

9. An insulator conducts heat and electricity. _____

   ANS: does not conduct   DIF: B   OBJ: 16-4

10. Water is transported in a plant through the arteries. _____

    ANS: xylem   DIF: B   OBJ: 16-4

7. Automobiles may slide off the road when attempting to stop on a muddy surface due to _____.
   a. increased friction
   b. decreased friction
   c. increased inertia
   d. decreased inertia

   ANS: B   DIF: A   OBJ: 17-6

8. When a machine exerts a force through a distance, _____ is done.
   a. energy
   b. work
   c. power
   d. MA

   ANS: B   DIF: B   OBJ: 17-4

9. Which situation has the least amount of work done?
   a. Jane slides a 100-N block of ice up a 2-m-high inclined plane.
   b. Jane lifts a 100-N block of ice 2 m.
   c. Jane pushes a 50-N block of ice 4 m horizontally.
   d. Jane holds a 50-N block of ice 1 m above the floor.

   ANS: D   DIF: A   OBJ: 17-4

10. Work is done when _____.
    a. a force causes an object to move
    b. an object is at rest
    c. a force is applied to an object
    d. the forces on an object are balanced

    ANS: A   DIF: A   OBJ: 17-4

11. The SI unit of power is the _____.
    a. joule
    b. meter
    c. second
    d. watt

    ANS: D   DIF: B   OBJ: 17-5

12. Moving at 2 m/s, which has the greatest inertia—a bowling ball, a baseball, or a table-tennis ball?
    a. bowling ball
    b. baseball
    c. table-tennis ball
    d. can't tell without more information

    ANS: A   DIF: A   OBJ: 17-1

13. A pulley and a rope system having two pulleys would be classified as a(n) _____ machine.
    a. simple
    b. complex
    c. compound
    d. ideal

    ANS: C   DIF: B   OBJ: 17-7

14. Which of the following is NOT a lever?
    a. wheelbarrow
    b. playground teeter-totter
    c. ramp
    d. crowbar

    ANS: C   DIF: B   OBJ: 17-7

15. Which is NOT classified as a lever?
    a. pulley
    b. wedge
    c. teeter-totter
    d. wheel-and-axle

    ANS: B   DIF: B   OBJ: 17-8

16. When a hammer is slid spinning across a level, frictionless tabletop, its center of gravity follows _____.
    a. a straight-line path
    b. a wobbly path mostly in a straight line
    c. a curved path
    d. a completely unpredictable path

    ANS: A   DIF: A   OBJ: 17-2

17. The center of gravity of a baseball bat is located _____.
    a. in the more massive end of the bat
    b. halfway up the bat
    c. in the thinner part of the bat
    d. where the batter grips it

    ANS: A   DIF: A   OBJ: 17-2

18. A student strikes a nail with a hammer. During the interaction of the hammer and nail, _____.
    a. there is a force on the nail, but not on the hammer
    b. there is a force on the hammer, but not on the nail
    c. there is a force on the hammer and on the nail
    d. the hammer is inanimate and exerts no force

    ANS: C   DIF: A   OBJ: 17-3

COMPLETION

1. An object has the same _____ on Earth as it does on the moon.

   ANS: mass   DIF: B   OBJ: 17-1

2. The product of force and the distance that an object moves in the direction of the force is _____.

   ANS: work   DIF: B   OBJ: 17-4

3. Once a hammer is moving, it tends to keep moving because of ___

ANS: inertia   DIF: B   OBJ: 17-3

4. An object will balance if its ___ is supported.

ANS: center of gravity   DIF: B   OBJ: 17-2

5. Newton's third law of motion is sometimes called the ___.

ANS: law of action and reaction   DIF: B   OBJ: 17-3

6. Work is the product of ___ and the distance that the object moves in the same direction as the ___.

ANS: force, force   DIF: B   OBJ: 17-5

7. The force due to gravity acting on an object is called the ___ of an object.

ANS: weight   DIF: B   OBJ: 17-1

8. The amount of work done on a 20-N rock that you lift 2.0 m is ___ J.

ANS: 40   DIF: A   OBJ: 17-4

9. The amount of power produced by a person doing 110 J of work to lift a box in 5.0 seconds is ___ watts.

ANS: 22   DIF: A   OBJ: 17-5

10. Power is the ___ at which work is done.

ANS: rate   DIF: B   OBJ: 17-5

11. The force exerted by a machine is called the ___.

ANS: resistance force   DIF: B   OBJ: 17-6

12. The ___ of a machine is the ratio of its output work to its input work.

ANS: efficiency   DIF: B   OBJ: 17-6

13. In order to calculate the work done on an object, multiply the force by the ___

ANS: distance the object moved in the direction of the force   DIF: B   OBJ: 17-4

14. A kilowatt is equal to ___ watts.

ANS: 1000   DIF: B   OBJ: 17-5

MATCHING

Match each item with the correct statement below. Write the answer in the space provided.

a. compound machine
b. mechanical advantage
c. newton
d. Newton's third law of motion
e. work
f. efficiency
g. center of gravity
h. forces

1. ___ SI unit of weight
2. ___ force times distance
3. ___ the law of action and reaction
4. ___ the number of times a machine multiplies the size of an effort force
5. ___ describes how well a machine converts work input into work output
6. ___ This multiplies and can change the direction of a force.
7. ___ the center of an object's weight distribution
8. ___ These always occur in pairs.

1. ANS: c   DIF: B   OBJ: 17-1
2. ANS: e   DIF: B   OBJ: 17-5
3. ANS: d   DIF: B   OBJ: 17-3
4. ANS: b   DIF: B   OBJ: 17-6
5. ANS: f   DIF: B   OBJ: 17-6
6. ANS: a   DIF: B   OBJ: 17-7
7. ANS: g   DIF: B   OBJ: 17-2
8. ANS: h   DIF: B   OBJ: 17-3

SHORT ANSWER

1. How much power does a 1200-N person produce in climbing stairs carrying a 300-N box if it takes 10 s to climb 1.6 meters?

ANS: $P = (F \times d)/t = (1500 \text{ N} \times 1.6 \text{ m})/10 \text{ s} = 240 \text{ W}$

DIF: B   OBJ: 17-5

2. How can a person produce more power in lifting a load up a flight of stairs?

ANS: Decrease the time it takes to climb the stairs.

DIF: B   OBJ: 17-5

3. Why do you push harder on the pedals of a single-speed bicycle to start it moving than to keep it moving at a constant speed?

ANS: The bike has inertia. Initially, the inertia must be overcome to get the bike moving. Once the bike is moving, inertia causes it to remain in motion.

DIF: A   OBJ: 17-3

4. Suppose you drop a rock from a cliff overlooking the ocean. The gravity of Earth pulls on the rock. According to the law of action and reaction, the rock must be also pulling Earth. Why don't we notice Earth moving upward?

ANS: Earth has enormous mass compared to the rock. Earth's pull on the rock causes much greater change in the rock's motion. The change in Earth's motion is too small for us to observe.

DIF: A   OBJ: 17-1

5. A piano must be moved onto a 3.0-m-high platform. A 4.0-m and a 6.0-m ramp are available. Compare the advantages and disadvantages of using each ramp length.

ANS: Using either ramp would require the same amount of work because the vertical height is the same for both ramps. The longer ramp will require less force but more distance to complete the task. In most instances it would be advantageous to use the longer ramp.

DIF: A   OBJ: 17-6

6. A nail gun rapidly propels nails into wood. Why is it correct to call a nail gun a powerful tool?

ANS: The rapid speed of driving the nails means that less time is required to do the work of nailing. A decrease in time means that power is increased.

DIF: A   OBJ: 17-5

7. High-performance tires are advertised to have excellent road grip and cornering ability. They do wear out faster than normal tires. Use the concept of friction to explain the characteristics of these tires.

ANS: High-performance tires are softer than other tires in order to have more friction with the road. This increase in friction causes the road to exert more force on the car. These tires wear out faster because of the greater force.

DIF: A   OBJ: 17-3

8. To move an 800-N barrel from ground level to a 1-m-high loading dock, describe the purpose of using some boards as a ramp.

ANS: An inclined plane multiplies the effort force, making it easier to move the barrel compared with lifting the barrel straight up.

DIF: A   OBJ: 17-8

9. How can the ideal mechanical advantage of a machine be increased?

ANS: Increase the ratio of the distance of the effort force/distance of the resistance force.

DIF: A   OBJ: 17-6

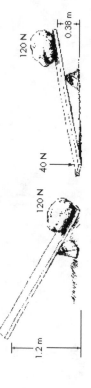

1.2 m   120 N   40 N   120 N   0.38 m

FIGURE 17-1

10. Use Figure 17-1 to determine the mechanical advantage of the lever used to lift the rock.

ANS: $MA = F_r/F_e = 120 \text{ N}/40 \text{ N} = 3$

DIF: A   OBJ: 17-6

11. Determine the efficiency of the lever shown in Figure 17-1.

ANS: $Eff = W_{out}/W_{in} = (120 \text{ N} \times 0.38 \text{ m})(40 \text{ N} \times 1.2 \text{ m}) \times 100\% = (45.6/48) \times 100\% = 95\%$

DIF: A   OBJ: 17-6

12. Explain why the lever in Figure 17-1 is not 100 percent efficient.

ANS: The lever may bend a little and there may be some friction at the fulcrum.

DIF: B   OBJ: 17-6

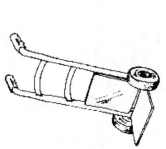

FIGURE 17-2

13. Identify the simple machines shown in Figure 17-2.

ANS: wedge, wheel-and-axle, and lever

DIF: B   OBJ: 17-8

14. How does each simple machine in Figure 17-2 make work easier?

ANS: By using a wedge, a hand truck can be slid under a load with less force. Using a lever enables someone to lift a load with less force.

DIF: B   OBJ: 17-7

15. What action-reaction forces are involved when the machine in Figure 17-2 is being used?

ANS: Load pushes down on wedge; wedge pushes up on load. Load pushes down on lever; lever pushes up on load. Wheels push against ground; ground pushes against wheels.

DIF: A   OBJ: 17-3

Table 17-1

Jose lifts a brick, a concrete block, and a board 1.0 meter vertically.

	Weight	Work	Time	Power
brick	35 N	**A**	4 s	**D**
concrete block	240 N	**B**	10 s	24 W
2 × 4 board	**E**	68 J	**C**	14 W

16. Using Table 17-1, find the work done, **A**, in lifting the brick 1.0 m.

ANS: 35 J   DIF: B   OBJ: 17-4

17. Using Table 17-1, find the work done, **B**, in lifting the concrete block 1.0 m.

ANS: 240 J   DIF: B   OBJ: 17-4

18. Using Table 17-1, calculate the power, **D**, required to lift the brick 1.0 m.

ANS: 9 W   DIF: B   OBJ: 17-5

19. Using Table 17-1, calculate the time, **C**, required to lift the board.

ANS: 5 s   DIF: B   OBJ: 17-5

20. Using Table 17-1, calculate the weight, **E**, of the board that was lifted 1.0 m.

ANS: 68 N   DIF: B   OBJ: 17-4

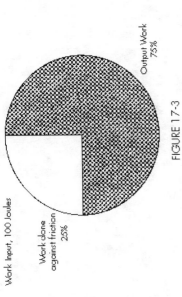

Work Input, 100 Joules

Work done against friction 25%

Output Work 75%

FIGURE 17-3

21. In Figure 17-3, how much energy is used to do work on the shingles?

ANS: According to the graph, about 3/4 of the work input is converted to work output, which is 75 J.

DIF: B   OBJ: 17-4

22. In Figure 17-3, how much energy goes to overcome the force of friction between the shingles and the roof?

ANS: According to the graph, about 1/4 of the input energy is used to overcome friction, or 25 J.

DIF: B   OBJ: 17-3

23. In Figure 17-3, calculate the efficiency of using the roof as a ramp.

ANS: $Eff = 75\% = Work_{out}/Work_{in} \times 100\% = 75\ J/100\ J \times 100\%$

DIF: A   OBJ: 17-6

24. In Figure 17-3, if the roof has an IMA of 2.0, what is the MA?

ANS: $MA = efficiency \times IMA = 0.75 \times 2.0 = 1.5$

DIF: A   OBJ: 17-6

25. For Figure 17-3, identify the type of machine being used.

ANS: inclined plane

DIF: B   OBJ: 17-8

OTHER

If the underscored word or phrase makes the sentence true, write "true" in the space provided. If the underscored word or phrase makes the sentence false, write the correct term or phrase in the space provided.

1. Friction is a force that opposes motion between two surfaces that are touching.

   ANS: true   DIF: B   OBJ: 17-3

2. The SI unit of power is the horsepower.

   ANS: watt   DIF: B   OBJ: 17-5

3. Two simple machines that are part of a bicycle are a(n) lever and wheel-and-axle.

   ANS: true   DIF: A   OBJ: 17-7

4. The mechanical advantage of a simple machine is always more than the ideal mechanical advantage of that machine.

   ANS: less than   DIF: B   OBJ: 17-6

5. The force of gravity affects an object's mass.

   ANS: weight   DIF: B   OBJ: 17-1

6. A brick will tip over when its center of gravity extends beyond its base of support.

   ANS: true   DIF: A   OBJ: 17-2

7. A rocket is pushed forward by the gases that are forced out the back of the rocket.

   ANS: true   DIF: B   OBJ: 17-3

8. The point located at the center of an object's weight distribution is called the lever.

   ANS: center of gravity   DIF: B   OBJ: 17-2

9. Power is mechanical advantage divided by time.

   ANS: work   DIF: B   OBJ: 17-5

10. The amount of power produced is measured in joules.

   ANS: watts   DIF: B   OBJ: 17-5

11. The force of gravity affects an object's inertia.

   ANS: weight   DIF: B   OBJ: 17-1

12. The force that opposes motion between two surfaces that are touching is called "friction."

   ANS: true   DIF: B   OBJ: 17-3

13. An object has the same weight in outer space as it does on Earth.

   ANS: mass   DIF: A   OBJ: 17-1

CHAPTER 18—TRANSFER OF THERMAL ENERGY

MULTIPLE CHOICE

1. R-values do NOT _____
   a. relate to insulation values
   b. relate to a material's ability to stop the flow of heat
   c. are higher for more heat-resistant materials
   d. help determine evaporation rates

   ANS: D   DIF: A   OBJ: 18-3

2. A heat pump does NOT _____
   a. work through radiant heating
   b. move heat two directions
   c. in cold weather transfer heat from cold air outside to warm the inside of a house
   d. work as an air conditioner to transfer heat outside the house

   ANS: A   DIF: A   OBJ: 18-5

3. OPEC does NOT _____
   a. include 11 member nations
   b. control 63 percent of Earth's oil reserves
   c. use the 42-gallon barrel as a unit of measure
   d. always act as a united group

   ANS: D   DIF: A   OBJ: 18-6

4. Active solar heating does NOT _____
   a. usually depend on solar collectors
   b. work without any moving parts
   c. work with a fan blowing warm air around
   d. work with warm water running through a house

   ANS: B   DIF: B   OBJ: 18-6

5. Which has a higher specific heat, steel or water?
   a. steel
   b. water
   c. Neither, they are both the same.
   d. Steel and water don't have specific heats.

   ANS: B   DIF: A   OBJ: 18-7

6. Water, when compared to most other substances, has _____
   a. a low specific heat
   b. an average specific heat
   c. a high specific heat
   d. no specific heat

   ANS: C   DIF: B   OBJ: 18-7

7. Which contains the most energy?
   a. a gallon of water at 90°F
   b. a gallon of water at 70°F
   c. a quart of water at 95°F
   d. a quart of water at 90°F

   ANS: A   DIF: A   OBJ: 18-1

8. When air is compressed, its temperature _____
   a. will remain the same
   b. will go lower
   c. will go higher
   d. will be converted

   ANS: C   DIF: A   OBJ: 18-5

9. Styrofoam is a good thermal _____
   a. radiator
   b. conductor
   c. insulator
   d. absorber

   ANS: C   DIF: B   OBJ: 18-2

10. Heat pumps can _____
    a. transfer heat from indoors to outdoors
    b. transfer heat from outdoors to indoors
    c. neither A nor B
    d. both A and B

    ANS: D   DIF: B   OBJ: 18-4

11. Solar-heating systems utilizing pumped-water systems to circulate hot water are described as _____
    a. passive
    b. active
    c. passive-active
    d. convective

    ANS: B   DIF: B   OBJ: 18-6

12. Which is NOT a method of heat transfer?
    a. convection
    b. radiation
    c. insulation
    d. conduction

    ANS: C   DIF: B   OBJ: 18-1

13. Which method of heating does NOT require matter to be present?
    a. conduction
    b. convection
    c. radiation
    d. compression

    ANS: C   DIF: A   OBJ: 18-1

14. To change radiant energy to thermal energy requires _____.
    a. absorption
    b. convection
    c. conduction
    d. radiation

    ANS: A   DIF: A   OBJ: 18-1

Table 18-1

Experiment	Substance	Mass	Temperature Change
1	water	300 g	increase 2.5°C
	steel	100 g	decrease 5°C
2	water	300 g	increase 5°C
	aluminum	100 g	decrease 70°C

Results of a hot metal being placed into 25°C (room temperature) water.

15. In Table 18-1, which material has the greatest change of temperature?
    a. water
    b. steel
    c. aluminum
    d. can't tell without more information

    ANS: B   DIF: A   OBJ: 18-7

16. In Table 18-1, what is the final temperature of the water when aluminum is added?
    a. 5°C
    b. 10°C
    c. 20°C
    d. 30°C

    ANS: D   DIF: A   OBJ: 18-1

17. In Table 18-1, what is the final temperature of the steel?
    a. 5°C
    b. 27°C
    c. 30°C
    d. 73°C

    ANS: B   DIF: B   OBJ: 18-7

18. In Table 18-1, which material would be the best choice for use as a heat-storage substance and to transport heat throughout a solar-heating system?
    a. steel
    b. aluminum
    c. water
    d. All are equally useful.

    ANS: C   DIF: A   OBJ: 18-7

19. Based on the data in Table 18-1, which material has the highest specific heat?
    a. steel
    b. aluminum
    c. water
    d. can't tell without more information

    ANS: C   DIF: A   OBJ: 18-7

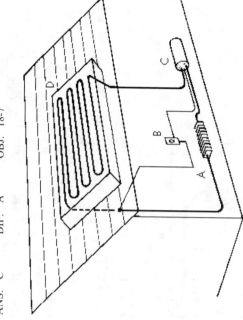

FIGURE 18-1

20. In Figure 18-1, part D represents the _____.
    a. thermostat
    b. heat exchanger
    c. circulating pump
    d. solar collector

    ANS: D   DIF: A   OBJ: 18-6

21. In Figure 18-1, part A represents the _____.
    a. thermostat
    b. heat exchanger
    c. circulating pump
    d. solar collector

    ANS: B   DIF: B   OBJ: 18-6

22. In Figure 18-1, water circulates in a direction _____.
   a. A-C-D
   b. D-C-A
   c. A-B-C
   d. A-C-B

   ANS: A   DIF: A   OBJ: 18-6

23. In Figure 18-1, identify the thermostat control.
   a. A
   b. B
   c. C
   d. D

   ANS: B   DIF: B   OBJ: 18-6

COMPLETION

1. A hot-water heater is an example of _____.

   ANS: convection   DIF: B   OBJ: 18-1

2. Sunbathing is an example of _____ heating.

   ANS: radiation   DIF: B   OBJ: 18-1

3. Placing your foot on a tile floor and feeling cool tiles is an example of _____.

   ANS: conduction   DIF: B   OBJ: 18-1

4. Goose down is a _____.

   ANS: thermal insulator   DIF: B   OBJ: 18-2

5. Metals are _____.

   ANS: thermal conductors   DIF: B   OBJ: 18-2

6. Materials that are poor conductors of heat are called _____.

   ANS: thermal insulators   DIF: B   OBJ: 18-1

7. Air conditioners work using the process of evaporation and _____.

   ANS: condensation   DIF: B   OBJ: 18-5

8. Sweat cools your body due to _____.

   ANS: evaporation   DIF: B   OBJ: 18-5

9. The method of solar heating in which radiant energy from the sun is absorbed and then slowly radiated is called _____.

   ANS: passive solar   DIF: B   OBJ: 18-6

10. A heat pump must do _____ in order to transfer heat from outdoors to indoors.

    ANS: work   DIF: A   OBJ: 18-5

11. Heat pumps are able to transfer heat through circulation of _____.

    ANS: refrigerant   DIF: B   OBJ: 18-5

12. A greater insulating value for a material is indicated by _____.

    ANS: a larger R-value   DIF: B   OBJ: 18-3

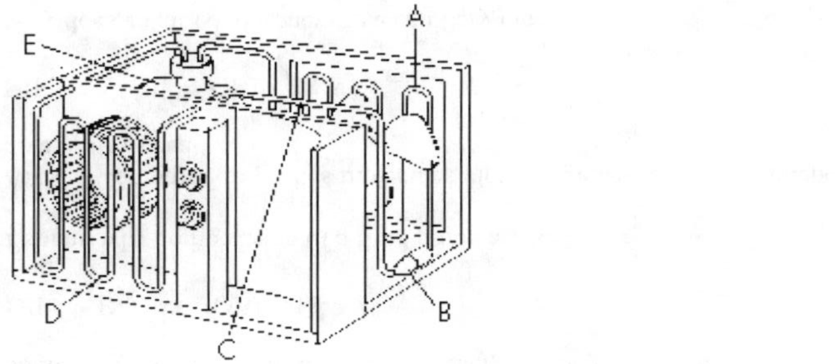

FIGURE 18-2

13. In Figure 18-2, where is heat removed from the area to be cooled?

    ANS: D   DIF: B   OBJ: 18-5

14. In Figure 18-2, where is the refrigerant compressed?

    ANS: E   DIF: A   OBJ: 18-5

15. Where in Figure 18-2 is the heat given off to the outside?

    ANS: A   DIF: B   OBJ: 18-5

16. Where in Figure 18-2 does the refrigerant expand?

    ANS: C   DIF: A   OBJ: 18-5

MATCHING

Match each item with the correct statement below. Write the answer in the space provided.

a. evaporation
b. specific heat
c. condensation
d. thermal insulators
e. active solar heating
f. insulator
g. heat
h. convection
i. radiation
j. passive solar heating
k. conduction
l. forced-air
m. heating
n. cooling
o. baseboard radiator
p. thermal conductor

1. _____ a change from gas to liquid
2. _____ energy that flows from something hotter to something colder
3. _____ slows the flow of heat
4. _____ transfers heat through space
5. _____ atoms vibrate and pass along energy while in the same position
6. _____ changing from liquid to gas—used in cooling
7. _____ transfer of heat from one place to another by moving fluid
8. _____ the amount of heat it takes to raise the temperature of a substance one kelvin
9. _____ In the northern hemisphere, large south-facing windows and heavily insulated walls are characteristic of this.
10. _____ This incorporates circulating water or antifreeze.
11. _____ temperature change caused by compressing a gas
12. _____ temperature change caused by letting air expand as it leaves a confined place
13. _____ heating system utilizing a heat exchanger and cold-air return
14. _____ heating system utilizing hot water
15. _____ materials forming a layer to prevent loss of heat
16. _____ substance that transfers heat easily

1. ANS: c   DIF: B   OBJ: 18-5
2. ANS: g   DIF: B   OBJ: 18-1
3. ANS: f   DIF: B   OBJ: 18-3
4. ANS: i   DIF: B   OBJ: 18-1
5. ANS: k   DIF: B   OBJ: 18-1
6. ANS: a   DIF: B   OBJ: 18-5
7. ANS: h   DIF: B   OBJ: 18-1
8. ANS: b   DIF: B   OBJ: 18-7
9. ANS: j   DIF: B   OBJ: 18-6
10. ANS: e   DIF: B   OBJ: 18-5
11. ANS: m   DIF: A   OBJ: 18-5
12. ANS: n   DIF: A   OBJ: 18-4
13. ANS: l   DIF: B   OBJ: 18-4
14. ANS: o   DIF: B   OBJ: 18-2
15. ANS: d   DIF: B   OBJ: 18-2
16. ANS: p   DIF: B   OBJ: 18-2

SHORT ANSWER

1. Why are R-values in colder climates higher for ceilings than those for walls?

   ANS: Because warm air rises, more heat transfer takes place through ceilings than through walls.

   DIF: A   OBJ: 18-3

2. Why do liquids and gases transfer heat by convection and not conduction?

   ANS: The energetic molecules of gases and liquids are not near enough to each other to transfer energy from molecule to molecule. Instead, energetic molecules flow towards areas with less heat.

   DIF: A   OBJ: 18-1

3. Which insulation is a better buy: one with an R-value of 88 and a cost of $1 per square meter or one with an R-value of 44 and a cost of $.75 per square meter?

   ANS: You get more insulation per dollar with the R-value of 88 insulation.

   DIF: B   OBJ: 18-3

4. Why is the high specific heat of water valuable?

   ANS: Because water can absorb and retain a lot of energy while increasing its temperature only slightly, it can be used to transfer heat energy through a system.

   DIF: B   OBJ: 18-7

5. Explain why compression of a fluid produces heat.

   ANS: Compression pushes molecules closer together; as a consequence, they lose energy and give it off as heat.

   DIF: A   OBJ: 18-5

6. Why does an air conditioner use a capillary tube?

   ANS: The capillary tube allows the refrigerant to expand and absorb energy from the surroundings.

   DIF: A   OBJ: 18-5

7. Why does evaporative cooling not work when the humidity is high?

   ANS: Water does not evaporate as quickly because the air is near the saturation point.

   DIF: A   OBJ: 18-5

8. Why is the word "radiator" in reference to radiator heating systems really the wrong word to use to describe what a radiator does?

ANS: The word "radiator" implies radiation, but a radiator heating system works through conduction and convection.

DIF: A   OBJ: 18-4

9. Explain why the ocean temperature in a given place does not vary much from one season to another.

ANS: The water has a high specific heat and holds a great deal of heat.

DIF: A   OBJ: 18-7

10. Explain why a piece of metal feels cooler to the touch than a piece of lumber at the same temperature.

ANS: The metal is a better conductor of heat; therefore, it takes heat away from your fingers more quickly, thus making them feel colder.

DIF: A   OBJ: 18-1

11. Describe the movement of heat between objects.

ANS: Heat flows from an object at a higher temperature to something at a lower temperature.

DIF: A   OBJ: 18-1

12. Explain how insulation reduces heat loss.

ANS: Small pockets in the insulating material trap air, which reduces heat loss by convection currents. The insulator material conducts heat poorly.

DIF: A   OBJ: 18-3

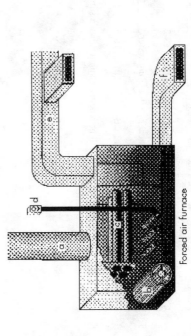

Forced air furnace

FIGURE 18-3

13. Identify the elements of the forced-air furnace shown in Figure 18-3.

ANS: a. chimney; b. blower; c. heat exchanger; d. thermostat; e. heat vent; f. cold-air return

DIF: B   OBJ: 18-4

14. Compare and contrast active and passive solar-heating systems.

ANS: In a passive solar-heating system, radiant energy is absorbed and converted to thermal energy and transferred to the surroundings as heat. In an active solar-heating system, thermal energy is transferred from one place to another by a circulating mechanism.

DIF: A   OBJ: 18-6

15. Explain how convection currents are created.

ANS: When one part of a gas or liquid is heated, convection currents are formed. The denser, cooler material moves downward while warmer, less dense material is displaced upward, creating a convection current.

DIF: A   OBJ: 18-1

16. Explain the advantage of a heat pump compared to a forced-air furnace.

ANS: A forced-air furnace is only able to heat, while a heat pump is a two-way heat mover that can both heat and cool.

DIF: A   OBJ: 18-4

17. Identify three examples of insulating materials used in homes.

ANS: fiberglass, wood, drywall, siding, air, foam

DIF: B   OBJ: 18-3

OTHER

If the underscored word or phrase makes the sentence true, write "true" in the space provided. If the underscored word or phrase makes the sentence false, write the correct term or phrase in the space provided.

1. Heat transfer by <u>convection</u> occurs when vibrating atoms bump into neighboring, slower-moving atoms.

ANS: conduction   DIF: B   OBJ: 18-1

2. Transfer of heat by <u>conduction</u> occurs when atoms in liquids and gases move from place to place.

ANS: convection   DIF: B   OBJ: 18-1

3. Something that reflects heat well is usually a poor absorber of heat. _____

   ANS: true   DIF: B   OBJ: 18-1

4. Heat can move easily through a thermal insulator. _____

   ANS: conductor   DIF: B   OBJ: 18-2

5. Passive solar heating systems transfer heat by circulating water. _____

   ANS: Active solar heating   DIF: B   OBJ: 18-6

6. A substance having an R-value of 5 will be a better insulator than a substance having an R-value of 12. _____

   ANS: poorer   DIF: A   OBJ: 18-3

CHAPTER 19—ELECTRICAL ENERGY

MULTIPLE CHOICE

1. What unit measures potential difference?
   a. ampere
   b. volt
   c. watt
   d. kilowatt

   ANS: B   DIF: A   OBJ: 19-2

2. What unit measures current?
   a. ampere
   b. volt
   c. watt
   d. kilowatt

   ANS: A   DIF: B   OBJ: 19-2

3. What moves through a circuit and is measured by current?
   a. number of volts per second
   b. number of watts per second
   c. amount of charge per second
   d. power

   ANS: C   DIF: B   OBJ: 19-2

4. What is the rate at which electrical energy is used?
   a. electric potential
   b. electrical power
   c. electric current
   d. ampere

   ANS: B   DIF: B   OBJ: 19-2

5. What property of a conductor inhibits the flow of current?
   a. voltage
   b. ampere
   c. resistance
   d. watt

   ANS: C   DIF: B   OBJ: 19-3

6. A difference in potential energy for each unit of charge is measured in _____.
   a. amperes
   b. watts
   c. volts
   d. hertz

   ANS: C   DIF: B   OBJ: 19-2

7. Electrical energy is measured in _____.
   a. volts
   b. kilowatts
   c. kilowatt-hours
   d. amperes

   ANS: C   DIF: B   OBJ: 19-2

8. Wires that are _____ and _____ have the least resistance.
   a. short, thin
   b. short, thick
   c. long, thin
   d. long, thick

   ANS: B   DIF: B   OBJ: 19-3

9. Current from a battery is _____.
   a. DC
   b. AC
   c. transformed by a transformer
   d. opposite in direction to current from a generator

   ANS: A   DIF: B   OBJ: 19-1

10. The electrical resistance of a thin wire of material X is _____ the electrical resistance of a thick wire of material X.
    a. greater than
    b. less than
    c. the same as
    d. Can't answer. Depends on material of wires.

    ANS: A   DIF: B   OBJ: 19-3

11. Alternating current is produced by _____.
    a. batteries
    b. alternating the voltage and resistance
    c. alternating a battery and a generator
    d. alternating the voltage direction at the generator

    ANS: D   DIF: A   OBJ: 19-1

12. The resistance of an open circuit is _____.
    a. zero
    b. small
    c. nearly infinite
    d. 1 ohm

    ANS: C   DIF: A   OBJ: 19-3

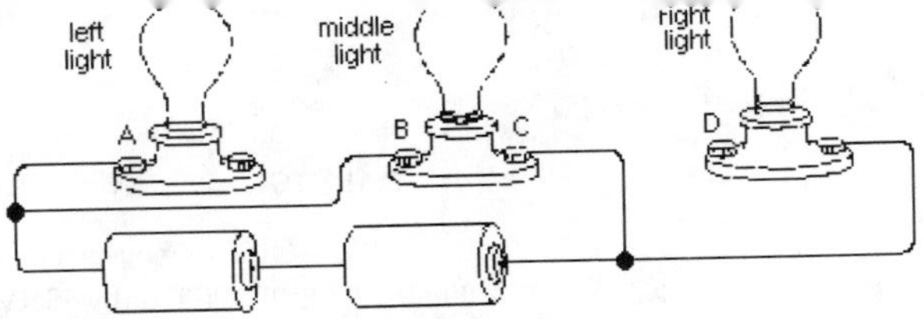

FIGURE 19-4

13. In Figure 19-4, if a wire is hooked between points A and D and the left lightbulb burns out,
    a. the right lightbulb will remain lit
    b. the middle lightbulb will go out
    c. the right lightbulb will go out
    d. both the middle and right lightbulbs will go out

    ANS: C   DIF: A   OBJ: 19-4

14. In Figure 19-4, the middle light is considered to be _____ with the batteries.
    a. in parallel
    b. in series
    c. a capacitor
    d. a transformer

    ANS: B   DIF: B   OBJ: 19-4

15. In Figure 19-4, to wire the left light in parallel with another light, place wire(s) between point A and _____.
    a. point B
    b. point C
    c. point D
    d. points B and C

    ANS: B   DIF: B   OBJ: 19-4

16. In Figure 19-4, to wire two lights in series with the batteries, place wire(s) from point D to _____.
    a. point A
    b. point B
    c. point C
    d. points B and C

    ANS: B   DIF: A   OBJ: 19-4

17. In Figure 19-4, in order to connect all three lights in parallel with the batteries, the left light at point A must be wired to point _____, and the right light at point D must be wired to point _____.
    a. B, C
    b. C, B
    c. D, B
    d. C, C

    ANS: B   DIF: A   OBJ: 19-4

COMPLETION

1. A battery converts _____ energy into electrical energy, whereas an electrical generator converts _____ energy into electrical energy.

   ANS: chemical, mechanical   DIF: B   OBJ: 19-1

2. _____ current flows in only one direction in a closed circuit, whereas _____ current goes through a cycle and flows in both directions.

   ANS: DC, AC   DIF: B   OBJ: 19-1

3. A battery produces DC current because it maintains its terminals at a _____ potential difference.

   ANS: constant   DIF: B   OBJ: 19-1

4. An electric generator that produces AC current maintains one terminal at 0 volts while the other terminal rapidly changes back and forth between _____ and _____ potential difference.

   ANS: positive, negative   DIF: A   OBJ: 19-1

5. The volt is a unit of _____.

   ANS: electrical potential difference   DIF: B   OBJ: 19-1

6. The amount of power used by a 3.0 V flashlight that uses 0.5 A of current is _____.

   ANS: 1.5 W   DIF: B   OBJ: 19-2

7. Electrical devices in our homes are connected in _____.

   ANS: parallel   DIF: B   OBJ: 19-4

8. A transformer allows _____ electrical energy to be increased or decreased in potential difference.

   ANS: AC, or alternating current   DIF: A   OBJ: 19-1

9. The total current in a parallel circuit is the sum of the currents in the separate _____.

   ANS: paths   DIF: B   OBJ: 19-4

10. A _____ is an automatic switch that will turn off the current if a circuit is overloaded.

    ANS: circuit breaker   DIF: B   OBJ: 19-4

11. It is impractical to wire appliances in your home in _____.

    ANS: series   DIF: B   OBJ: 19-4

MATCHING

Match each item with the correct statement below. Write the answer in the space provided.

a. volt
b. circuit breaker
c. generator
d. switch
e. ampere
f. series circuit
g. resistance
h. watt
i. parallel circuit
j. power
k. fuse

1. _____ only one path for current to flow
2. _____ multiple paths for current
3. _____ inhibits flow of current
4. _____ opens and closes circuits
5. _____ unit of potential difference
6. _____ unit of current
7. _____ unit for rate of energy usage
8. _____ product of voltage and current
9. _____ a component that protects equipment by melting when excess current flows through it
10. _____ a switch, made of two metal strips, that turns off when unsafe amounts of current flow through it
11. _____ is used to produce alternating current

1. ANS: f   DIF: B   OBJ: 19-4
2. ANS: i   DIF: B   OBJ: 19-4
3. ANS: g   DIF: B   OBJ: 19-3
4. ANS: d   DIF: B   OBJ: 19-3
5. ANS: a   DIF: B   OBJ: 19-1
6. ANS: e   DIF: B   OBJ: 19-1
7. ANS: h   DIF: B   OBJ: 19-2
8. ANS: j   DIF: B   OBJ: 19-2
9. ANS: k   DIF: B   OBJ: 19-3
10. ANS: b   DIF: B   OBJ: 19-3
11. ANS: c   DIF: B   OBJ: 19-1

SHORT ANSWER

1. How much power is used by a household appliance that is linked to a 240-volt line and has 10 amperes of current flowing through it?

   ANS: 2400 watts (240 volts × 10 amperes = 2400 watts)

   DIF: B   OBJ: 19-2

2. If a 2400-watt appliance is used 20 hours a month, how many kilowatt-hours of energy are used?

   ANS: 480 kilowatt-hours (2400 watts = 2.4 kilowatts. 2.4 kilowatts × 20 hours = 480 kilowatt-hours.)

   DIF: A   OBJ: 19-2

FIGURE 19-1

3. If several appliances are linked up in a series circuit, what can be said of the current that flows in each appliance?

   ANS: Each appliance in the series circuit will have the same current flowing through it.

   DIF: B   OBJ: 19-4

4. If several appliances are linked up in a parallel circuit, what can be said of the current that flows in each appliance?

   ANS: Each appliance in the parallel circuit will have a different current flowing through it. The specific current in each appliance depends on its wattage.

   DIF: B   OBJ: 19-4

5. What happens to the potential energy of a charge as it passes through a battery?

   ANS: The energy increases.

   DIF: A   OBJ: 19-2

6. Calculate the total power used in a kitchen by a 120-V blender consuming 5.0 A, a light using 1.0 A, and a toaster using 10 A.

   ANS: $P = I \times V = (5\ A + 1\ A + 10\ A)(120\ V) = 1920\ W$

   DIF: A   OBJ: 19-2

7. Calculate the power used by a 120-V hair dryer that uses 10 A of current.

   ANS: $P = I \times V = 10\ A \times 120\ V = 1200\ W$

   DIF: B   OBJ: 19-2

8. Calculate the total potential difference of three 1.5-V batteries wired in series.

   ANS: $V = 1.5\ V + 1.5\ V + 1.5\ V = 4.5\ V$

   DIF: A   OBJ: 19-1

9. A circuit consists of two batteries in series with a lightbulb. In order to reduce the intensity of the light, what should be done?

   ANS: remove one of the batteries

   DIF: B   OBJ: 19-2

10. Explain what will result when the resistance in a series circuit is reduced.

    ANS: The electrical current flowing in the circuit will increase.

    DIF: A   OBJ: 19-3

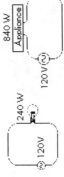

FIGURE 19-2

11. What is the total voltage across the flashlight bulb in Figure 19-1?

    ANS: 6 volts (2 + 2 + 2 = 6 volts)

    DIF: A   OBJ: 19-2

12. In Figure 19-1, how much current flows through the flashlight bulb?

    ANS: 1 ampere ($P = IV$; therefore, $I = P/V$. Current = 6 watts divided by 6 volts = 1 ampere.)

    DIF: A   OBJ: 19-2

13. What is the amount of current that flows through the lightbulb in Figure 19-2?

    ANS: 2 amperes (240 watts/120 volts = 2 amperes)

    DIF: B   OBJ: 19-2

14. If the cost of electricity is $0.10 per kilowatt-hour, what does it cost to burn the light in Figure 19-2 for 10 hours?

    ANS: $0.24. (240 watts = 0.24 kilowatts × 10 hours = 2.4 kilowatt-hours × $0.10 = $0.24)

    DIF: A   OBJ: 19-2

15. In the circuit shown in Figure 19-2, what would happen to the current and the brightness of the lightbulb if another lightbulb were added?

    ANS: The current would go down and the lightbulb would become dimmer.

    DIF: B   OBJ: 19-4

16. How much current will flow through the appliance in Figure 19-2 when it is turned on?

    ANS: 7 A (840 watts/120 volts = 7 A)

    DIF: A   OBJ: 19-4

21. Using Table 19-1, calculate the power, **A**, used by the night-light.

ANS: $P = V \times I = 120\ V \times 0.06\ A = 7.2\ W$ DIF: B   OBJ: 19-2

22. Using Table 19-1, find the amount of current, **B**, the television uses.

ANS: $I = P/V = 240\ W/120\ V = 2\ A$ DIF: B   OBJ: 19-2

23. Using Table 19-1, calculate the power, **C**, used by the microwave oven.

ANS: $P = V \times I = 120\ V \times 7.5\ A = 900\ W$ DIF: B   OBJ: 19-2

24. In Table 19-1, at what potential difference, **D**, does the clothes dryer operate?

ANS: $V = P/I = 3600\ W/15\ A = 240\ V$ DIF: A   OBJ: 19-2

25. In Table 19-1, if the clothes dryer is used for 3 hours, how many total kilowatt-hours are used?

ANS: $E = P \times t = 3600\ W \times 3\ h = 10.8\ kW\text{-}h$ DIF: A   OBJ: 19-2

26. What is the purpose of transformers?

ANS: Transformers increase or decrease efficiently the voltage or potential of alternating current that is carried long distances by power lines.

DIF: B   OBJ: 19-1

27. What is the function of resistance and how can it be applied in an electrical circuit?

ANS: Resistance inhibits the flow of current in an electrical circuit. As resistance increases, current will decrease. Resistance can be used to control current in an electric circuit.

DIF: B   OBJ: 19-3

OTHER

If the underscored word or phrase makes the sentence true, write "true" in the space provided. If the underscored word or phrase makes the sentence false, write the correct term or phrase in the space provided.

1. In a circuit containing a battery and a lightbulb, current flows from the <u>negative</u> terminal of the battery into the circuit and returns to the negative battery terminal. _____

ANS: positive   DIF: B   OBJ: 19-1

2. When a <u>potential difference</u> is applied between the ends of a conductor, charges will move through it. _____

ANS: true   DIF: B   OBJ: 19-2

---

17. If a 15-A circuit breaker is added to the circuit in Figure 19-2, how many appliances can run at one time? Explain why.

ANS: Two appliances can run at one time. If all three appliances were turned on, 21 A of current would flow through the circuit, and this would trip the 15-A circuit breaker. If two appliances were used, 14 A of current would flow, and this is lower than the 15-A circuit breaker.

DIF: A   OBJ: 19-4

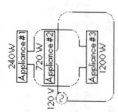

FIGURE 19-3

18. What is the total current in the circuit in Figure 19-3?

ANS: 18 A

DIF: B   OBJ: 19-2

19. In Figure 19-3, when appliances 1 and 2 are both running and appliance 2 is turned off, what happens to the current in appliance 1?

ANS: Nothing. These appliances are in a parallel circuit.

DIF: B   OBJ: 19-4

20. If a 15-A circuit breaker is put into the circuit shown in Figure 19-3, indicate by writing "yes" or "no" whether the breaker would trip when the following combinations of appliances are turned on: a. appliances 1, 2, and 3; b. appliances 1 and 2; c. appliances 1 and 3; d. appliances 2 and 3.

ANS: a. yes; b. no; c. no; d. yes

DIF: A   OBJ: 19-4

Table 19-1

Appliance	Potential Difference	Current	Power
night-light	120 V	0.06 A	**A**
television	120 V	**B**	240 W
microwave oven	120 V	7.5 A	**C**
clothes dryer	**D**	15 A	3600 W

MULTIPLE CHOICE

1. An example of homeostasis would be _____.
   a. keeping body temperature constant
   b. leg cramps
   c. widely varying body temperature
   d. a broken bone

   ANS: A   DIF: B   OBJ: 20-1

2. Body organs used to keep a person cool include _____.
   a. blood capillaries
   b. the hypothalamus
   c. both a and b
   d. neither a nor b

   ANS: C   DIF: A   OBJ: 20-1

3. Hereditary diseases are _____.
   a. communicable
   b. noncommunicable
   c. passed from child to parent
   d. dependent on a person's lifestyle

   ANS: B   DIF: B   OBJ: 20-6

4. Examples of hereditary diseases would include _____.
   a. sickle-cell anemia and hemophilia
   b. melanoma and heart disease
   c. cystic fibrosis and emphysema
   d. flu and meningitis

   ANS: A   DIF: B   OBJ: 20-6

5. The terms describing the gene alleles TT, Tt, and tt in the order shown would be _____.
   a. homozygous, heterozygous, heterozygous
   b. heterozygous, homozygous, heterozygous
   c. homozygous, homozygous, heterozygous
   d. homozygous, heterozygous, homozygous

   ANS: D   DIF: A   OBJ: 20-6

---

3. The unit of electric current is the volt. _____

   ANS: ampere   DIF: B   OBJ: 19-2

4. Electrical energy that continuously varies with time is termed alternating current. _____

   ANS: true   DIF: B   OBJ: 19-1

5. When one lightbulb burns out in a series circuit containing several lightbulbs, all of the other lights go out. _____

   ANS: true   DIF: B   OBJ: 19-4

6. A fuse or circuit breaker would be placed in parallel with the device in a circuit. _____

   ANS: series   DIF: B   OBJ: 19-4

7. In a parallel circuit, the current is the same everywhere. _____

   ANS: series   DIF: B   OBJ: 19-4

10. To complete spaces **B** and **C** of Table 20-2, which diseases require vectors for their spread?
    a. Lyme disease and malaria
    b. giardiasis and dysentery
    c. hepatitis and influenza
    d. AIDS and the common cold

    ANS: A   DIF: B   OBJ: 20-3

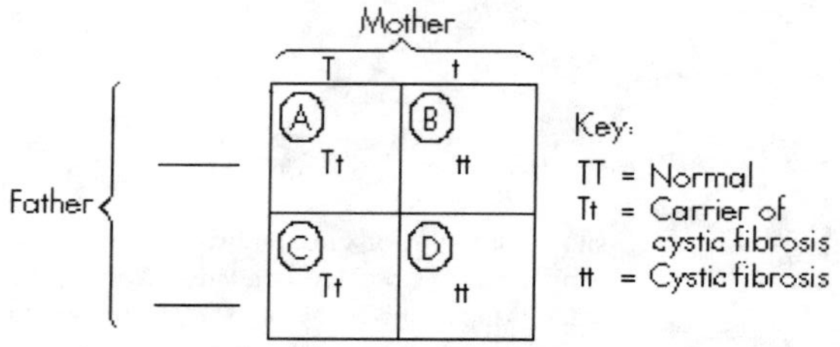

FIGURE 20-2

Key:
TT = Normal
Tt = Carrier of cystic fibrosis
tt = Cystic fibrosis

11. The father's genes in Figure 20-2 would have to be _____.
    a. TT
    b. Tt
    c. tt
    d. tT

    ANS: C   DIF: A   OBJ: 20-6

12. The child whose genes are shown in box A of Figure 20-2 would _____.
    a. be normal
    b. be a carrier of cystic fibrosis
    c. have cystic fibrosis
    d. none of the above

    ANS: B   DIF: B   OBJ: 20-6

13. The child whose genes are shown in box B of Figure 20-2 would _____.
    a. be normal
    b. be a carrier of cystic fibrosis
    c. have cystic fibrosis
    d. none of the above

    ANS: C   DIF: B   OBJ: 20-6

14. If the child whose genes are shown in box C of Figure 20-2 eventually marries a mate having the genes TT, they could expect a _____.
    a. 50% chance of having a child with cystic fibrosis
    b. 25% chance of having a child with cystic fibrosis
    c. 100% chance of having a child with cystic fibrosis
    d. 0% chance of having a child with cystic fibrosis

    ANS: D   DIF: A   OBJ: 20-6

Table 20-2

Route of Transmission	Examples of Disease
A _____	dysentery giardiasis
vectors	**B** _____ **C** _____
D _____	food poisoning hepatitis
direct contact	AIDS **E** _____
air	measles **F** _____

6. To complete space **D** of Table 20-2, what route of infection is involved in the spread of food poisoning?
    a. direct contact
    b. contaminated object
    c. vector
    d. all of the above

    ANS: B   DIF: B   OBJ: 20-3

7. To complete space **E** of Table 20-2, which disease can be spread by direct contact?
    a. malaria
    b. Lyme disease
    c. common cold
    d. botulism

    ANS: C   DIF: B   OBJ: 20-3

8. To complete space **F** of Table 20-2, which disease can be spread via the air?
    a. influenza
    b. syphilis
    c. dysentery
    d. giardiasis

    ANS: A   DIF: B   OBJ: 20-3

9. To complete space **A** of Table 20-2, what route of infection is involved in the spread of dysentery and giardiasis?
    a. direct contact
    b. air
    c. vectors
    d. water

    ANS: D   DIF: B   OBJ: 20-3

COMPLETION

1. Bacteria are often pathogens and may be found _____

    ANS: on your body (or: in air, inside your body, in soil, everywhere)

    DIF: B OBJ: 20-3

2. Syphilis, gonorrhea, and AIDS are all examples of diseases that may be transmitted _____

    ANS: sexually

    DIF: B OBJ: 20-3

3. Lyme disease is carried by a tick but is actually caused by a _____

    ANS: bacterium

    DIF: A OBJ: 20-3

4. The protist organism responsible for malaria is passed from organism to organism by a _____

    ANS: mosquito (or Anopheles mosquito)

    DIF: B OBJ: 20-3

5. Viruses cause disease when they reproduce within a host cell and cause its _____

    ANS: destruction

    DIF: B OBJ: 20-3

6. Pathogens such as influenza can be spread through the air in droplets when a person _____

    ANS: sneezes (or coughs)

    DIF: B OBJ: 20-3

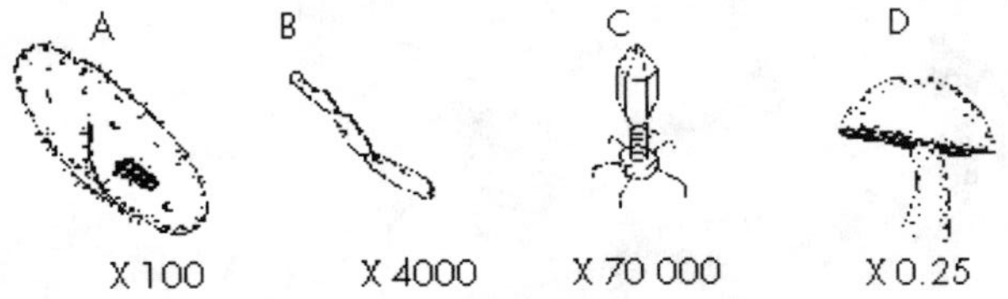

A   B   C   D

X 100   X 4000   X 70 000   X 0.25

FIGURE 20-1

7. The letter in Figure 20-1 that best matches an organism in Kingdom Eubacteria would be _____

    ANS: B DIF: A OBJ: 20-4

8. The letter in Figure 20-1 that best matches an organism in Kingdom Fungi would be _____

    ANS: D DIF: A OBJ: 20-4

9. The letter in Figure 20-1 that best matches an organism in Kingdom Protista would be _____

    ANS: A DIF: A OBJ: 20-4

10. The letter in Figure 20-1 that best matches an organism that may be one cell in size or as large as a many-celled seaweed would be _____

    ANS: A DIF: A OBJ: 20-4

11. The letter in Figure 20-1 that best matches a pathogen that can only reproduce within a living cell would be _____

    ANS: C DIF: A OBJ: 20-4

12. The letter in Figure 20-1 that best matches a pathogen that lacks a cell structure would be _____

    ANS: C DIF: A OBJ: 20-4

13. The letter in Figure 20-1 that best matches an organism that is only unicellular would be _____

    ANS: B DIF: A OBJ: 20-4

14. The letter in Figure 20-1 that best matches an organism type that causes tuberculosis or Lyme disease would be _____

    ANS: C DIF: A OBJ: 20-4

15. The letter in Figure 20-1 that best matches an organism type that causes malaria or amoebic dysentery would be _____

    ANS: B DIF: A OBJ: 20-4

16. The letter in Figure 20-1 that best matches an organism type that causes ringworm or athlete's foot would be _____

    ANS: A DIF: A OBJ: 20-4

17. _____

    ANS: D DIF: B OBJ: 20-4

MATCHING

Match each item with the correct statement below. Write the answer in the space provided.

a. communicable disease   f. homozygous
b. homeostasis   g. noncommunicable disease
c. vector   h. virus
d. heterozygous   i. disease
e. allele   j. pathogen

1. _____ stable internal environment
2. _____ disruption of homeostasis
3. _____ spreads from person to person
4. _____ cause of disease
5. _____ carries disease that infects another

3. In Figure 20-3, what role does the tsetse fly play in the transmission of both types of sleeping sickness?

ANS: The tsetse fly is the vector of both types of sleeping sickness. As such, it transfers the disease from one animal or human to another.

DIF: B   OBJ: 20-3

4. From Figure 20-3, infer how humans in East Africa reduce their risk of becoming infected with sleeping sickness.

ANS: Humans in East Africa could reduce their risk of becoming infected with sleeping sickness by avoiding contact with wild animal populations and by taking steps to prevent being bitten by tsetse flies, such as using screens on windows and doors and keeping arms and legs covered.

DIF: A   OBJ: 20-3

5. Based on Figure 20-3, what do you think would happen if human populations took over areas presently inhabited by wild animals in East Africa?

ANS: There would probably be an increase in the transmission of sleeping sickness to humans because humans would then have more contact with wild animals and their pathogens.

DIF: A   OBJ: 20-3

Table 20-1
Functions of Major Organs and Systems of the Human Body

System	Major Organs	Function
A ___	brain, spinal cord	B ___
muscular	C ___	D ___
		E ___
urinary	F ___	maintains water and salt balance, removes waste from blood
circulatory	G ___	circulates blood through body, delivers needed substances to cells
digestive	H ___	breaks food down into building blocks used by body

6. Name the system represented by space A in Table 20-1.

ANS: nervous   DIF: B   OBJ: 20-2

---

6. ___ not caused by pathogens
7. ___ alternate form of a gene
8. ___ having two identical alleles
9. ___ having two different alleles
10. ___ inorganic pathogen

1. ANS: b   DIF: B   OBJ: 20-1
2. ANS: i   DIF: B   OBJ: 20-1
3. ANS: a   DIF: B   OBJ: 20-3
4. ANS: j   DIF: B   OBJ: 20-4
5. ANS: c   DIF: B   OBJ: 20-3
6. ANS: g   DIF: B   OBJ: 20-5
7. ANS: e   DIF: B   OBJ: 20-6
8. ANS: f   DIF: A   OBJ: 20-6
9. ANS: d   DIF: A   OBJ: 20-6
10. ANS: h   DIF: B   OBJ: 20-4

SHORT ANSWER

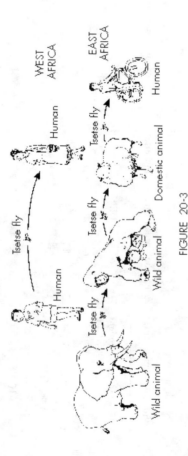

FIGURE 20-3

1. Based on Figure 20-3, what type of disease is African sleeping sickness—communicable or noncommunicable? How do you know?

ANS: African sleeping sickness is a communicable disease because it can be spread from one individual to another via a vector.

DIF: B   OBJ: 20-3

2. According to Figure 20-3, what seems to be the major difference in the spread of the two types of sleeping sickness?

ANS: Sleeping sickness infects only humans in West Africa whereas in East Africa it infects wild game animals and domestic animals as well as humans.

DIF: A   OBJ: 20-3

15. Explain this apparent contradiction: "The cells of people with diabetes are starved for sugar, yet diabetics must strictly limit the amount of sugar they eat."

ANS: Diabetics are unable to get sugar into their cells, either because they lack insulin or because their cells are not responsive to insulin. Instead, any sugar from the food they eat remains circulating in the blood until it is removed by the kidneys and excreted. If they eat too much sugar, their blood sugar levels may get dangerously high.

DIF: A   OBJ: 20-6

16. Write a list of guidelines for preventing the spread of diseases that are transferred from person to person by direct contact. What diseases would your guidelines help prevent?

ANS: Cover the mouth when coughing or sneezing; wash hands frequently; keep fingers and objects away from the mouth; and sanitize doorknobs and other objects that are handled frequently. The guidelines will help prevent diseases spread by direct contact, such as colds and influenza.

DIF: A   OBJ: 20-3

17. Analyze factors that led to the shift from communicable to noncommunicable diseases as major causes of death since 1900.

ANS: Vaccines, antibiotics, and other medical advances were primarily responsible for the decline in communicable disease death rates since the year 1900. As people survived these diseases, they lived longer. This exposed them for a longer period of time to environmental and lifestyle factors that led to the development of noncommunicable diseases, such as heart disease and cancer.

DIF: A   OBJ: 20-3

18. Discuss the roles of genetic versus lifestyle factors in the development of noncommunicable diseases, using heart disease as an example.

ANS: Lifestyle choices, such as the amount of fat we eat and the amount of exercise we get, for example, are important factors determining whether or not we develop heart disease. Some people, however, inherit a tendency to develop cardiovascular problems.

DIF: A   OBJ: 20-5

OTHER

If the underscored word or phrase makes the sentence true, write "true" in the space provided. If the underscored word or phrase makes the sentence false, write the correct term or phrase in the space provided.

1. Over time, the inner lining of arteries may narrow due to the formation of plaques.

_____

ANS: true   DIF: B   OBJ: 20-5

---

7. Name the function represented by space **B** in Table 20-1.

ANS: regulates most body activities (or: receives and responds to nerve information, causes muscle movement)

DIF: B   OBJ: 20-2

8. Name the organs represented by space **C** in Table 20-1.

ANS: muscles

DIF: B   OBJ: 20-2

9. Name the function represented by space **D** in Table 20-1.

ANS: allows body to move (or: moves materials through body, produces body heat)

DIF: B   OBJ: 20-2

10. Name the function represented by space **E** in Table 20-1.

ANS: moves materials through body (or: allows body to move, produces body heat)

DIF: B   OBJ: 20-2

11. Name the organs represented by space **F** in Table 20-1.

ANS: kidneys (or: bladder)

DIF: B   OBJ: 20-2

12. Name the organs represented by space **G** in Table 20-1.

ANS: heart (or: blood vessels)

DIF: B   OBJ: 20-2

13. Name the organs represented by space **H** in Table 20-1.

ANS: mouth (or: esophagus, stomach, intestines, liver)

DIF: B   OBJ: 20-2

14. Identify the processes that help maintain a constant internal body temperature in cold weather.

ANS: When the body gets cold, three processes come into play to increase body temperature. The hypothalamus stimulates an increase in metabolism, which leads to the production of more body heat. Shivering, or involuntary muscle contractions, also increases the amount of heat produced by the body. Contraction of capillaries in the arms, legs, hands, and feet conserves heat at the body's core.

DIF: A   OBJ: 20-1

2. The risk for heart disease increases if your diet is high in nonfatty foods. ____________________

ANS: fatty foods DIF: B OBJ: 20-5

3. Heart muscle that is deprived of oxygen due to blocked arteries may result in a stroke. ____________________

ANS: heart attack DIF: B OBJ: 20-5

4. Sunlight wavelengths that are responsible for skin cancer are infrared. ____________________

ANS: UV (or ultraviolet) DIF: B OBJ: 20-5

5. Skin that receives sunlight may have cells that form damaged genetic material. ____________________

ANS: true DIF: A OBJ: 20-5

6. Cells that destroy neighboring tissue by reproducing much more quickly than their surrounding cells are known as normal cells. ____________________

ANS: cancer DIF: B OBJ: 20-5

7. Malignant melanoma develops in the upper portions of the lungs. ____________________

ANS: skin DIF: B OBJ: 20-5

8. A diabetic experiences dehydration as excess blood sugar adds water to body cells. ____________________

ANS: removes water from DIF: B OBJ: 20-1

9. Glucose levels in blood will drop in response to normal release of insulin. ____________________

ANS: true DIF: B OBJ: 20-1

10. A drop in blood glucose triggers the pancreas to start insulin production. ____________________

ANS: stop DIF: A OBJ: 20-1

11. Diabetes upsets the homeostasis of the circulatory and digestive system. ____________________

ANS: true DIF: A OBJ: 20-1

12. A diabetic who does not receive insulin tends to have blood glucose levels that are too low. ____________________

ANS: too high DIF: B OBJ: 20-1

Family A

Father \ Mother	T	t
	TT	Tt
	TT	Tt

Family B

Father \ Mother	T	t
	TT	Tt
	Tt	tt

FIGURE 20-5

13. In Figure 20-5, the mother in family A is a carrier of the abnormal trait. ____________________

ANS: true DIF: B OBJ: 20-6

14. The parents in family B in Figure 20-5 are both homozygous for the trait. ____________________

ANS: heterozygous DIF: A OBJ: 20-6

15. All of the potential children in family A in Figure 20-5 can be expected to inherit the disease. ____________________

ANS: None DIF: A OBJ: 20-6

16. Each child in family B in Figure 20-5 has a 50 percent chance of inheriting the disease. ____________________

ANS: 25 DIF: A OBJ: 20-6

17. In Figure 20-5, half the potential children in both families can be expected to be carriers of the trait. ____________________

ANS: true DIF: B OBJ: 20-6

CHAPTER 21—PREVENTING AND TREATING DISEASE

MULTIPLE CHOICE

1. Your body producing antibodies against a disease is an example of _____.
   a. passive immunity
   b. the inflammatory response
   c. active immunity
   d. an autoimmune response

   ANS: C   DIF: B   OBJ: 21-3

2. Natural active immunity occurs when you _____.
   a. receive a vaccination for a disease
   b. receive antibodies for a disease
   c. get a booster shot
   d. catch a disease

   ANS: D   DIF: B   OBJ: 21-3

3. Passive immunity occurs when antibodies are produced by _____.
   a. receiving a vaccine
   b. another source
   c. first catching a disease
   d. both a and c are correct

   ANS: B   DIF: B   OBJ: 21-3

4. Once you have the measles, you rarely have them again. This illustrates _____.
   a. active natural immunity
   b. active artificial immunity
   c. passive natural immunity
   d. the value of a vaccination

   ANS: A   DIF: B   OBJ: 21-3

5. Antibodies pass from mother to fetus by way of _____.
   a. breast milk
   b. the placenta
   c. pathogens
   d. both a and b are correct

   ANS: D   DIF: A   OBJ: 21-3

6. Pathogens are destroyed in cellular immunity by the action of _____.
   a. antibodies
   b. lysozyme
   c. T cells
   d. plasma cells

   ANS: C   DIF: A   OBJ: 21-5

7. A patient receives a kidney transplant. The body responds by calling upon _____.
   a. an antibody immune response
   b. a cellular immunity response
   c. B cells
   d. a response of pathogens

   ANS: B   DIF: A   OBJ: 21-5

8. In cellular immunity, the body uses _____.
   a. B and T cells
   b. only macrophages
   c. macrophages and then plasma cells
   d. macrophages and then T cell types

   ANS: D   DIF: A   OBJ: 21-5

9. In rheumatoid arthritis, T cells and antibodies attack the _____.
   a. nerve coverings
   b. site where nerves and muscles meet
   c. membranes that protect joints
   d. body's muscles

   ANS: C   DIF: A   OBJ: 21-6

10. An autoimmune disease caused by the body destroying a nerve's outer covering would be _____.
    a. multiple sclerosis
    b. myasthenia gravis
    c. Type I diabetes
    d. AIDS

    ANS: A   DIF: A   OBJ: 21-6

11. The autoimmune disease called myasthenia gravis attacks _____.
    a. the pancreas
    b. where nerves and muscles meet
    c. helper T cells
    d. nerve coverings

    ANS: B   DIF: A   OBJ: 21-6

12. HIV (human immunodeficiency virus) brings about disease by _____.
    a. destroying the immune system
    b. destroying helper T cells
    c. both a and b are correct
    d. neither a nor b is correct

    ANS: C   DIF: B   OBJ: 21-6

13. Autoimmune diseases result when the body's immune system cannot _____.
    a. produce enough T cells
    b. produce enough B cells
    c. recognize pathogens
    d. recognize its own cells

    ANS: D   DIF: B   OBJ: 21-6

14. Doctors monitoring the ongoing health and treatment of an AIDS patient would be interested in their patient's _____.
    a. insulin levels
    b. helper T cell numbers
    c. virus numbers per cell
    d. method of catching the disease

    ANS: B   DIF: A   OBJ: 21-6

Table 21-2
Types of Immunity

	Passive	Active
Natural	measles	chicken pox
Artificial	rabies	polio

15. According to Table 21-2, how can a child acquire passive natural immunity to measles?
    a. by receiving an injection of dead measles virus
    b. by receiving antibodies from his or her mother during pregnancy
    c. by receiving an injection of measles antibodies
    d. by having the disease

    ANS: B   DIF: A   OBJ: 21-3

16. Based on Table 21-2, how would passive artificial immunity to rabies be acquired?
    a. by injection with antibodies to the rabies virus
    b. by injection with dead rabies virus
    c. by infection with the rabies virus through an animal bite
    d. by transmission of antibodies to the rabies virus via breast milk

    ANS: A   DIF: B   OBJ: 21-3

17. Which of the following diseases should be placed in the same box in Table 21-2 as polio?
    a. the common cold
    b. botulism
    c. diphtheria
    d. AIDS

    ANS: C   DIF: A   OBJ: 21-3

18. Which of the following diseases should be placed in the same box in Table 21-2 as chicken pox?
    a. smallpox
    b. AIDS
    c. tetanus
    d. the common cold

    ANS: D   DIF: A   OBJ: 21-3

19. Which types of immunities shown in Table 21-2 are longer lasting than the others?
    a. artificial active and natural active
    b. artificial passive and natural passive
    c. natural passive and natural active
    d. artificial passive and artificial active

    ANS: A   DIF: B   OBJ: 21-3

COMPLETION

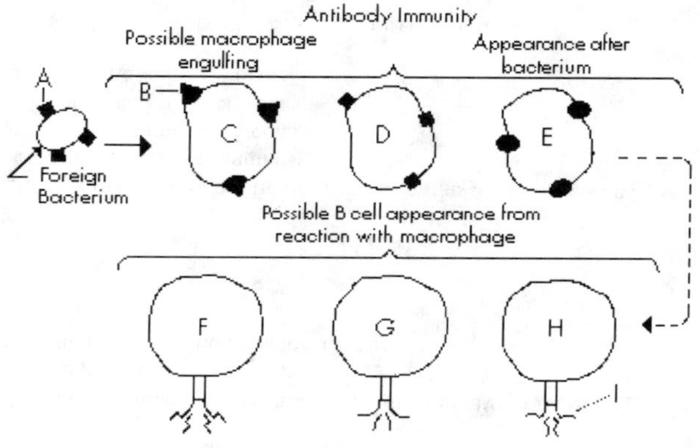

FIGURE 21-1

1. Label A of Figure 21-1 would represent a(n) _____

    ANS: antigen   DIF: B   OBJ: 21-4

2. Label B of Figure 21-1 would represent a(n) _____

    ANS: antigen   DIF: B   OBJ: 21-4

3. Using choices C, D, or E from Figure 21-1, the correct appearance of the macrophage would be _____

    ANS: D   DIF: A   OBJ: 21-4

4. Using choices F, G, or H from Figure 21-1, the correct appearance of the B cell would be _____

    ANS: G   DIF: A   OBJ: 21-4

5. Other cells are involved in the step from macrophage to B cell in Figure 21-1. These other cells are called _____

    ANS: helper T cells   DIF: B   OBJ: 21-4

MATCHING

Match each item with the correct statement below. Write the answer in the space provided.

a. epidermis
b. macrophage
c. T cells
d. antibodies
e. cellular immunity
f. vaccines
g. antibody immunity
h. analgesics
i. dermis
j. B cells

___ 1. contains melanin-filled cells
___ 2. contains sweat glands
___ 3. involved in phagocytosis
___ 4. produce antibodies
___ 5. produce chemicals that attract macrophages
___ 6. destroys pathogens found outside cells
___ 7. destroys pathogens found inside cells
___ 8. produce artificial active immunity
___ 9. produced from molds or other microorganisms
___ 10. relieve pain

1. ANS: a   DIF: B   OBJ: 21-1
2. ANS: i   DIF: B   OBJ: 21-1
3. ANS: b   DIF: B   OBJ: 21-1
4. ANS: j   DIF: B   OBJ: 21-5
5. ANS: c   DIF: B   OBJ: 21-4
6. ANS: g   DIF: B   OBJ: 21-5
7. ANS: e   DIF: B   OBJ: 21-5
8. ANS: f   DIF: B   OBJ: 21-7
9. ANS: d   DIF: B   OBJ: 21-8
10. ANS: h   DIF: B   OBJ: 21-8

SHORT ANSWER

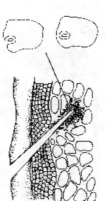

FIGURE 21-3

1. Identify the two responses shown in Figure 21-3. What readily observed signs in the patient show that the two responses are occurring?

ANS: the inflammatory response and phagocytosis: redness and swelling show inflammation; pus in the wound shows that phagocytosis is occurring

DIF: A   OBJ: 21-2

---

6. Label I in Figure 21-1 represents a(n) _____

ANS: antibody   DIF: A   OBJ: 21-4

7. B cells in Figure 21-1 go on to form memory and _____

ANS: plasma cells   DIF: A   OBJ: 21-4

CELLULAR IMMUNITY

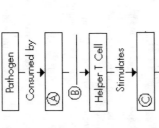

FIGURE 21-2

8. Space A of Figure 21-2 should contain the cell name _____

ANS: macrophage   DIF: B   OBJ: 21-5

9. Space B of Figure 21-2 should contain the process title _____

ANS: binds to   DIF: B   OBJ: 21-5

10. Space C of Figure 21-2 should contain the cell name _____

ANS: killer T cell   DIF: B   OBJ: 21-5

11. Space D of Figure 21-2 should contain the term _____

ANS: pathogen, bacterium, or virus   DIF: B   OBJ: 21-5

12. Space E in Figure 21-2 should contain the cell name _____

ANS: memory T cell   DIF: B   OBJ: 21-5

2. What triggers the response shown on the left in Figure 21-3?

ANS: histamine triggers inflammation, the damaged tissue releases it

DIF: A   OBJ: 21-2

3. In Figure 21-3, how is the response shown on the right related to the response shown on the left?

ANS: Phagocytosis, on the right, is promoted by the inflammatory response, shown on the left. Inflammation increases blood flow to the injury, carrying phagocytes that surround and consume foreign particles.

DIF: A   OBJ: 21-2

4. Explain what indicates that the wound shown in Figure 21-3 has become infected.

ANS: the presence of pus, which is a combination of tissue fluid, phagocytes, and dead pathogens

DIF: B   OBJ: 21-2

5. How will the body reestablish its first line of defense at the wound shown in Figure 21-3?

ANS: Blood will clot and form a scab to close the wound, reestablishing the barrier of skin, the body's first line of defense.

DIF: B   OBJ: 21-2

6. Explain how the inflammatory response helps rid the body of pathogens.

ANS: Damaged skin tissue produces chemicals, including the hormone histamine, that cause nearby blood vessels to expand and become porous. Blood flow to the area increases, increasing the pressure in the vessels and pushing fluids and white blood cells into the surrounding tissue. Macrophages and other phagocytes in the blood surround and engulf foreign particles and damaged tissue in the process of phagocytosis, which destroys the pathogens.

DIF: B   OBJ: 21-2

7. Compare and contrast active and passive immunity.

ANS: Active immunity occurs when the body is exposed to a pathogen and produces antibodies that destroy them. Passive immunity occurs when these antibodies are produced by another source, then transferred into the body. Active immunity may take time to develop, but it is usually long lasting. Passive immunity lasts for just a few weeks or months.

DIF: B   OBJ: 21-3

8. Sequence the steps involved in developing antibody immunity.

ANS: Pathogens invade the body and are engulfed and destroyed by macrophages. Antigens from the destroyed pathogens migrate to the surface of the macrophages, where helper T cells bind to them and activate. The activated helper T cells bind with B cells and the B cells divide to form plasma and memory cells. Plasma cells produce antibodies to the pathogen; memory cells retain the ability to produce additional antibodies if needed in the future.

DIF: B   OBJ: 21-4

9. Explain how vaccines stimulate the development of active immunity.

ANS: Vaccines consist of weakened or killed pathogens or a portion of a pathogen and stimulate the immune system to react as if the body had been infected by the pathogen. Memory B cells and T cells form, and produce antibodies that allow the immune system to destroy the pathogen if it attacks later.

DIF: B   OBJ: 21-7

10. Compare the effects on disease of antibiotics, radiation therapies, and pain relievers.

ANS: Antibiotics cure bacterial and fungal infections by killing the pathogens, but do not affect viruses. Chemotherapy attacks rapidly growing tumor cells and destroys them or stops their reproduction. Pain-relieving drugs only alleviate pain, and in some cases reduce fever and inflammation. Radiation in the form of X rays is used to destroy cancer cells or their DNA with high-energy particles. It may also be used to diagnose disease.

DIF: B   OBJ: 21-8

OTHER

If the underscored word or phrase makes the sentence true, write "true" in the space provided. If the underscored word or phrase makes the sentence false, write the correct term or phrase in the space provided.

1. Skin and an inflammatory response are part of the body's specific defense. _____

ANS: nonspecific   DIF: B   OBJ: 21-2

2. Pus formation is the body's initial local healing reaction to infection. _____

ANS: The inflammatory response   DIF: B   OBJ: 21-2

3. An antigen is a physical barrier serving as the body's first line of defense. _____

ANS: Skin   DIF: B   OBJ: 21-1

4. Much like an inner skin, cilia form(s) a thick, sticky fluid. _____

ANS: the mucous membrane   DIF: A   OBJ: 21-1

5. Sweat and saliva contain an enzyme called mucus that destroys bacterial cell walls. _____

ANS: lysozyme   DIF: A   OBJ: 21-1

6. Skin is made up of dermis composed of both a living and dead layer. _____

ANS: epidermis   DIF: B   OBJ: 21-1

7. Nerve fibers and blood vessels are present in the <u>epidermis</u> layer of skin. _____

ANS: dermis   DIF: A   OBJ: 21-1

8. <u>Cilia</u> are tiny, hairlike structures that line the throat. _____

ANS: true   DIF: B   OBJ: 21-1

9. Macrophages are a type of cell called a <u>phagocyte</u>. _____

ANS: true   DIF: A   OBJ: 21-2

10. Macrophages are capable of engulfing and thus getting rid of <u>antibodies</u>. _____

ANS: antigens, bacteria, viruses, or pathogens   DIF: A   OBJ: 21-2

11. Antibiotics can be used to treat diseases caused by <u>viruses</u>. _____

ANS: bacteria, fungi, or protists   DIF: B   OBJ: 21-8

12. Chemotherapeutic drugs are often used to stop the growth of <u>normal</u> cells. _____

ANS: abnormal or cancerous   DIF: B   OBJ: 21-8

13. <u>Aspirin</u> is a common analgesic. _____

ANS: true   DIF: B   OBJ: 21-8

14. Radiation knocks electrons from a cell's DNA, thus causing the cell to <u>expand</u> when it divides. _____

ANS: die   DIF: A   OBJ: 21-8

15. AZT, or zidovudine, works to slow AIDS because it causes cells to form incorrect <u>HIV</u>. _____

ANS: DNA (or: thymine within DNA)   DIF: A   OBJ: 21-8

16. The type of white blood cells that develop in the thymus are called <u>B cells</u>. _____

ANS: T cells   DIF: B   OBJ: 21-4

17. The type of immunity in which pathogens are destroyed by antigens is called <u>cellular immunity</u>. _____

ANS: antibody   DIF: B   OBJ: 21-5

18. Stem cells, from which both B cells and T cells develop, are located in the <u>spleen</u>. _____

ANS: bone marrow   DIF: B   OBJ: 21-4

19. The formation of both types of immunity is triggered by the action of a <u>macrophage</u>. _____

ANS: true   DIF: B   OBJ: 21-5

20. Memory cells play an important role in antibody immunity <u>but not</u> in cellular immunity. _____

ANS: and   DIF: B   OBJ: 21-5

Refer to Table 21-1. If the underscored word or phrase makes the sentence true, write "true" in the space provided. If the underscored word or phrase makes the sentence false, write the correct term or phrase in the space provided.

Table 21-1
Reported Cases of Three Diseases in the U.S.

Disease	1901–1940	1941–1980	1981–2020
A	7842	12 046	18 557
B	12 993	15 128	306
C	45 807	47 231	46 869

21. The numbers in Table 21-1 could support evidence that a vaccine <u>was used</u> to prevent disease A during the years 1941–1980. _____

ANS: was not used   DIF: A   OBJ: 21-7

22. The numbers in Table 21-1 could support evidence that a vaccine <u>was used</u> to prevent disease B during the years 1981–2020. _____

ANS: true   DIF: A   OBJ: 21-7

23. The numbers in Table 21-1 could support evidence that a vaccine <u>was used</u> to prevent disease C during the years 1901–1940. _____

ANS: was not used   DIF: A   OBJ: 21-7

24. It is possible that disease A in Table 21-1 does have a vaccine. However, individuals <u>may not</u> have received booster shots for the disease. _____

ANS: true   DIF: A   OBJ: 21-7

CHAPTER 22—DETECTING DISEASE

MULTIPLE CHOICE

1. The shape of a microscope lens is _____.
   a. flat
   b. plane
   c. curved
   d. refracted and then reflected

   ANS: C   DIF: A   OBJ: 22-8

2. Bending of light rays is called _____.
   a. refraction
   b. reflection
   c. absorption
   d. compound magnification

   ANS: A   DIF: B   OBJ: 22-8

3. Operation of a compound microscope depends on use of _____.
   a. a mirror and eyepiece
   b. X rays
   c. differences in material density
   d. lenses and light rays

   ANS: D   DIF: A   OBJ: 22-8

4. A lens can _____.
   a. change the direction of light rays passing through it
   b. decrease the size of an object
   c. detect the presence of virus pathogens
   d. reflect light, causing it to alter its natural color

   ANS: A   DIF: B   OBJ: 22-8

5. A CAT (computerized axial tomography) scan uses _____.
   a. visible light
   b. X rays
   c. sound waves
   d. electricity and magnetism

   ANS: B   DIF: B   OBJ: 22-9

6. Images that are more detailed than those seen with CAT scans and X rays best describe _____.
   a. ultrasound
   b. the light microscope
   c. MRI
   d. sonograms

   ANS: C   DIF: B   OBJ: 22-9

7. Sound waves reflecting off of body parts describes _____.
   a. ultrasound
   b. MRI
   c. CAT scans
   d. X rays

   ANS: A   DIF: B   OBJ: 22-9

8. A two-dimensional image of bones or organ placement is achieved through _____.
   a. MRI
   b. X rays
   c. sonograms
   d. CAT scans

   ANS: B   DIF: B   OBJ: 22-9

9. Three-dimensional images and cross-sectional views of internal body structures result from _____.
   a. X rays
   b. electrophoresis
   c. ultrasound
   d. CAT scans

   ANS: D   DIF: B   OBJ: 22-9

10. Body tissues containing different amounts of water form the basis for _____.
    a. X rays
    b. ultrasound
    c. CAT scans
    d. an MRI

    ANS: D   DIF: A   OBJ: 22-9

11. The way to determine which pathogen causes a particular disease is _____.
    a. to calculate the percent of white blood cells
    b. to infect healthy humans
    c. to isolate the pathogen from an infected host and use it to infect a healthy animal
    d. to isolate bacterial or viral proteins by electrophoresis

    ANS: C   DIF: B   OBJ: 22-3

12. One reason communicable diseases spread rapidly throughout the world is _____.
    a. the diseases are often endemic in the population
    b. people travel
    c. pathogens reproduce easily
    d. symptoms are not treated soon enough

    ANS: B   DIF: B   OBJ: 22-4

13. Visible light ___
    a. is a form of electromagnetic radiation
    b. is reflected from specific body tissues
    c. can damage DNA, causing mutations or cancer
    d. all of the above

ANS: A   DIF: B   OBJ: 22-8

14. Magnetic resonance imaging ___
    a. uses a computer to compile different X ray images to form a three-dimensional image
    b. uses ionizing radiation to align atomic nuclei
    c. is based on differential absorption of electromagnetic waves by different types of tissue
    d. is based on the different amounts of time it takes for atomic nuclei of different tissues to respond to a magnetic field

ANS: D   DIF: B   OBJ: 22-9

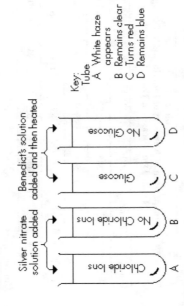

Key:
Tube
A White haze appears
B Remains clear
C Turns red
D Remains blue

Silver nitrate solution added   Benedict's solution added and then heated

A Chloride Ions   B No Chloride Ions   C Glucose   D No Glucose

FIGURE 22-2

15. The urine from a person is tested for glucose. The tube turns red after Benedict's solution is added and heated. Using the information in Figure 22-2, you can conclude that the person may have ___
    a. cystic fibrosis
    b. Lyme disease
    c. diabetes
    d. both diabetes and cystic fibrosis

ANS: C   DIF: B   OBJ: 22-5

16. Sweat from a person is tested for salt. The tube turns a hazy white after silver nitrate solution is added. Using the information in Figure 22-2, you can conclude that the person ___
    a. may have diabetes
    b. may not have diabetes
    c. has chloride ions in his or her sweat
    d. has no chloride ions in his or her sweat

ANS: C   DIF: B   OBJ: 22-5

---

17. Sweat from a person is tested for glucose. The tube remains blue after Benedict's solution is added and then heated. Using the information in Figure 22-2, you can conclude that the person is ___
    a. may have cystic fibrosis
    b. may not have cystic fibrosis
    c. may not have diabetes
    d. may not have glucose in his or her sweat

ANS: D   DIF: A   OBJ: 22-5

18. Kidneys filter salt in the form of ions from the blood. According to the information in Figure 22-2, the appearance of a normal urine sample receiving silver nitrate solution will ___
    a. have a white haze
    b. remain clear
    c. turn red
    d. remain blue

ANS: A   DIF: A   OBJ: 22-5

ELECTROPHORESIS GEL OF 3 MOLECULES
At Start of Experiment

A
B
C

20 minutes Later

A   B

C

Direction of Current Flow

FIGURE 22-3

19. Molecule A in Figure 22-3 is ___
    a. larger than B
    b. larger than C
    c. smaller than B but larger than C
    d. smaller than C but larger than B

ANS: D   DIF: B   OBJ: 22-7

20. Molecule B in Figure 22-3 is ___
    a. larger than A and C
    b. smaller than A and C
    c. similar in size to A
    d. similar in size to C

ANS: B   DIF: B   OBJ: 22-7

21. Molecule C in Figure 22-3 is _____.
   a. smaller than A
   b. smaller than B
   c. the largest of the three samples
   d. the smallest of the three samples

ANS: C   DIF: B   OBJ: 22-7

22. Using the data from Figure 22-3, it would be correct to say _____.
   a. molecule size is identical for each sample
   b. molecule size differs for each sample
   c. exact molecule size can be determined from the results
   d. exact molecule size could be determined if the experiment were continued for 1 hour

ANS: B   DIF: B   OBJ: 22-7

23. Using the data from Figure 22-3 and assuming that A, B, and C were actually pathogens, it would be correct to say that _____.
   a. one could determine the specific names of the pathogens from the data
   b. one could not determine the specific names of the pathogens from the data
   c. all three pathogens are closely related
   d. all three pathogens were taken from the same diseased person

ANS: B   DIF: A   OBJ: 22-7

Table 22-1
Comparison of Numbers of Individuals Suffering From Two Diseases in Three Countries

Country	Disease	1960	1970	1980	1990	2000
China	X	11 248	70 652	10 814	9850	10 417
	Y	27 518	28 901	28 562	27 844	27 750
Australia	X	6117	5877	6004	6054	5932
	Y	10 088	10 559	10 484	10 196	10 381
United States	X	8765	8945	9101	9187	8884
	Y	1746	3984	7168	25 824	6077

24. Using Table 22-1 and comparing disease X to Y in China in 1970, it would be correct to say _____.
   a. X is endemic, Y is epidemic
   b. X is epidemic, Y is endemic
   c. both are epidemic
   d. both are endemic

ANS: B   DIF: B   OBJ: 22-4

25. Using Table 22-1 and comparing disease Y in China and Australia, it would be correct to say _____.
   a. Y in China is endemic but epidemic in Australia
   b. Y in China is epidemic but endemic in Australia
   c. both are epidemic
   d. both are endemic

ANS: D   DIF: B   OBJ: 22-4

26. Using Table 22-1 and comparing disease X to Y in the United States, it would be correct to say _____.
   a. X is endemic, Y is epidemic
   b. X is epidemic, Y is endemic
   c. both are epidemic
   d. both are endemic

ANS: A   DIF: B   OBJ: 22-4

27. Using Table 22-1 and comparing disease X in China to Y in the United States, it would be correct to say _____.
   a. X is endemic, Y is epidemic
   b. X is epidemic, Y is endemic
   c. both are epidemic
   d. both are endemic

ANS: C   DIF: B   OBJ: 22-4

28. In Table 22-1, the years in Australia that best show an epidemic occurring are _____.
   a. 1960–1980
   b. 1970–1990
   c. 1990–2000
   d. none of the above

ANS: D   DIF: A   OBJ: 22-4

COMPLETION

1. Blood pressure is the force exerted by blood pressing _____.

ANS: against artery walls   DIF: B   OBJ: 22-2

2. High blood pressure may result from factors such as _____.

ANS: heredity, obesity, heart problems, plaque buildup, or chemical imbalances

   DIF: B   OBJ: 22-2

3. Blood pressure rises when heart ventricles _____.

ANS: contract   DIF: B   OBJ: 22-2

16. A nonrandom distribution that shows many cases of a disease in a particular area is an example of a ____.

ANS: disease cluster   DIF: B   OBJ: 22-4

17. The underlying idea of ____ is that a pathogen from a diseased organism will cause the disease in another organism.

ANS: Koch's postulates   DIF: B   OBJ: 22-3

18. Particles are pumped from areas of lower to higher concentration by ____.

ANS: active transport   DIF: B   OBJ: 22-6

19. During an influenza ____, many people become ill will influenza.

ANS: epidemic   DIF: B   OBJ: 22-4

20. A ____ uses light rays and lenses to enlarge the image of an object.

ANS: light microscope   DIF: B   OBJ: 22-8

21. ____ uses electricity and magnetism to reveal healthy and diseased tissue.

ANS: Magnetic resonance imaging, or MRI   DIF: B   OBJ: 22-9

Steps used to test if a disease is caused by a specific organism

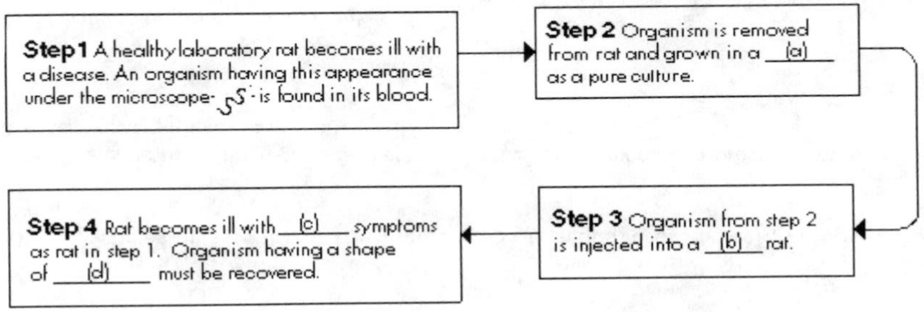

Step 1 A healthy laboratory rat becomes ill with a disease. An organism having this appearance under the microscope "S" is found in its blood.

Step 2 Organism is removed from rat and grown in a __(a)__ as pure culture.

Step 3 Organism from step 2 is injected into a __(b)__ rat.

Step 4 Rat becomes ill with __(c)__ symptoms as rat in step 1. Organism having a shape of __(d)__ must be recovered.

FIGURE 22-1

22. The steps outlined in Figure 22-1 are known as ____.

ANS: Koch's postulates   DIF: B   OBJ: 22-3

23. The term that best completes space a in step 2 of Figure 22-1 would be ____.

ANS: laboratory or sterile dish   DIF: A   OBJ: 22-3

---

4. Blood pressure drops when heart ventricles ____.

ANS: relax (or: are about to contract)   DIF: B   OBJ: 22-2

5. The higher of the two values in blood pressure is called ____.

ANS: systolic pressure   DIF: A   OBJ: 22-2

6. Passive transport ____ require cell energy in order to take place.

ANS: does not   DIF: B   OBJ: 22-6

7. During diffusion, ions will move from regions of greater concentration toward regions of ____ concentration.

ANS: lesser   DIF: B   OBJ: 22-6

8. Lipid molecules can pass through the lipid layers of a cell's ____.

ANS: membrane   DIF: A   OBJ: 22-6

9. Active transport relies on the presence of gate or ____ proteins in a cell membrane.

ANS: carrier   DIF: A   OBJ: 22-6

10. Active transport gets its name from the fact that cell ____ is needed for the process.

ANS: energy   DIF: B   OBJ: 22-6

11. During ____, molecules move from regions of lower to greater concentration.

ANS: active transport   DIF: B   OBJ: 22-6

12. A disease always present is ____.

ANS: endemic   DIF: B   OBJ: 22-4

13. ____ requires no energy to move particles across a membrane.

ANS: Passive transport   DIF: B   OBJ: 22-6

14. Visible light has longer wavelengths and less energy than ____.

ANS: X rays   DIF: B   OBJ: 22-8

15. A method to identify substances on the basis of molecular size and electrical charge is ____.

ANS: electrophoresis   DIF: B   OBJ: 22-7

24. The term that best completes space b in step 3 of Figure 22-1 would be _____.

ANS: healthy   DIF: B   OBJ: 22-3

25. The term that best completes space c in step 4 of Figure 22-1 would be _____.

ANS: same   DIF: B   OBJ: 22-3

26. If the disease is caused by the same organism in step 1, then the shape of a recovered organism in step 4 space d of Figure 22-1 should have a shape resembling a _____.

ANS: spiral or corkscrew   DIF: A   OBJ: 22-3

SHORT ANSWER

1. Does it matter how many fields of view you count on the microscope slide to figure out the percentage of white blood cells? Explain.

ANS: more fields counted result in more accurate calculation as cells may be clumped in some fields, making the distribution uneven

DIF: A   OBJ: 22-5

2. If you wanted to know the number of red blood cells and white blood cells per microliter of blood, what information would you need?

ANS: the volume of the sample on the slide, the dilution factor, and the fraction of the slide counted

DIF: B   OBJ: 22-5

3. In what ways is MRI considered better than a CAT scan?

ANS: MRI is safer: it does not use ionizing radiation; a computer assigns different colors to tissues whose nuclei respond differently, giving a more detailed image that the simple black and white of a CAT scan.

DIF: A   OBJ: 22-9

4. What causes fever and what purpose, if any, does it serve?

ANS: Macrophages rush to an infected area and release chemicals causing chills and fever. The higher body temperature slows the reproduction of viruses or bacteria.

DIF: A   OBJ: 22-1

5. Why is energy required for active transport? Where does the energy come from?

ANS: To move substances against a concentration gradient, from low to high, is similar to swimming against a current. The energy needed for active transport comes from the breakdown of food.

DIF: A   OBJ: 22-6

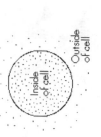

FIGURE 22-5

6. How will particles in Figure 22-5 move if no energy is involved?

ANS: from the inside of the cell to the outside by passive diffusion

DIF: B   OBJ: 22-6

7. If the particles outside the cell in Figure 22-5 are required by the cell, how will they be transported?

ANS: Active transport will carry them across the cell membrane, a process requiring energy. Carrier or gate proteins may be involved in the transport.

DIF: B   OBJ: 22-6

8. How is the transport of insulin regulated?

ANS: An insulin molecule acts as a signal and combines with a type of carrier protein called a gate protein to open and allow insulin into the cell.

DIF: A   OBJ: 22-6

Table 22-2

	Red	White	Total
Field 1			
Field 2			
Field 3			
Total			

FIGURE 22-6

9. Figure 22-6 shows three different fields of a microscope slide of blood cells. Use the information in the figure to complete Table 22-2. Hint: white blood cells have nuclei, red blood cells do not.

ANS:

Table 22-2

	Red	White	Total
Field 1	6	1	7
Field 2	7	1	8
Field 3	5	0	5
Total	18	2	20

DIF: B   OBJ: 22-5

10. Calculate the percentage of white blood cells you observe in Figure 22-6. This blood sample was diluted to make the cells easier to count. Does it change the percentage? Explain.

ANS: The percentage of white blood cells is 2/20 = 10%. Diluting the sample does not change the percent. The total number is less, but proportions are the same.

DIF: A   OBJ: 22-5

11. If a healthy person has approximately 6 million red blood cells and 10 000 white blood cells per microliter of blood, does the sample shown in Figure 22-6 represent a healthy or diseased blood sample? Explain.

ANS: Healthy blood is less than 0.2% white blood cells; therefore the sample indicates infection.

DIF: A   OBJ: 22-5

12. Describe and name the technique shown in Figure 22-4.

ANS: The technique, electrophoresis, is used to identify substances according to differences in molecular size and electrical charge.

DIF: B   OBJ: 22-7

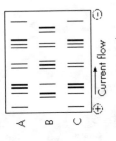

FIGURE 22-4

13. How could the technique shown in Figure 22-4 be used to determine whether a patient has a certain virus?

ANS: By using electrophoresis to analyze a sample of the patient's DNA and then comparing that banding pattern with the patterns of samples from patients with known viruses, electrophoresis could determine whether a patient has a particular virus.

DIF: A   OBJ: 22-7

14. If sample A in Figure 22-4 is from a patient with an unknown virus, and patients B and C each have a different identified virus, what can we learn from the patterns in the figure?

ANS: Patient A has the same virus as patient C.

DIF: A   OBJ: 22-7

15. What information does a blood pressure reading give? Why is it important?

ANS: The lower measurement, or diastolic pressure, gives the blood pressure between heartbeats. The higher measurement, or systolic pressure, gives the pressure when the heart muscle is contracting. Blood pressure is the force of blood pushing against artery walls. If it's too high, stroke, heart attack, or kidney failure can result.

DIF: B   OBJ: 22-2

16. Explain why universal precautions for health-care workers include wearing gloves and, in some cases, masks.

ANS: Body fluids and even breath are vehicles for pathogens. One may come into contact with infected body fluids and become infected if he or she has a cut or, in the case of an airborne pathogen, inhales the pathogen.

DIF: A   OBJ: 22-3

OTHER

If the underscored word or phrase makes the sentence true, write "true" in the space provided. If the underscored word or phrase makes the sentence false, write the correct term or phrase in the space provided.

1. An infection will usually result in an increase in the number of red blood cells.

ANS: white blood cells   DIF: A   OBJ: 22-1

2. A general disease symptom always shows up as a(n) decrease in fatigue.

ANS: increase   DIF: B   OBJ: 22-1

CHAPTER 23—PHYSICS OF FLIGHT

MULTIPLE CHOICE

1. A plane can fly upside down and still get lift because of _____.
   a. the Bernoulli effect
   b. the Coanda effect
   c. the angle of attack
   d. all of the above

   ANS: C   DIF: B   OBJ: 23-9

2. Which one of the following does NOT produce thrust?
   a. propeller
   b. wing
   c. jet engine
   d. car pulling a glider

   ANS: B   DIF: A   OBJ: 23-4

3. When an object in free-fall has not reached terminal speed, then each second the object falls, it falls _____.
   a. a greater distance than in the second before
   b. the same distance as in the second before
   c. with the same speed as before
   d. with increased acceleration

   ANS: A   DIF: A   OBJ: 23-7

4. When the thrust of an airplane is tripled and all other forces remain constant, the airplane's acceleration _____.
   a. decreases 9 times as much
   b. increases 3 times as much
   c. increases 9 times as much
   d. decreases 3 times as much

   ANS: B   DIF: A   OBJ: 23-8

5. When a steel ball, a baseball, and a Styrofoam ball are dropped from an airplane at the same time, what happens?
   a. All three will hit the ground at the same time because they all have the same terminal speed.
   b. The steel ball will hit first because it will reach terminal speed later than the others.
   c. The baseball will hit first because it will reach terminal speed later than the others.
   d. The Styrofoam ball will hit first because it will reach terminal speed later than the others.

   ANS: B   DIF: A   OBJ: 23-7

---

3. Release of hormones by macrophages may result in fever and chills. _____

   ANS: true   DIF: A   OBJ: 22-1

4. The appearance of a red, bull's-eye rash is a typical symptom of influenza.

   ANS: Lyme disease   DIF: A   OBJ: 22-1

5. Your body usually shows an increase in appetite when infected by a pathogen.

   ANS: decrease   DIF: B   OBJ: 22-1

6. Which has more momentum: a glider moving at 200 miles per hour, a small jet fighter traveling at 200 miles per hour, or a jumbo jet traveling at 200 miles per hour?
   a. the glider
   b. the jumbo jet
   c. the fighter jet
   d. They all have the same momentum.

   ANS: B   DIF: B   OBJ: 23-3

7. Which has the greater momentum—a bicyclist moving at 10 m/s or a train moving at 10 m/s?
   a. the bicyclist
   b. the train
   c. both have the same momentum
   d. unknown–not enough information is provided to decide

   ANS: B   DIF: B   OBJ: 23-3

8. The acceleration produced by an unbalanced force on a ball is _____.
   a. in the opposite direction of the unbalanced force
   b. directly proportional to the unbalanced force
   c. directly proportional to the mass of the object
   d. all of the above

   ANS: B   DIF: A   OBJ: 23-2

9. If an object's mass remains the same but its momentum changes, what might be happening to the object?
   a. It is accelerating.
   b. A force is acting on it.
   c. Its velocity is changing.
   d. All of the above could be happening.

   ANS: D   DIF: A   OBJ: 23-3

10. If the force supplied by a car's engine equals the force of friction with the road and air drag, then _____.
    a. the car's speed will be decreasing
    b. the car's speed will be constant
    c. the car's speed will be increasing

    ANS: B   DIF: B   OBJ: 23-1

11. In a moving stream, if the stream narrows, the water will move _____.
    a. slower
    b. the same speed
    c. faster

    ANS: C   DIF: B   OBJ: 23-9

12. In order for a plane to have a large amount of lift and a small amount of drag, _____.
    a. the angle of attack should be zero
    b. the angle of attack should be moderate
    c. the angle of attack should be large

    ANS: B   DIF: A   OBJ: 23-8

13. As air flows over an aircraft wing, the greater air pressure occurs _____.
    a. on the bottom of the wing
    b. on top of the wing
    c. behind the wing

    ANS: A   DIF: B   OBJ: 23-9

14. In order for a plane to begin to descend, _____.
    a. the lift force should be increased
    b. the drag force should be decreased
    c. the lift force should be decreased
    d. the thrust force should be increased

    ANS: C   DIF: A   OBJ: 23-1

15. Saturn's atmosphere is more dense than Earth's. How would the terminal speed of a falling satellite on Saturn compare with one falling on Earth?
    a. less than on Earth
    b. the same as on Earth
    c. greater than on Earth
    d. not able to be compared because no satellite has been observed falling to Saturn

    ANS: A   DIF: A   OBJ: 23-7

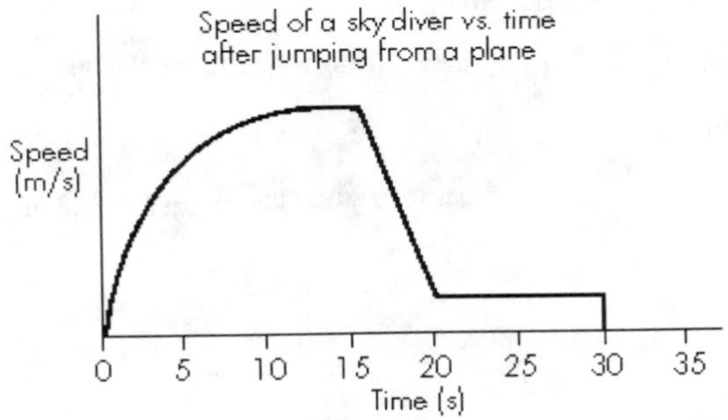

Speed of a skydiver vs. time after jumping from a plane

FIGURE 23-2

16. In Figure 23-2, during which interval of time does the skydiver reach terminal velocity?
    a. between 0 and 5 seconds
    b. between 5 and 10 seconds
    c. between 10 and 15 seconds
    d. between 15 and 20 seconds

    ANS: C   DIF: A   OBJ: 23-7

17. In Figure 23-2, during which interval of time was the skydiver's speed changing the fastest?
   a. between 0 and 5 seconds
   b. between 5 and 10 seconds
   c. between 10 and 15 seconds
   d. between 20 and 25 seconds

   ANS: A   DIF: A   OBJ: 23-5

18. In Figure 23-2, during which interval of time was the parachute open?
   a. between 5 and 10 seconds
   b. between 10 and 15 seconds
   c. between 15 and 30 seconds
   d. between 30 and 35 seconds

   ANS: C   DIF: A   OBJ: 23-2

19. In Figure 23-2, at which time did the skydiver most likely land?
   a. 5 seconds
   b. 10 seconds
   c. 20 seconds
   d. 30 seconds

   ANS: D   DIF: A   OBJ: 23-2

COMPLETION

1. _____ is a measurement of the gravitational force acting on an object.

   ANS: Weight   DIF: B   OBJ: 23-6

2. In order for a cart to travel at a constant speed, the forces acting on it must be _____

   ANS: balanced   DIF: B   OBJ: 23-1

3. _____ results when an object experiences unbalanced forces.

   ANS: Acceleration   DIF: B   OBJ: 23-1

4. _____ is a noncontact force that acts on a car.

   ANS: Gravity   DIF: B   OBJ: 23-4

5. When the drag of the air equals the force of gravity on a falling ball, the ball is said to have reached its _____

   ANS: terminal velocity   DIF: B   OBJ: 23-7

6. A hovering helicopter is producing 10 000 N of lift. The weight of the helicopter and occupants is _____

   ANS: 10 000 N   DIF: A   OBJ: 23-6

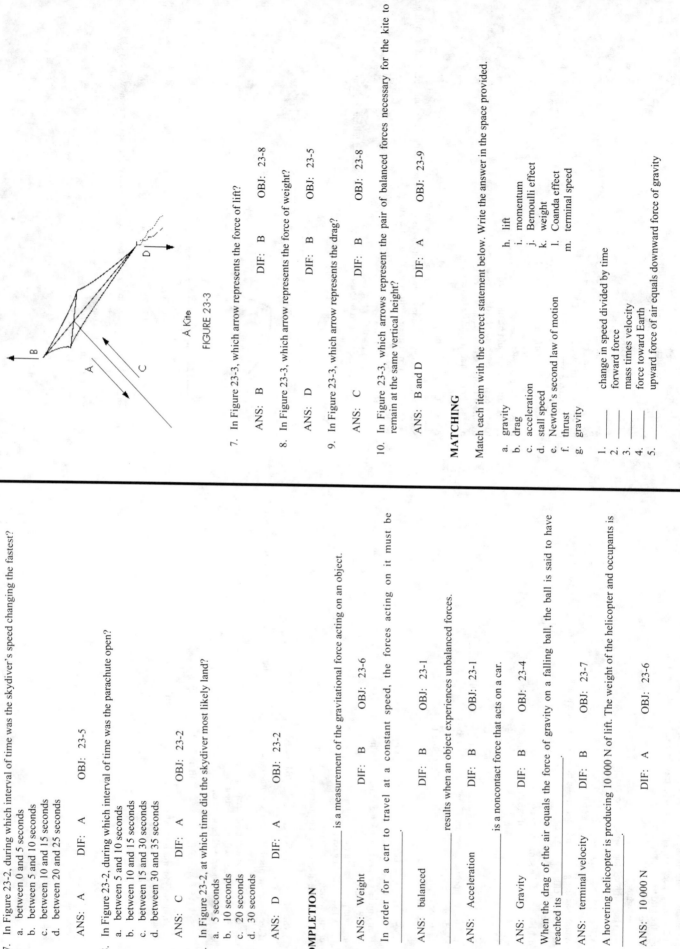

A Kite

FIGURE 23-3

7. In Figure 23-3, which arrow represents the force of lift?

   ANS: B   DIF: B   OBJ: 23-8

8. In Figure 23-3, which arrow represents the force of weight?

   ANS: D   DIF: B   OBJ: 23-5

9. In Figure 23-3, which arrow represents the drag?

   ANS: C   DIF: B   OBJ: 23-8

10. In Figure 23-3, which arrows represent the pair of balanced forces necessary for the kite to remain at the same vertical height?

   ANS: B and D   DIF: A   OBJ: 23-9

MATCHING

Match each item with the correct statement below. Write the answer in the space provided.

a. gravity
b. drag
c. acceleration
d. stall speed
e. Newton's second law of motion
f. thrust
g. gravity

h. lift
i. momentum
j. Bernoulli effect
k. weight
l. Coanda effect
m. terminal speed

1. ____ change in speed divided by time
2. ____ forward force
3. ____ mass times velocity
4. ____ force toward Earth
5. ____ upward force of air equals downward force of gravity

23-4

23-5

6. _____ air resistance
7. _____ faster moving air exerts less pressure
8. _____ the relationship among force, mass, and acceleration
9. _____ lift equals the plane's weight
10. _____ downward force due to an object's mass
11. _____ an upward force on an airplane
12. _____ a force that results from the weak interaction between a surface and a moving fluid such as air or water
13. _____ a noncontact force that pulls objects downward

1. ANS: c   DIF: B   OBJ: 23-2
2. ANS: f   DIF: B   OBJ: 23-4
3. ANS: i   DIF: B   OBJ: 23-3
4. ANS: a   DIF: B   OBJ: 23-7
5. ANS: m   DIF: B   OBJ: 23-7
6. ANS: b   DIF: B   OBJ: 23-5
7. ANS: j   DIF: B   OBJ: 23-9
8. ANS: e   DIF: B   OBJ: 23-2
9. ANS: d   DIF: B   OBJ: 23-9
10. ANS: k   DIF: B   OBJ: 23-6
11. ANS: h   DIF: B   OBJ: 23-9
12. ANS: l   DIF: B   OBJ: 23-9
13. ANS: g   DIF: B   OBJ: 23-4

SHORT ANSWER

1. In order for a girl pulling a sled to increase her speed, what force must be increased most?

ANS: the force of the girl pushing against the ground

DIF: A   OBJ: 23-2

2. Explain which vehicle would experience the greater force during a head-on collision—a garbage truck or a small sports car.

ANS: Neither—both would experience the same force (equal and opposite).

DIF: A   OBJ: 23-3

3. When a skydiver reaches her terminal speed, what does the air resistance equal?

ANS: It is equal to the force on her due to gravity, or weight.

DIF: A   OBJ: 23-7

4. Explain what causes a sheet of paper that is held flat with air blowing across it to rise.

ANS: The velocity of air over the top surface is greater than the air below. Downward air pressure on the top is reduced, and higher pressure below causes an unbalanced upward force, making the paper rise.

DIF: A   OBJ: 23-9

5. Describe gravity.

ANS: Gravity is a force toward Earth due to an object's mass.

DIF: A   OBJ: 23-4

6. Compare a contact and noncontact force.

ANS: A force resulting from touching, such as a push on a wagon, is a contact force, while a force that occurs without physical touching, such as gravity, is a noncontact force.

DIF: A   OBJ: 23-4

7. During equal increments of time, describe what happens to a falling ball.

ANS: It falls greater and greater distances.

DIF: A   OBJ: 23-5

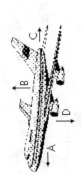

FIGURE 23-1

8. Which arrow in Figure 23-1 represents drag?

ANS: C   DIF: B   OBJ: 23-4

9. Which arrow in Figure 23-1 represents lift?

ANS: B   DIF: B   OBJ: 23-4

10. Which arrow in Figure 23-1 represents thrust?

ANS: A   DIF: B   OBJ: 23-4

11. Which arrow in Figure 23-1 represents gravity?

ANS: D   DIF: B   OBJ: 23-4

Table 23-2

Time Interval (s)	Starting Speed (m/s)	Ending Speed (m/s)	Average Speed (m/s)	Distance (m)
0–5	0	16	___	___
5–10	16	26	___	___
10–15	26	32	___	___
15–20	32	34	___	___

12. What is the average speed for each time interval shown in Table 23-2?

ANS: 8, 21, 29, 33   DIF: A   OBJ: 23-2

13. Using $d = v \times t$, calculate the distance traveled during each time interval in Table 23-2.

ANS: 40, 105, 145, 165   DIF: A   OBJ: 23-2

14. Based on the information in Table 23-2, what is your estimate for the total distance needed for take-off?

ANS: 455 m   DIF: A   OBJ: 23-2

15. During your work with the investigation "How does air drag depend on the falling object?" what factors affected the drag due to air resistance of an airplane?

ANS: Answers could include shape of plane, size of plane, density of air, type of wing, amount of thrust, and wind speed.

DIF: B   OBJ: 23-8

16. Explain why a paper airplane flies longer than the wad of paper.

ANS: A paper airplane's wing produces lift.

DIF: B   OBJ: 23-9

17. Under what conditions will an airplane undergo a constant speed?

ANS: When the forces of lift and gravity are equal and opposite, and thrust and drag are equal and opposite.

DIF: B   OBJ: 23-1

---

18. Why is angle of attack important in flying an airplane?

ANS: The proper angle of attack gives the best lift. If the angle of attack is too steep, lift is greatly decreased and the plane will stall.

DIF: A   OBJ: 23-9

19. Explain what must happen for a plane to take off.

ANS: The plane must have enough thrust to overcome drag. This is done by accelerating it. Enough speed is also needed so that lift is greater than the weight of the plane.

DIF: B   OBJ: 23-9

Table 23-1

Object	Mass	Initial Velocity	Final Velocity	Time	Acceleration	Force
ice skater	50 kg	0.45 m/s	5.0 m/s	3.0 s	**A**	**B**
hockey puck	0.5 kg	**C**	40 m/s	0.5 s	80 m/s/s	**D**

20. Using Table 23-1, calculate the acceleration, **A**, of the ice skater.

ANS: 1.5 m/s/s   DIF: B   OBJ: 23-5

21. Using Table 23-1, find the force, **B**, that the ice skater supplied to accelerate himself.

ANS: 75 N   DIF: B   OBJ: 23-2

22. Using Table 23-1, determine the initial velocity, **C**, of the hockey puck.

ANS: 0 m/s   DIF: B   OBJ: 23-2

23. Using Table 23-1, determine the force the ice skater applied to the hockey puck, **D**.

ANS: 40 N   DIF: A   OBJ: 23-2

24. Explain what must happen for a plane to land safely.

ANS: The engine speed must be decreased and the nose pointed down. Weight adds to the forward force. Flaps are used to increase wing area, allowing the plane to fly slower without dropping below the stall speed. As the wheels touch the ground, it reaches stall speed.

DIF: B   OBJ: 23-9

MULTIPLE CHOICE

1. Several different types of plants have dropped seeds on a driveway. With a gentle breeze blowing, which of the following is least likely to be further dispersed?
   a. cottonwood
   b. maple
   c. dandelion
   d. milkweed

   ANS: B   DIF: A   OBJ: 24-8

2. In order to increase the aspect ratio of an airplane wing, one could _____.
   a. decrease wing length and width
   b. decrease wing width and increase length
   c. increase wing width and increase length
   d. decrease wing length

   ANS: B   DIF: A   OBJ: 24-3

3. The control surfaces of an airplane allow it to _____.
   a. tilt up or down
   b. roll from side to side
   c. turn right or left
   d. all of the above

   ANS: D   DIF: B   OBJ: 24-3

4. In order to decrease stall speed, birds _____.
   a. decrease lift
   b. increase lift
   c. decrease weight
   d. increase weight

   ANS: B   DIF: A   OBJ: 24-3

5. Jet engines burn _____.
   a. gasoline
   b. alcohol
   c. kerosene
   d. all of the above

   ANS: C   DIF: B   OBJ: 24-6

6. Seeds from a _____ tree help increase widespread dispersal.
   a. maple
   b. oak
   c. walnut
   d. redbud

   ANS: A   DIF: B   OBJ: 24-7

---

25. When driving a car on a two-lane road, you notice that the car veers toward the middle of the road when a large truck passes. Why does this happen?

    ANS: The Bernoulli effect and the Coanda effect cause the car and the truck to move toward the middle of the road due to lower air pressure between the two vehicles.

    DIF: A   OBJ: 23-9

OTHER

If the underscored word or phrase makes the sentence true, write "true" in the space provided. If the underscored word or phrase makes the sentence false, write the correct term or phrase in the space provided.

1. If an unbalanced force acts on an object, the object's <u>momentum</u> will change. _____

   ANS: true   DIF: B   OBJ: 23-3

2. The speed of an object dropped in air will <u>never</u> stop increasing. _____

   ANS: eventually   DIF: B   OBJ: 23-7

3. If the force acting on a cart is doubled, the acceleration will <u>quadruple</u>. _____

   ANS: double   DIF: B   OBJ: 23-2

4. Bernoulli's effect states that when air moves faster, the pressure it exerts is <u>greater</u>. _____

   ANS: less   DIF: B   OBJ: 23-9

5. Gravity is described as a <u>noncontact</u> force. _____

   ANS: true   DIF: B   OBJ: 23-4

6. A falling tissue box will experience <u>more</u> drag than a baseball. _____

   ANS: true   DIF: A   OBJ: 23-8

Table 24-1

Bird	Wing Length (m)	Wing Width (m)	Wing Area (m²)	Weight (N)	Wing Loading	Aspect Ratio
bird X	0.15	0.01	0.0014	0.05	**A**	**B**
bird Y	2.5	0.30	0.75	80	**C**	**D**
bird Z	1.6	0.20	0.32	16	**E**	**F**

7. Which of the following forces that act on an airplane is also important to the dispersal of plumed seeds?
   a. lift
   b. thrust
   c. drag
   d. all of the above

   ANS: C   DIF: B   OBJ: 24-7

8. The term describing how an airplane's nose moves left or right is _____.
   a. pitch
   b. roll
   c. yaw
   d. tilt

   ANS: C   DIF: B   OBJ: 24-3

9. Which of the following features do birds not manipulate to change their direction of flight?
   a. wing position
   b. foot position (nonwebbed)
   c. rolling
   d. tail feather position

   ANS: B   DIF: A   OBJ: 24-1

10. During a landing, planes extend flaps, while birds _____.
    a. roll
    b. move their wings backwards
    c. spread their feathers
    d. lift their heads

    ANS: C   DIF: B   OBJ: 24-2

11. Which do birds not use to obtain thrust?
    a. thermal air currents
    b. wings
    c. gravity
    d. clouds

    ANS: D   DIF: B   OBJ: 24-4

12. A hawk, while hunting and capturing a rabbit, would most likely not use which of the following?
    a. downdrafts
    b. fast forward flight
    c. slow forward flight
    d. thermals

    ANS: A   DIF: A   OBJ: 24-4

13. In Table 24-1, the wing loading, **A**, for bird X is _____.
    a. 5
    b. 36
    c. 50
    d. 80

    ANS: B   DIF: B   OBJ: 24-2

14. In Table 24-1, the wing loading, **C**, for bird Y is _____.
    a. 36
    b. 50
    c. 80
    d. 107

    ANS: D   DIF: B   OBJ: 24-2

15. In Table 24-1, the wing loading, **E**, for bird Z is _____.
    a. 50
    b. 80
    c. 107
    d. 266

    ANS: A   DIF: B   OBJ: 24-2

16. In Table 24-1, the aspect ratio, **B**, for bird X is _____.
    a. 2
    b. 8
    c. 8.3
    d. 15

    ANS: D   DIF: B   OBJ: 24-2

17. In Table 24-1, the aspect ratio, **D**, for bird Y is _____.
    a. 2
    b. 8
    c. 8.3
    d. 15

    ANS: C   DIF: B   OBJ: 24-2

18. In Table 24-1, the aspect ratio, **F**, for bird Z is _____.
   a. 2
   b. 8
   c. 8.3
   d. 15

   ANS: B   DIF: B   OBJ: 24-2

19. In Table 24-1, which bird has the greatest wing loading?
   a. bird X
   b. bird Y
   c. bird Z
   d. can't tell from data provided

   ANS: B   DIF: A   OBJ: 24-2

20. In Table 24-1, which bird has the greatest aspect ratio?
   a. bird X
   b. bird Y
   c. bird Z
   d. can't tell from data provided

   ANS: A   DIF: A   OBJ: 24-2

COMPLETION

1. When gliding, a bird is able to use part of the force of gravity acting on it to provide _____.

   ANS: thrust   DIF: B   OBJ: 24-4

2. Birds are able to use _____ air currents to allow them to soar.

   ANS: rising   DIF: B   OBJ: 24-4

3. In order for effective seed dispersal by maple trees, the seeds have adapted _____.

   ANS: wings   DIF: B   OBJ: 24-8

4. Plants growing near the ground are likely to have a _____ type of seeds to aid in dispersal.

   ANS: parachute   DIF: B   OBJ: 24-8

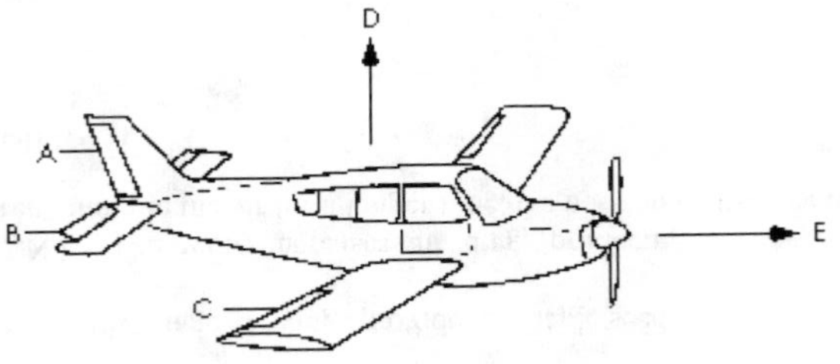

FIGURE 24-1

5. In Figure 24-1, structure B represents a(n) _____.

   ANS: elevator   DIF: B   OBJ: 24-3

6. In Figure 24-1, structure C represents a(n) _____.

   ANS: aileron   DIF: B   OBJ: 24-3

7. In Figure 24-1, the _____ is indicated by the control surface labeled A.

   ANS: rudder   DIF: B   OBJ: 24-3

8. In Figure 24-1, the force associated with E represents _____.

   ANS: thrust   DIF: B   OBJ: 24-6

9. In Figure 24-1, force D represents _____.

   ANS: lift   DIF: B   OBJ: 24-3

MATCHING

Match each item with the correct statement below. Write the answer in the space provided.

a. by spreading feathers to increase wing area
b. by holding wings closer to their body, thus reducing wing area
c. by flexing primary wing feathers or tails
d. wing loading
e. aspect ratio
f. wingspan
g. soaring
h. pitch
i. yaw
j. dispersal
k. elevator
l. by raising wings higher above bodies
m. by moving wings forward or back or flexing tail feathers
n. rudder
o. roll

1. _____ weight divided by wing area
2. _____ distance between wing tips
3. _____ wingspan divided by average wing width
4. _____ spread of seeds over a wide area
5. _____ flying with motionless wings
6. _____ motion made as nose of plane turns left or right
7. _____ motion as nose of plane points up or down
8. _____ tilting motion as one wing dips lower than the other
9. _____ movable flap on a plane's vertical tail fin
10. _____ movable flap on a plane's horizontal tail surface
11. _____ Birds change pitch
12. _____ Birds change yaw
13. _____ Birds change roll
14. _____ Birds land
15. _____ Birds increase speed

1. ANS: d   DIF: B   OBJ: 24-1
2. ANS: f   DIF: B   OBJ: 24-1
3. ANS: e   DIF: B   OBJ: 24-1
4. ANS: j   DIF: B   OBJ: 24-7
5. ANS: g   DIF: B   OBJ: 24-2
6. ANS: i   DIF: B   OBJ: 24-3
7. ANS: h   DIF: B   OBJ: 24-3
8. ANS: o   DIF: B   OBJ: 24-3
9. ANS: n   DIF: B   OBJ: 24-1
10. ANS: k   DIF: B   OBJ: 24-1
11. ANS: m   DIF: B   OBJ: 24-3
12. ANS: l   DIF: B   OBJ: 24-3
13. ANS: c   DIF: B   OBJ: 24-3
14. ANS: a   DIF: B   OBJ: 24-3
15. ANS: b   DIF: B   OBJ: 24-3

SHORT ANSWER

1. What is the flight analogy for a spinning maple seed?

   ANS: the rotating blades of a helicopter

   DIF: B   OBJ: 24-7

2. What is the flight analogy for a dandelion seed?

   ANS: a parachute

   DIF: B   OBJ: 24-7

3. What is the result of fungus spores having very small terminal speeds?

   ANS: these particles are carried long distances by the slightest breeze or thermal current

   DIF: B   OBJ: 24-7

4. Explain the survival advantage of winged seeds.

   ANS: The mature seeds carry the embryo for the next generation of plants. If all seeds fell directly under the plant, they would crowd each other out and never grow into mature plants. Winged seeds can be dispersed over a wider area than seeds without wings.

   DIF: B   OBJ: 24-7

5. How do you calculate how far from the parent tree a spinning maple seed will travel?

   ANS: distance = wind velocity × time in the air

   DIF: A   OBJ: 24-7

6. How do planes decrease their stall speed?

   ANS: Planes extend flaps and other wing parts to increase lift and decrease stall speed.

   DIF: A   OBJ: 24-2

7. Describe the energy transfer in a bird's muscles.

   ANS: About 80% of the energy turns into heat, while 20% does work.

   DIF: A   OBJ: 24-5

8. Compare the amount of thrust produced by gasoline and kerosene.

   ANS: Energy released per kilogram is the same, but kerosene is denser; thus, more energy can be stored per tankful.

   DIF: A   OBJ: 24-6

9. Compare the feathers in a bird that function like an airplane's ailerons and flaps.

   ANS: Birds move their wings forward, backward, up, or down to control their direction. Tail feather position can be adjusted to alter the bird's pitch.

   DIF: A   OBJ: 24-1

10. Compare and contrast three basic thrust methods used in different airplane designs.

    ANS: Propeller-driven aircraft were standard for the earliest planes and for planes needing to travel slowly. Early jets expelled hot gases to produce thrust but have been replaced by quieter and more efficient turbo-fan jet engines.

    DIF: A   OBJ: 24-6

11. What advantage do wings provide for maple seeds?

    ANS: The wing increases air drag, producing a slower terminal velocity. With the seed remaining in the air for a longer time, the horizontal distance the seed travels increases.

    DIF: A   OBJ: 24-7

12. Explain the disadvantage for dandelions to have winged seeds like maple trees.

ANS: Winged seeds are designed to spin as they fall so they can travel horizontally by the wind to increase dispersal. A winged seed near ground level would be unable to achieve the necessary lift to effectively disperse it.

DIF: B   OBJ: 24-8

Bird

Airplane

FIGURE 24-2

13. Refer to Figure 24-2 and list three structural features that are the same for birds and airplanes.

ANS: wings, streamlined shape, light weight, rigid skeleton

DIF: B   OBJ: 24-1

14. What feature shown in Figure 24-2 provides lift in both birds and airplanes?

ANS: wings   DIF: B   OBJ: 24-1

15. What feature shown in Figure 24-2 allows air to flow around the bird or airplane with less drag?

ANS: streamlined shape   DIF: A   OBJ: 24-1

16. What characteristics of wings affect lift?

ANS: wing area, shape, and angle   DIF: B   OBJ: 24-2

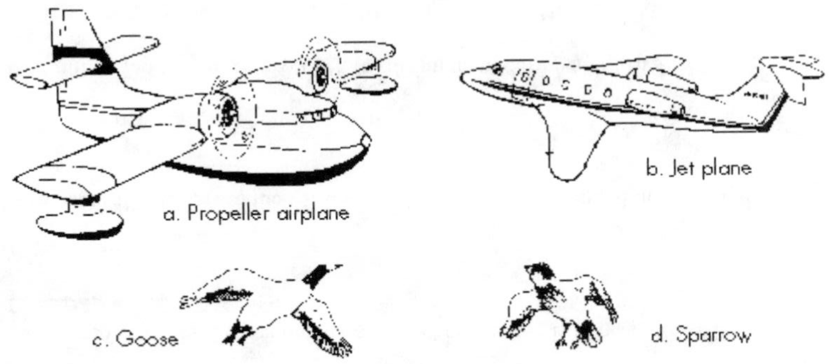

b. Jet plane

a. Propeller airplane

c. Goose

d. Sparrow

FIGURE 24-3

---

17. For each item in Figure 24-3, list what provides thrust.

ANS: a. propeller, b. jet engine, c. wings, d. wings

DIF: B   OBJ: 24-6

18. For each item in Figure 24-3, list the energy source.

ANS: a. gasoline, b. kerosene, c. fat, d. carbohydrates

DIF: B   OBJ: 24-6

Table 24-2

Bird	Wing Length (m)	Wing Width (m)	Wing Area (m^2)	Weight (N)
Andean condor	3.00	0.38	1.14	115
Brown pelican	2.10	0.214	0.45	26
Wren	0.17	0.025	0.0042	0.10

19. Sequence the birds listed in Table 24-2 in order of wing loading (lowest to highest).

ANS: wren, brown pelican, Andean condor

DIF: A   OBJ: 24-2

20. Which bird listed in Table 24-2 can fly most slowly?

ANS: wren

DIF: A   OBJ: 24-2

21. Which bird listed in Table 24-2 can turn more quickly? Explain.

ANS: Wren; its aspect ratio, 6.8, is smaller than the other birds'.

DIF: A   OBJ: 24-2

22. If all the birds listed in Table 24-2 fly at the same speed, which bird's wings produces the greatest lift? Explain.

ANS: Brown pelican; its aspect ratio, 9.8, is greater than the other birds'.

DIF: A   OBJ: 24-2

CHAPTER 25—PHYSICS OF SPACE FLIGHT

MULTIPLE CHOICE

1. Which of these wavelengths from the electromagnetic spectrum is NOT used for communication?
   a. ultraviolet
   b. microwave
   c. shortwave radio
   d. UHF and VHF

   ANS: A   DIF: B   OBJ: 25-1

2. The color red in Landsat satellite wavelength bands _____.
   a. distinguishes soil from plants
   b. picks out different types of vegetation
   c. indicates moisture content
   d. finds heated water

   ANS: B   DIF: A   OBJ: 25-1

3. Which is higher above Earth: polar or geostationary satellites?
   a. polar
   b. geostationary
   c. The height varies.
   d. Both are the same height.

   ANS: B   DIF: A   OBJ: 25-1

4. Landsat does NOT give data for _____.
   a. tracking hurricanes
   b. distinguishing soil from plants
   c. mapping shorelines
   d. distinguishing rock types

   ANS: A   DIF: A   OBJ: 25-1

5. Why is a space telescope such as Hubble such a tremendous advantage over Earth-based telescopes?
   a. Hubble is above the filtering effects of UV, IR, and visible light by Earth's atmosphere.
   b. Hubble is free of the effects of the shifting gases of Earth's atmosphere.
   c. Astronomers using Hubble can observe planets more clearly in the UV and IR bands.
   d. both b and c

   ANS: D   DIF: B   OBJ: 25-2

6. What is the unit of measure for specific impulse?
   a. Newton × second
   b. Newton × meter
   c. astronomical unit
   d. second

   ANS: D   DIF: A   OBJ: 25-4

OTHER

If the underscored word or phrase makes the sentence true, write "true" in the space provided. If the underscored word or phrase makes the sentence false, write the correct term or phrase in the space provided.

1. The purpose of a bird spreading its wings while landing is to decrease stall speed.

   ANS: true   DIF: B   OBJ: 24-2

2. Swans are able to spread their feathers, which decreases their lift during landing. _____

   ANS: increases   DIF: B   OBJ: 24-2

3. Bird utilize food stores of glycogen to sustain them during short flights. _____

   ANS: true   DIF: B   OBJ: 24-5

4. Chickens use their muscles for only short bursts, thus enabling them to burn fat.

   ANS: carbohydrates   DIF: A   OBJ: 24-5

5. During inhalation in a bird, the majority of air enters the lungs.

   ANS: air sacs   DIF: B   OBJ: 24-5

6. The term "roll" describes the tilting motion made by an airplane as one of its wings dips lower than the other. _____

   ANS: true   DIF: B   OBJ: 24-3

7. Spreading flight feathers is similar to moving the rudder on an aircraft. _____

   ANS: ailerons   DIF: B   OBJ: 24-1

8. To achieve better dispersal, ground plants have adapted by making winged seeds.

   ANS: parachute   DIF: A   OBJ: 24-7

7. Which is NOT an advantage of a solid-fueled rocket over a liquid-fueled rocket?
   a. Solid fuel does not have to be stored at very cold temperatures.
   b. The thrust of solid-fuel rockets can be turned on and off.
   c. Solid-fuel rockets are cheaper.
   d. Solid fuel can be stored for long periods of time.

   ANS: B   DIF: B   OBJ: 25-4

8. Space-based observations of Earth are useful for _____.
   a. natural resources
   b. navigation
   c. communications
   d. weather
   e. all of the above

   ANS: E   DIF: B   OBJ: 25-1

9. The satellite that is best used to study Earth's natural resources is the _____.
   a. weather satellite
   b. GPS
   c. Landsat satellite
   d. communication satellite

   ANS: C   DIF: B   OBJ: 25-1

10. The space shuttle utilizes a _____ propulsion system.
    a. liquid-fuel
    b. solid-fuel
    c. both a and b
    d. neither a nor b

    ANS: C   DIF: B   OBJ: 25-4

11. Measuring the distance to the stars is best done in _____.
    a. meters
    b. kilometers
    c. AUs
    d. light-years

    ANS: D   DIF: B   OBJ: 25-5

12. A rocket is made of all of the following except _____.
    a. payload
    b. body
    c. superstructure
    d. propellant

    ANS: C   DIF: B   OBJ: 25-3

13. Uses of a permanent space station in orbit include _____
    a. manufacturing in a weightless environment
    b. observation of Earth and space
    c. manufacturing in a vacuum environment
    d. all of the above

    ANS: D   DIF: B   OBJ: 25-1

14. The _____ of the space shuttle is/are reused.
    a. liquid-fuel tank
    b. solid rocket boosters
    c. *Saturn V* booster
    d. all of the above

    ANS: B   DIF: B   OBJ: 25-3

15. Robert Goddard's early liquid-fuel rocket utilized _____ and liquid oxygen as a fuel.
    a. liquid hydrogen
    b. hydrazine
    c. kerosene
    d. gasoline

    ANS: D   DIF: B   OBJ: 25-4

16. From Landsat, lakes and oceans appear _____.
    a. gray
    b. blue
    c. black
    d. red

    ANS: C   DIF: B   OBJ: 25-1

17. A glowing cloud of gas and dust is best described as a _____.
    a. galaxy
    b. planet
    c. nebula
    d. local group

    ANS: C   DIF: B   OBJ: 25-2

18. Which does not belong?
    a. Viking
    b. Magellan
    c. Landsat
    d. Mir

    ANS: D   DIF: B   OBJ: 25-2

COMPLETION

1. An example of a _____ in a rocket is hydrazine as the fuel and nitrogen tetroxide as the oxidizer.

   ANS: propellant   DIF: B OBJ: 25-4

2. The distance from the sun to Earth is 1 _____, or about 150 million kilometers.

   ANS: astronomical unit   DIF: B OBJ: 25-5

3. Visible light and infrared and ultraviolet radiation are part of the _____

   ANS: electromagnetic spectrum   DIF: A OBJ: 25-2

4. Propellants are measured by _____, a ratio related to the exhaust speed of gases coming out of a rocket.

   ANS: specific impulse   DIF: A OBJ: 25-3

5. Many rockets are built in _____ so that when the fuel is used up, they can be discarded.

   ANS: stages   DIF: A OBJ: 25-3

6. While satellites in polar orbit can view the weather in greater detail, _____, remaining above the same location on Earth, can see overall weather patterns.

   ANS: geostationary satellites   DIF: B OBJ: 25-1

7. Satellites are able to view Earth by observing the ultraviolet, infrared, and visible forms of _____ waves.

   ANS: electromagnetic   DIF: B OBJ: 25-1

MATCHING

Match each item with the correct statement below. Write the answer in the space provided.

a. GPS
b. light-year
c. impulse
d. polar orbiting
e. Saturn V
f. specific impulse
g. AU
h. space shuttle
i. geostationary

1. _____ useful in estimating distance to nearby galaxies
2. _____ low-altitude weather satellites used for observing storm detail
3. _____ meteorological satellites useful for observing cloud patterns and weather changes
4. _____ useful in pinpointing a person's location on Earth

5. _____ the average distance from Earth to the sun
6. _____ a change in momentum
7. _____ a change of momentum divided by weight
8. _____ a staged rocket used for the moon missions
9. _____ utilizes both solid and liquid fuels

1. ANS: b   DIF: B   OBJ: 25-2
2. ANS: d   DIF: B   OBJ: 25-1
3. ANS: i   DIF: B   OBJ: 25-1
4. ANS: a   DIF: B   OBJ: 25-1
5. ANS: g   DIF: B   OBJ: 25-2
6. ANS: c   DIF: B   OBJ: 25-3
7. ANS: f   DIF: A   OBJ: 25-3
8. ANS: e   DIF: B   OBJ: 25-4
9. ANS: h   DIF: B   OBJ: 25-4

SHORT ANSWER

1. Write the sequence of these related rocket systems or discoveries from oldest to youngest: Robert Goddard, space shuttle, Chinese, Saturn V.

   ANS: Chinese, Robert Goddard, Saturn V, space shuttle

   DIF: B   OBJ: 25-3

2. Write the correct sequence in which these space shuttle events occur: jettison fuel tank, liftoff, flies as a glider, solid rocket booster fires, fires rockets to slow and move to lower orbit.

   ANS: solid rocket booster fires, liftoff, jettison fuel tank, fires rockets to slow and move to lower orbit, flies as a glider

   DIF: B   OBJ: 25-5

3. Put the following choices in order of size from largest to smallest: 1 million kilometers, AU, light-year.

   ANS: light-year, AU, 1 million kilometers

   DIF: B   OBJ: 25-2

4. Rank the following from smallest to largest: solar system, local group, Milky Way, universe.

   ANS: solar system, Milky Way, local group, universe

   DIF: B   OBJ: 25-2

Table 25-1

Rocket	Fuel	Specific Impulse (s)
Saturn V	liquid oxygen/kerosene	260
Atlas-Centauri	liquid oxygen/liquid hydrogen	444
space shuttle main engine	liquid oxygen/liquid hydrogen	455
space shuttle solid rocket booster	solid metal fuels	242
space shuttle reaction control system	hydrazine/nitrogen tetroxide	270
space shuttle orbital maneuvering system	hydrazine/nitrogen tetroxide	313

5. According to Table 25-1, the _____ engine will have the greatest exhaust speed.

ANS: space shuttle main   DIF: B   OBJ: 25-5

6. According to Table 25-1, the _____ engine is able to be assembled and fueled and is ready to operate several months before the scheduled mission.

ANS: space shuttle solid rocket booster   DIF: B   OBJ: 25-4

7. According to Table 25-1, the _____ engine will produce the smallest engine gas exhaust speeds.

ANS: solid rocket booster   DIF: B   OBJ: 25-4

8. According to Table 25-1, the exhaust speed of the *Atlas-Centauri* rocket engine is _____.

ANS: 4350 m/s   DIF: A   OBJ: 25-5

9. According to Table 25-1, the exhaust speed of the nonliquid fuel booster is _____.

ANS: 2370 m/s   DIF: A   OBJ: 25-5

10. What scientific unit is appropriate to measure the distance between two cities in a state?

ANS: kilometer   DIF: B   OBJ: 25-5

11. What scientific unit is appropriate to measure distances within the solar system?

ANS: astronomical unit   DIF: B   OBJ: 25-5

12. What unit is appropriate to measure the distances between stars in the Milky Way Galaxy?

ANS: light-year   DIF: B   OBJ: 25-5

13. What is the velocity of a model rocket at take-off if the mass of the rocket is 0.3 kg, the mass of the propellant is 0.25 kg, and the velocity of the exhaust gas is 75 m/s?

ANS: $V_{rocket} = (m/M)V_{exhaust} = (0.25 \text{ kg}/0.3 \text{ kg})75 \text{ m/s} = 63$ m/s

DIF: A   OBJ: 25-3

14. The highest possible ratio of propellant-mass-to-body-mass is about 10/1. If a liquid fluorine and liquid hydrogen fuel could produce an exhaust speed of 3650 m/s, what would be the velocity of the rocket?

ANS: $V_{rocket} = (m/M)V_{exhaust} = (10/1)3650 \text{ m/s} = 36\,500$ m/s = 36.500 km/s

DIF: A   OBJ: 25-3

15. Why are units such as the astronomical unit and light-year needed in astronomy?

ANS: The great distances between planets in our solar system and stars in our galaxy are best handled by a unit of measure larger than kilometers.

DIF: A   OBJ: 25-5

16. Suppose that a fuel combination has an exhaust velocity of 2450 m/s. What is the velocity of a rocket at take-off if its propellant mass-to-fuel-mass ratio is 2/1?

ANS: $V_{exhaust} = (2/1)2450$ m/s = 4900 m/s, or 4.9 km/s

DIF: A   OBJ: 25-3

17. Why is interstellar space travel not very probable in our lifetime?

ANS: Distances to the stars are so vast that the time and energy needed to travel to them is impossible with our present technology.

DIF: A   OBJ: 25-5

18. Compare a geostationary and polar orbiting satellite.

ANS: Geostationary satellites orbit high above the equator and stay above the same position on Earth at all times. Polar orbiting satellites orbit Earth's poles closer to Earth's surface and only view a narrow strip of Earth during each pass.

DIF: A   OBJ: 25-1

19. What is the purpose of burning four molecules of hydrogen with one molecule of oxygen when you only two molecules of hydrogen are needed to combine with one oxygen?

ANS: A water molecule is formed by two hydrogens and one oxygen. The additional two hydrogens are expelled with the water to produce a greater exhaust speed.

DIF: A   OBJ: 25-3

20. What is necessary in addition to hydrogen in a liquid-fuel rocket?

ANS: An oxidizer is needed to combine with the hydrogen fuel.

DIF: A   OBJ: 25-5

21. Describe how a rocket is able to move forward in a vacuum.

ANS: The escaping gas exerts an equal and opposite force on the rocket, which moves it forward.

DIF: B   OBJ: 25-3

22. Describe the characteristics of rocket fuels that are most important in attaining the greatest exhaust speed.

ANS: It is important to have the least massive fuel.

DIF: A   OBJ: 25-5

23. Discuss advantages and disadvantages of solid- and liquid-fuel rocket propellants.

ANS: Solid fuel can be stored in the rocket for long periods of time, but once started, the rocket engines cannot be stopped. Liquid fuel can be placed in rockets only near the time they are to be used because of the extremely cold storage temperatures required. Liquid-fuel engines can be started and stopped easily.

DIF: A   OBJ: 25-4

24. What benefit is there to making observations of space from beyond Earth's atmosphere?

ANS: On Earth, light is distorted while passing through the atmosphere causing planets to twinkle, and a large amount of IR and UV light is blocked. Moving above the atmosphere will eliminate these problems.

DIF: A   OBJ: 25-2

25. Discuss how space-based observations could be used to look for evidence of life on a large scale.

ANS: On a large scale, one can look for major construction projects that may be viewed from space, such as The Great Wall of China or illuminated cities at night. Atmospheric gases, such as oxygen and methane, can be detected by instruments on satellites.

DIF: A   OBJ: 25-2

26. If you wish to observe and track a storm front as it moves across the country, describe why you would or would not choose images from Landsat.

ANS: Landsat takes photographs as it passes over an area and is best at looking for natural resources over a relatively cloud-free zone. A geostationary weather satellite takes pictures again a short time later, so it would be a better choice to track storm movements.

DIF: A   OBJ: 25-1

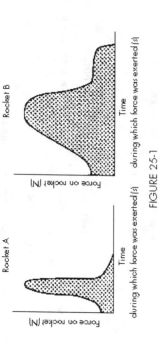

FIGURE 25-1

27. What is represented by the shaded areas in the graphs in Figure 25-1?

ANS: impulse   DIF: A   OBJ: 25-3

28. Which rocket in Figure 25-1 has the greater change in momentum?

ANS: Rocket B   DIF: A   OBJ: 25-3

29. Which rocket in Figure 25-1 could launch a payload into a higher orbit?

ANS: Rocket B   DIF: A   OBJ: 25-3

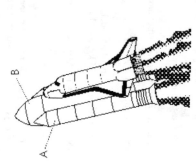

FIGURE 25-2

8. In order to overcome the difficulty of having a rocket that has a high fuel-mass-to-rocket-body-mass ratio, rockets are built with <u>one stage</u>.

ANS: several stages   DIF: B   OBJ: 25-5

9. The space shuttle uses its liquid fuel engines for maneuvering during <u>launch</u>.

ANS: orbit   DIF: B   OBJ: 25-3

10. Sending large telescopes as payloads on <u>interplanetary journeys</u> is not a good idea because they are too massive.

ANS: true   DIF: B   OBJ: 25-2

---

30. What do A and B represent in Figure 25-2?

ANS: A is the solid rocket booster. B is the container of the liquid fuel.

DIF: A   OBJ: 25-4

31. What is the major difference between the flight of the space shuttle and that of an airplane?

ANS: The space shuttle must endure the friction of reentering Earth's atmosphere.

DIF: B   OBJ: 25-3

OTHER

If the underscored word or phrase makes the sentence true, write "true" in the space provided. If the underscored word or phrase makes the sentence false, write the correct term or phrase in the space provided.

1. Landsat is used to map the mineral resources of <u>Mars.</u>

ANS: Earth   DIF: B   OBJ: 25-1

2. It is easier to predict the movement of hurricanes because of the use of <u>global positioning</u> satellites.

ANS: geostationary   DIF: B   OBJ: 25-1

3. A communications satellite receives and strengthens <u>electromagnetic waves</u> before sending them to a receiving station.

ANS: true   DIF: A   OBJ: 25-1

4. Astronomers study <u>comets</u> for the birth of stars.

ANS: nebulae   DIF: B   OBJ: 25-2

5. <u>Geostationary</u> satellites provide good details for storm observation.

ANS: Polar orbiting   DIF: B   OBJ: 25-1

6. In order to accelerate a rocket, when the engine fires, the exhaust gases push on the <u>air</u> to move it forward.

ANS: rocket   DIF: B   OBJ: 25-3

7. Spacecraft not achieving a speed of <u>7 km/s</u> will fall back to Earth rather than reach orbit.

ANS: true   DIF: B   OBJ: 25-5

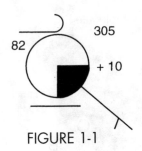

FIGURE 1-1

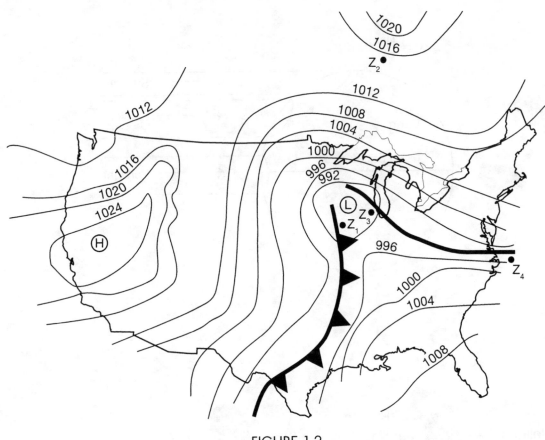

FIGURE 1-2

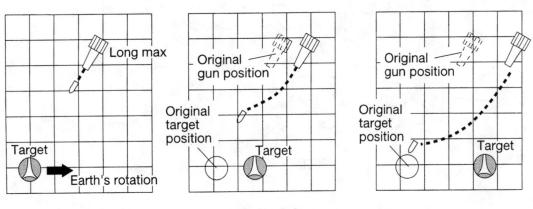

FIGURE 2-1

A Water Molecule

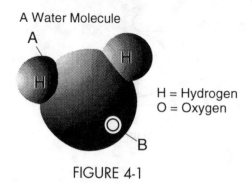

A

H

H

H = Hydrogen
O = Oxygen

B

FIGURE 4-1

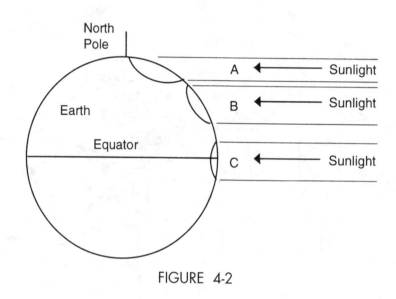

North
Pole

A ← Sunlight

B ← Sunlight

Earth

Equator

C ← Sunlight

FIGURE 4-2

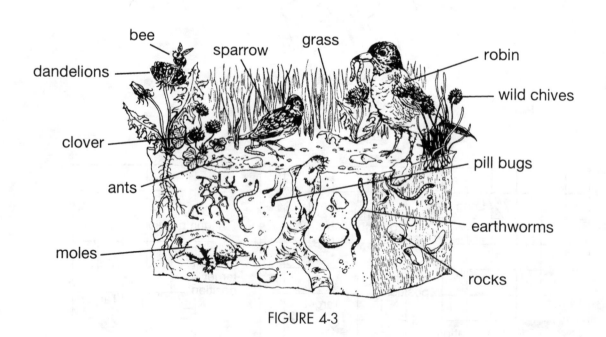

bee

sparrow

grass

robin

dandelions

wild chives

clover

pill bugs

ants

earthworms

moles

rocks

FIGURE 4-3

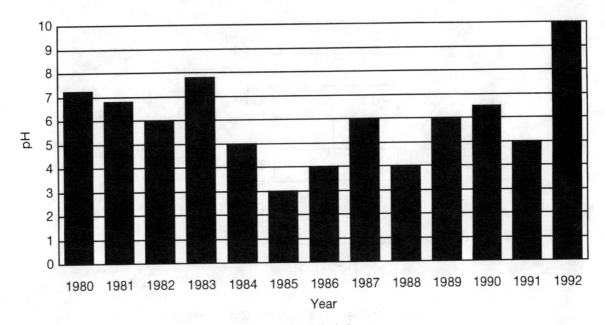

FIGURE 4-4

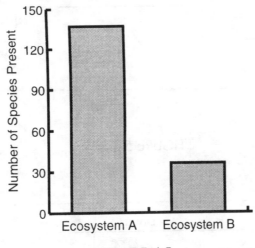

FIGURE 4-5

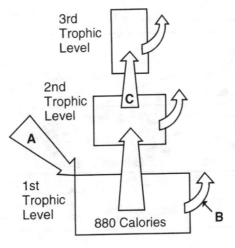

FIGURE 5-1

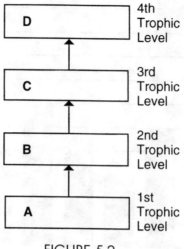

D	4th Trophic Level
C	3rd Trophic Level
B	2nd Trophic Level
A	1st Trophic Level

FIGURE 5-2

A Plant is Enclosed in an Airtight, Glass Container
and Placed Outdoors for 24 Hours.

Amount of
CO_2 in
Container
During
24 Hours

Time A   Time B   Time C

FIGURE 5-3

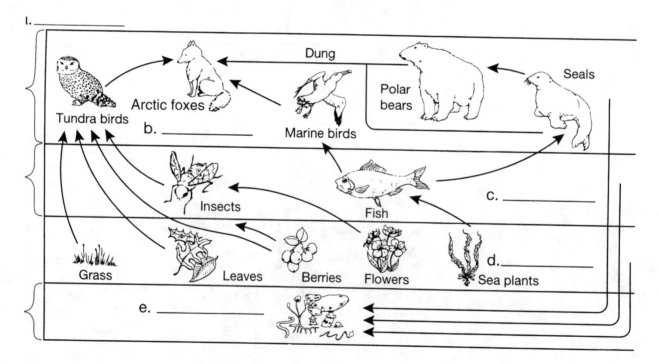

a. _____

Dung

Tundra birds   Arctic foxes   Polar bears   Seals

b. _____   Marine birds

Insects   Fish   c. _____

Grass   Leaves   Berries   Flowers   Sea plants   d. _____

e. _____

FIGURE 5-4

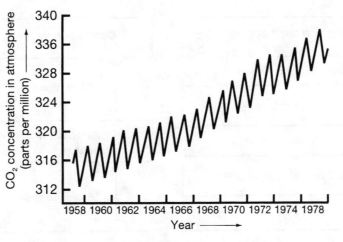

FIGURE 5-5

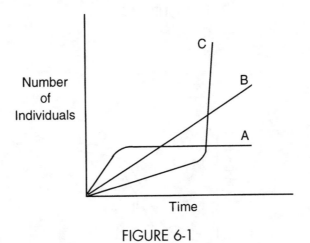

FIGURE 6-1

Weed Population Growth in May and June

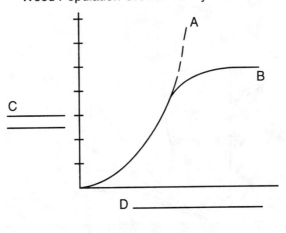

FIGURE 6-2

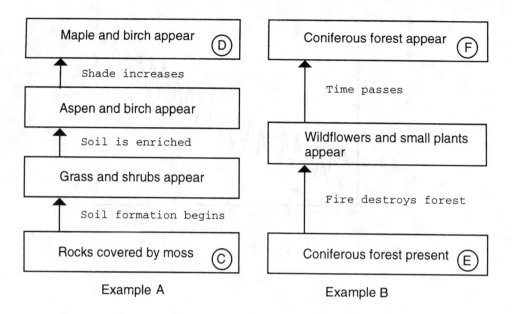

Example A

Example B

FIGURE 6-3

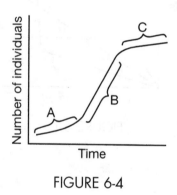

FIGURE 6-4

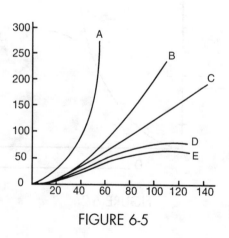

FIGURE 6-5

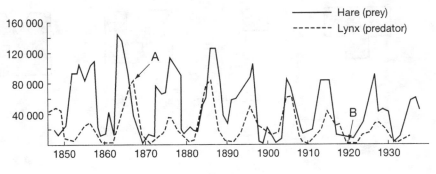

FIGURE 6-6

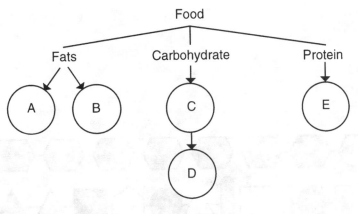

FIGURE 7-1

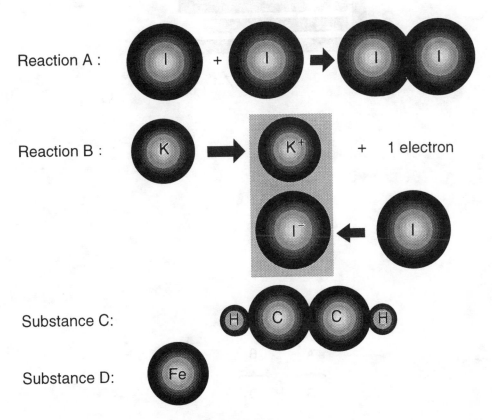

FIGURE 7-2

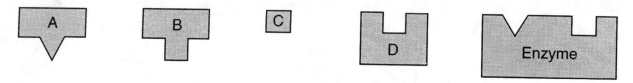

FIGURE 7-3

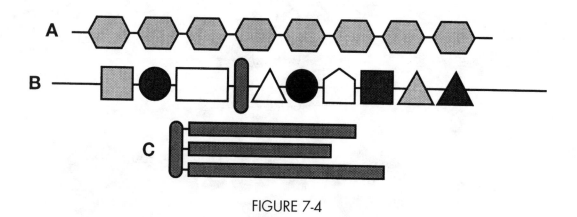

FIGURE 7-4

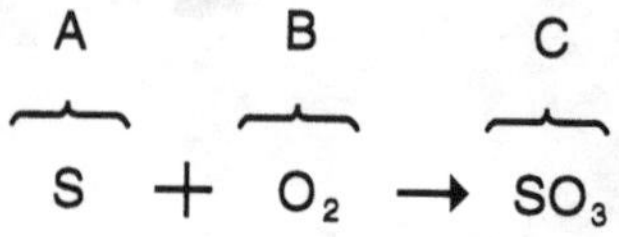

$$\underbrace{S}_{A} \; + \; \underbrace{O_2}_{B} \; \rightarrow \; \underbrace{SO_3}_{C}$$

FIGURE 8-1

The Nitrogen Cycle

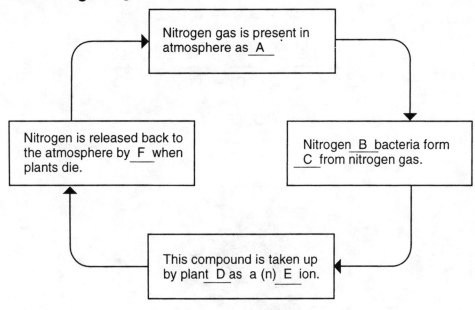

FIGURE 8-2

Events Occurring in Photosynthesis

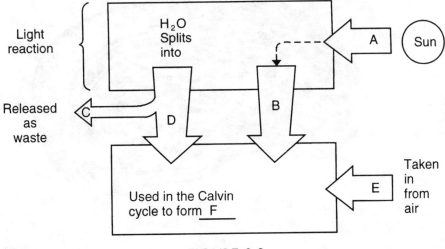

FIGURE 8-3

$$X \left\{ \overbrace{CO_2}^{A} + \overbrace{H_2O}^{B} \rightarrow \overbrace{C_6H_{12}O_6}^{C} + \overbrace{O_2}^{D} \right.$$

$$Y \left\{ \overbrace{C_6H_{12}O_6}^{E} + \overbrace{O_2}^{F} \rightarrow \overbrace{CO_2}^{G} + \overbrace{H_2O}^{H} \right.$$

FIGURE 8-4

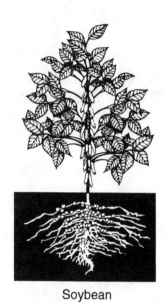

Soybean

FIGURE 8-5

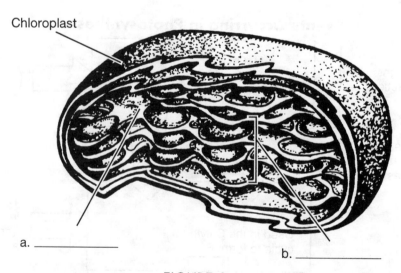

Chloroplast

a. _____

b. _____

FIGURE 8-6

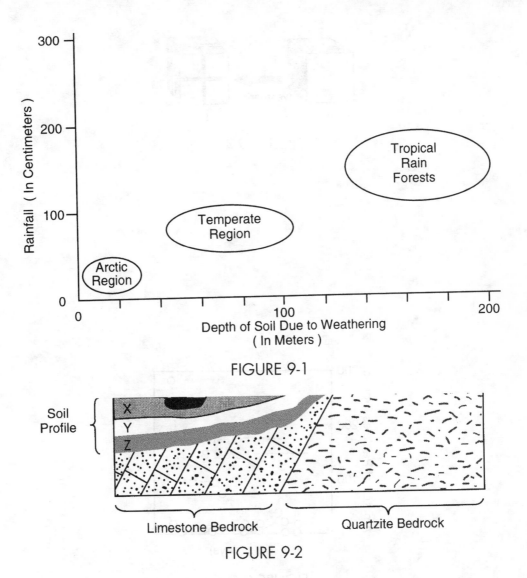

FIGURE 9-1

FIGURE 9-2

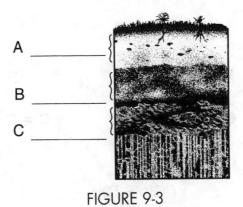

FIGURE 9-3

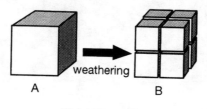

FIGURE 9-4

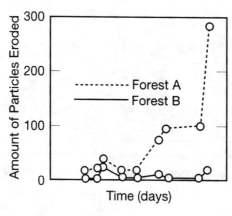

FIGURE 9-5

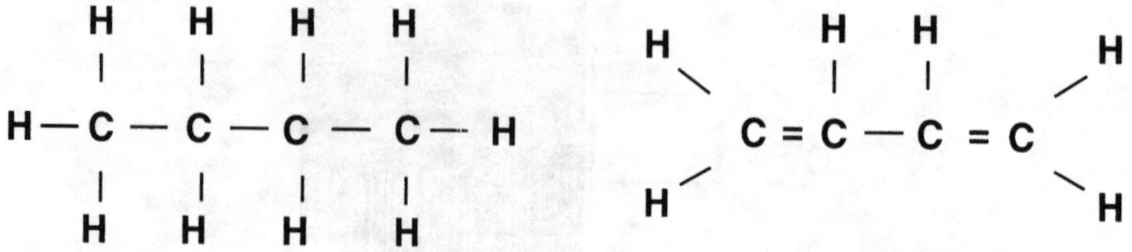

```
    H    H    H    H
    |    |    |    |
H — C — C — C — C — H
    |    |    |    |
    H    H    H    H
```

```
  H              H    H              H
   \             |    |             /
    C = C — C = C
   /    |              |    \
  H    H              H    H
```

FIGURE 10-1

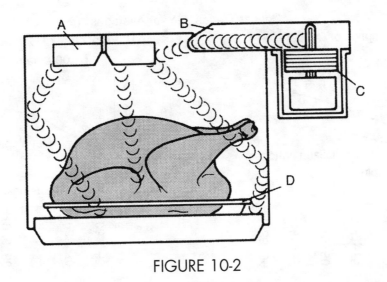

FIGURE 10-2

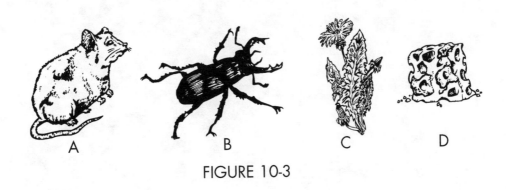

FIGURE 10-3

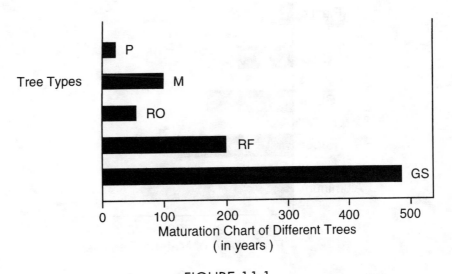

Maturation Chart of Different Trees
(in years)

FIGURE 11-1

Copper Trends, 5-Year Averages, 1961- 90

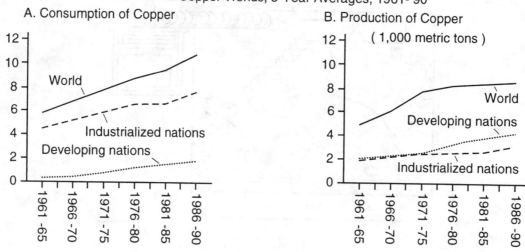

FIGURE 11-2

Recycling in the United States

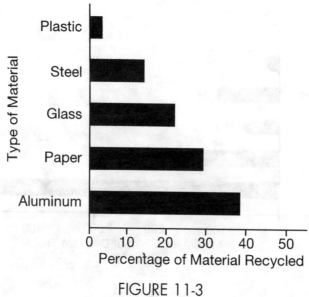

FIGURE 11-3

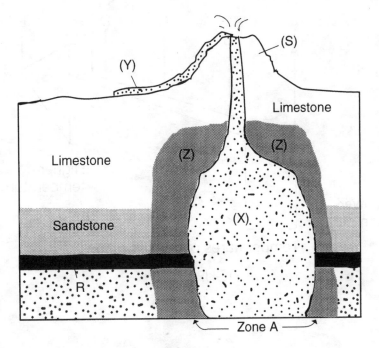

FIGURE 12-1

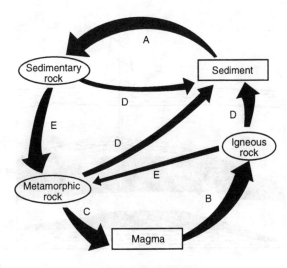

Figure 12-2

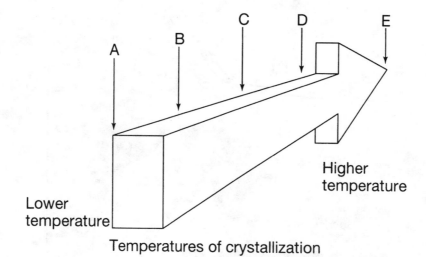

Lower temperature

Higher temperature

Temperatures of crystallization

FIGURE 12-3

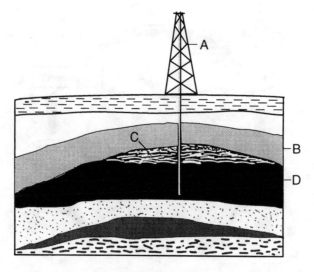

FIGURE 13-1

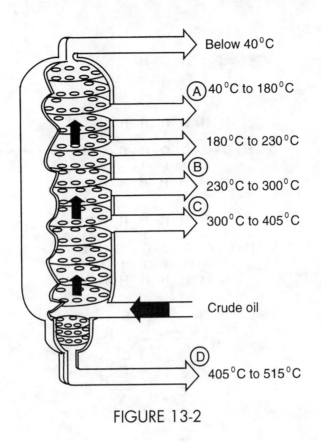

FIGURE 13-2

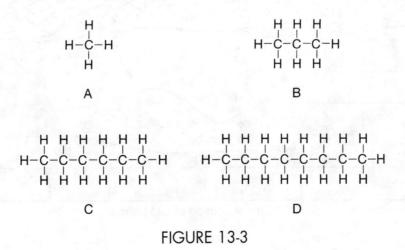

FIGURE 13-3

A   H
        |
    H - C - H
        |
        H

B   H H H H H H H
    | | | | | | |
H - C-C-C-C-C-C-C - H
    | | | | | | |
    H H H H H H H

C   H H H H H H H H H
    | | | | | | | | |
H - C-C-C-C-C-C-C-C-C - H
    | | | | | | | | |
    H H H H H H H H H

D
        H   H
        C - C
      /   \
   H-C   C-H
      \   /
   H-C   C-H
      \   /
        C - C
        H   H

FIGURE 13-4

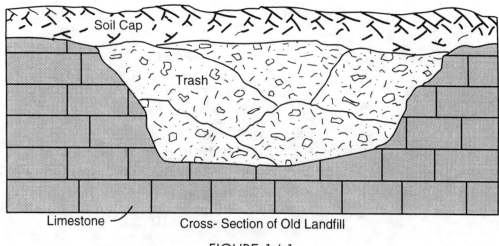

Limestone   Cross- Section of Old Landfill

FIGURE 14-1

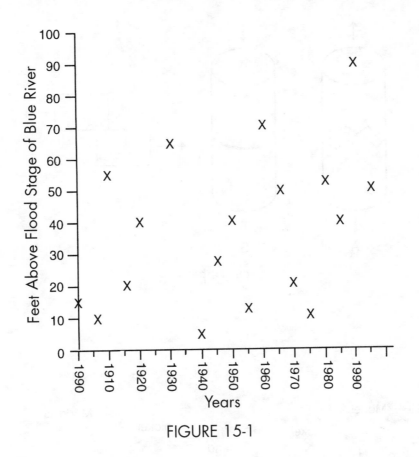

FIGURE 15-1

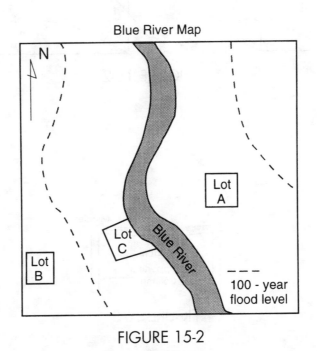

Blue River Map

FIGURE 15-2

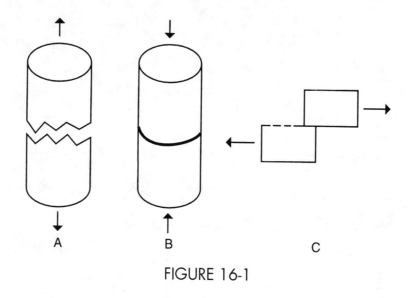

A   B   C

FIGURE 16-1

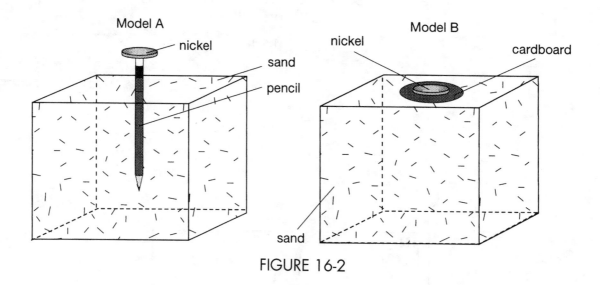

Model A

nickel
sand
pencil

Model B

nickel
cardboard

sand

FIGURE 16-2

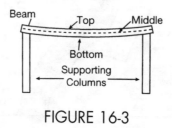

Beam   Top   Middle
Bottom
Supporting
Columns

FIGURE 16-3

Proposal A
Flat Roof
$1.0 million

Proposal B
Pitched Roof
$2.0 million

Proposal C
Domed Roof
$3.0 million

FIGURE 16-4

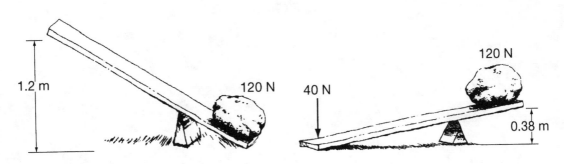

1.2 m

120 N

40 N

120 N

0.38 m

FIGURE 17-1

FIGURE 17-2

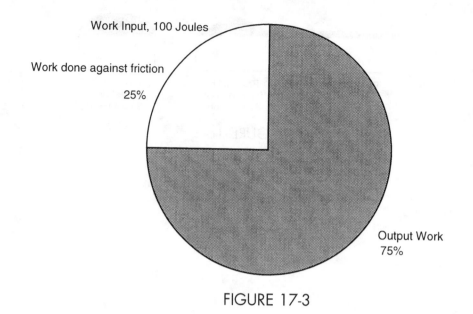

Work Input, 100 Joules

Work done against friction

25%

Output Work
75%

FIGURE 17-3

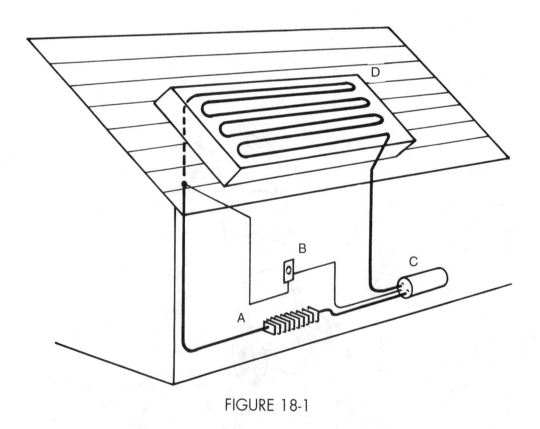

FIGURE 18-1

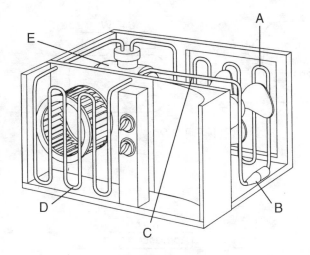

FIGURE 18-2

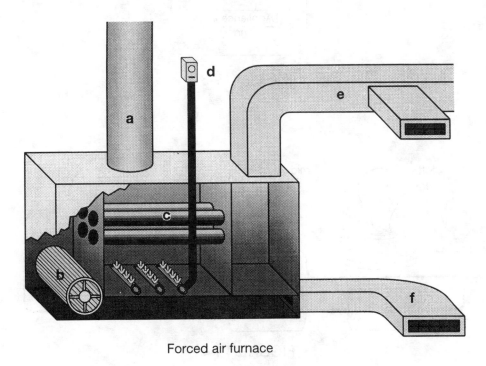

Forced air furnace

FIGURE 18-3

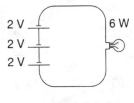

FIGURE 19-1

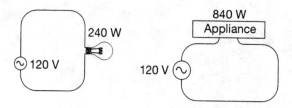

FIGURE 19-2

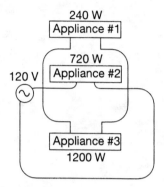

FIGURE 19-3

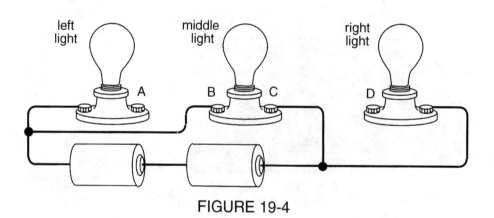

FIGURE 19-4

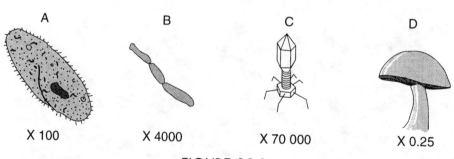

X 100   X 4000   X 70 000   X 0.25

FIGURE 20-1

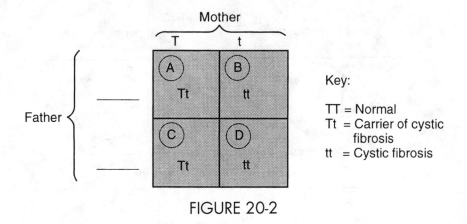

FIGURE 20-2

Key:

TT = Normal
Tt = Carrier of cystic fibrosis
tt = Cystic fibrosis

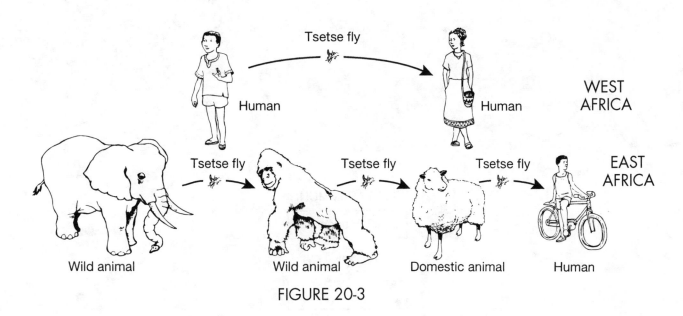

FIGURE 20-3

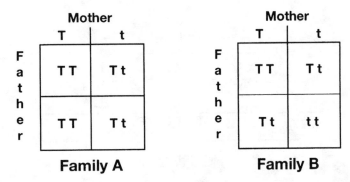

Figure 20-5

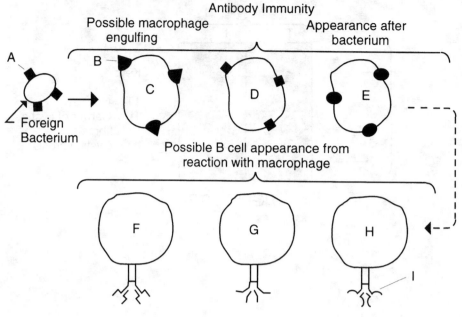

Antibody Immunity

Possible macrophage engulfing

Appearance after bacterium

Foreign Bacterium

Possible B cell appearance from reaction with macrophage

FIGURE 21-1

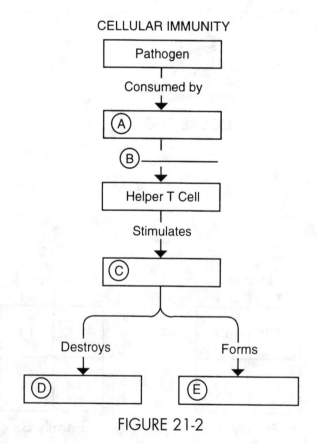

CELLULAR IMMUNITY

Pathogen

Consumed by

Ⓐ

Ⓑ

Helper T Cell

Stimulates

Ⓒ

Destroys

Forms

Ⓓ

Ⓔ

FIGURE 21-2

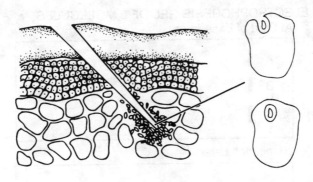

FIGURE 21-3

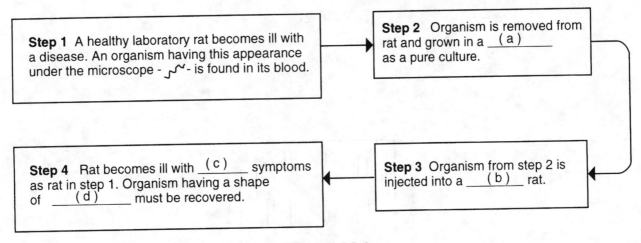

Steps used to test if a disease is caused by a specific organism

Step 1 A healthy laboratory rat becomes ill with a disease. An organism having this appearance under the microscope - ᔉᔧ- is found in its blood.

Step 2 Organism is removed from rat and grown in a __(a)__ as a pure culture.

Step 3 Organism from step 2 is injected into a ____(b)__ rat.

Step 4 Rat becomes ill with __(c)__ symptoms as rat in step 1. Organism having a shape of ____(d)____ must be recovered.

FIGURE 22-1

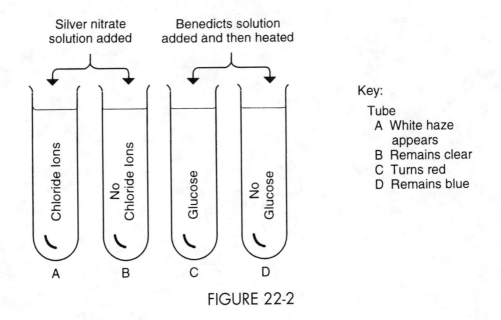

Silver nitrate solution added

Benedicts solution added and then heated

Chloride Ions

No Chloride Ions

Glucose

No Glucose

A   B   C   D

Key:

Tube
  A White haze appears
  B Remains clear
  C Turns red
  D Remains blue

FIGURE 22-2

ELECTROPHORESIS GEL OF 3 MOLECULES
At Start of Experiment

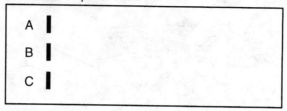

20 minutes Later

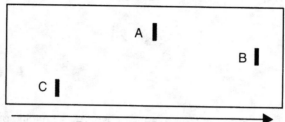

Direction of Current Flow

FIGURE 22-3

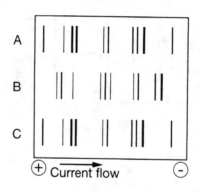

+ Current flow −

FIGURE 22-4

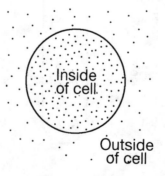

Inside of cell

Outside of cell

FIGURE 22-5

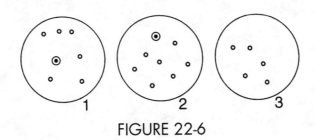

FIGURE 22-6

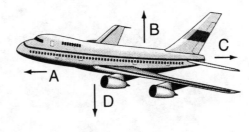

FIGURE 23-1

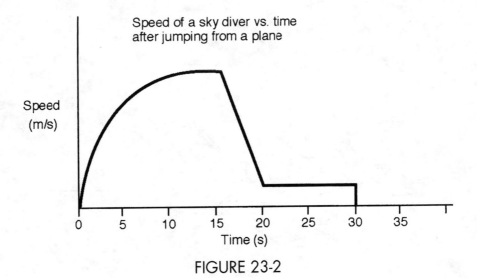

Speed of a sky diver vs. time
after jumping from a plane

FIGURE 23-2

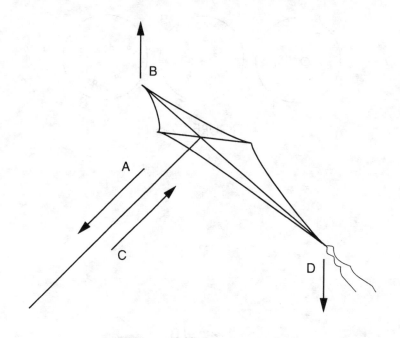

A Kite

FIGURE 23-3

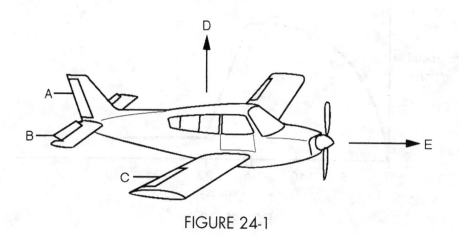

FIGURE 24-1

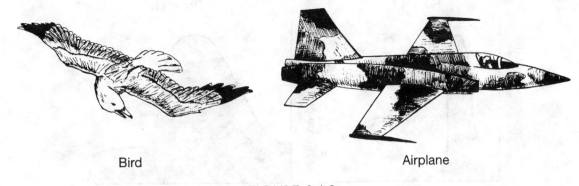

Bird

Airplane

FIGURE 24-2

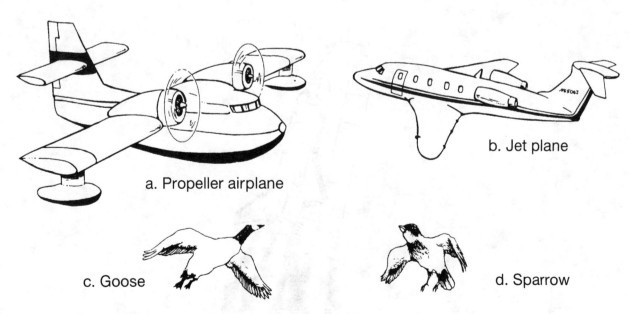

a. Propeller airplane

b. Jet plane

c. Goose

d. Sparrow

FIGURE 24-3

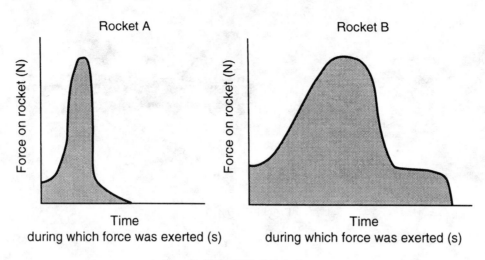

Rocket A — Force on rocket (N) vs. Time during which force was exerted (s)

Rocket B — Force on rocket (N) vs. Time during which force was exerted (s)

FIGURE 25-1

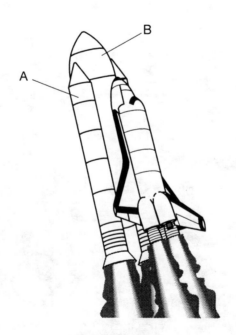

FIGURE 25-2